Revitalising language in Provence:
A critical approach

T0366883

Publications of the Philological Society, 48

WILEY
Blackwell

Revitalising language in Provence:
A critical approach

James Costa
Université Sorbonne Paris Cité

Publications of the Philological Society, 48

WILEY
Blackwell

This edition first published 2016
© 2016 The Philological Society

Blackwell Publishing was acquired by John Wiley & Sons in February 2007. Blackwell's publishing program has been merged with Wiley's global Scientific, Technical, and Medical business to form Wiley-Blackwell.

Registered Office
John Wiley & Sons Ltd, The Atrium, Southern Gate, Chichester, West Sussex, PO19 8SQ, United Kingdom

Editorial Offices
350 Main Street, Malden, MA 02148-5020, USA
9600 Garsington Road, Oxford, OX4 2DQ, UK
The Atrium, Southern Gate, Chichester, West Sussex, PO19 8SQ, UK

For details of our global editorial offices, for customer services, and for information about how to apply for permission to reuse the copyright material in this book please see our website at www.wiley.com/wiley-blackwell.

The right of James Costa to be identified as the author of this work has been asserted in accordance with the UK Copyright, Designs and Patents Act 1988.

Library of Congress Cataloging-in-Publication Data
Library of Congress Cataloging-in-Publication Data is available for this work. ISBN 978-1-1192-4353-3
A catalogue record for this book is available from the British Library.

Set in Times by SPS (P) Ltd., Chennai, India
Printed in Singapore

1 2016

REVITALISING LANGUAGE IN PROVENCE:

A CRITICAL APPROACH

James Costa
Université Sorbonne Paris Cité

Sorbonne Nouvelle
Institut de Linguistique et Phonétique Générales et Appliquées
19 rue des Bernardins
75005 Paris, France

james.costa@icloud.com

CONTENTS

ACKNOWLEDGEMENTS

This monograph derives from a PhD dissertation defended at the University of Grenoble in 2010 under the supervision of Professor Marinette Matthey. I wish to thank her for her advice and patience. I also wish to thank the members of the committee who evaluated my work: Professor Alexandre Duchêne, Professor Colette Grinevald, Professor Philippe Martel and Dr Julia Sallabank.

First and foremost I wish to express gratitude to those in the Occitan language movement who welcomed me nearly fifteen years ago and who made my life considerably richer on many levels. I think in particular of Joan Saubrement, who passed away as this book was being reviewed, Ana-Maria Poggio and many at the Institut d'Estudis Occitans in Provence and other parts of Occitania without whom I could never have completed this study.

This book would not have come to fruition without the support of those who suffered through years of crankiness and yet still talk to me. I wish to extend particular thanks to Michel Bert, Aurélie Bourdais, Yves Costa, Guri Bordal Steien, Sara Brennan, Janet Connor, Alfonso Del Percio, Aude Etrillard, Colette Grinevald, Monica Heller, Marie Huet, Alexandra Jaffe, Patricia Lambert, Pauline Martin, Salikoko Mufwene, Eric Negrel, Aneta Pavlenko, Bénédicte Pivot, Sue and Steve Watkins, and Karyn Wilson.

Finally, I wish to address special thanks to Susan M. Fitzmaurice for her extreme patience as series editor.

This book derives from research conducted while I was a researcher at ICAR research laboratory, based at the Ecole Normale Supérieure de Lyon (ENS-Lyon). However, while deriving from research conducted prior to my appointment at the University of Oslo, Norway, this work was largely written while working as a postdoctoral fellow at the Centre for Multilingualism in Society across the Lifespan (MultiLing) in Oslo. It would not have been completed without the more than ideal conditions afforded by the centre. This work was thus largely supported by the Research Council of Norway through its Centres of Excellence funding scheme (project number 223265), as well as by COST Action IS 1306, "New Speakers in a Multilingual Europe". This volume also represents a contribution to the Standards project, registered at the Research Council of Norway under project number 223265 and directed by Dr Pia Lane.

My grandmother, Josephine Wilson, died while I was working on an early draft of this book in the summer of 2014. It is for her.

PREFACE

James Costa's work comes at a time when language revitalisation programmes seem to be flourishing. In an odd sense, it would appear that it has never been a better time to undertake revitalisation, with a constellation of policies and ideologies that would apparently favour vibrant indigenous language use. International instruments include the United Nations Declaration on the Rights of Indigenous Peoples, UNESCO's *Convention for the Safeguarding of the Intangible Cultural Heritage,* and the *European Charter for Regional or Minority Languages,* to name just a few. At the same time attitudes toward indigenous and minority languages seems to have changed over the last few decades. More and more groups are seeking means to revitalize their languages. There is a general, and growing, sense of community among indigenous peoples worldwide that unites them in revitalisation efforts as they share best practices and learn from one another. What began as isolated pockets of revitalisation have become widespread programmes, seemingly united in their goals and challenges, if not in the details of their plans. And perhaps the attitudes of linguists have shifted the greatest of all: it is no longer acceptable to work in an endangered language community without giving back to the people, and giving back is generally equated with engaging in revitalisation projects.

Language revitalisation efforts are not new: Costa traces their origins to the early nineteenth century, with basic work on what today would be considered documentation dating as far back as the eighteenth century and the work of dialectologists of the time to record words and phrases from dialects in danger of disappearing. This was part of a larger fascination with collecting and preserving elements of vanishing culture. Costa finds the precursor to modern-day documentation in North American salvage anthropology of the early twentieth century, with a focus on collecting and rescuing authentic indigenous cultures and languages from external influences due to contact and colonisation. This is an undercurrent that runs through much documentation work even today, with many seeing a need to document the last speaker while we can still get a record of a supposedly pure and thus authentic and legitimate indigenous language.

There has been an explosion of attention to revitalisation in the last few decades, with speaker communities actively involved in creating language programmes, perhaps even insisting on programmes, and linguists and anthropologists working in minority language communities seeing it as an ethical obligation to engage in such efforts. Indeed, from the standpoint of external scholars, participating in revitalisation efforts is often construed as the only morally acceptable way to work with communities. Giving back to communities has *de facto* come to be interpreted as contributing to language revitalisation.

And yet, for all the emphasis on language revitalisation from the endangered language movement, at a fundamental level it is an unanalysed concept. Since the early 1990s, linguists have paid increasing attention to language shift and endangerment and, along with them, revitalisation. There has been significant growth in language documentation projects and archiving. The rate of loss, however, does not appear to have abated and, arguably, only a small number of revitalisation programmes have been successful (depending very much on how one defines success). This alone indicates the need for more discussion of revitalisation as an enterprise. While there is a general sense that we should revitalise, there is considerably less clarity about what, exactly, that means. Does language revitalisation mean creating new speakers? Does it mean creating pedagogical materials? Increasing the domains of usage? Learning greetings? What counts as a success? It is often presented as the solution to language shift and loss, as the means to combat linguistic and, incumbent with it, cultural erosion, and yet speakers continue to shift to majority languages.

Costa boldly asserts that language revitalisation is not about language. Rather, he situates it within other revitalisation movements as a type of social movement. This approach enables him to focus on the actors involved in revitalisation, assessing what is at stake and what people hope to achieve in revitalisation. In so doing, he moves the emphasis from language as an object to communities and people. Language revitalisation in this view becomes centred on relationships and the dynamics between the people involved in revitalisation movements. This fresh focus on the social actors themselves enables Costa to analyse revitalisation movements in terms of the core roles these actors play and how they interact. His discussion here provides insightful breakthroughs into the processes involved in revitalisation that often – perhaps inevitably – result in a classification of speakers as valid, authentic and legitimate, or not. More to the point, he demonstrates why this (re)classification occurs as a result of the social dynamics of the very process of revitalisation. This book comes at a timely moment in the development of revitalisation programmes and will do much to inform how communities might want to advance them, and how external linguists and anthropologies might want to engage with them.

Lenore A. Grenoble
The University of Chicago

1

RESEARCHING LANGUAGE REVITALISATION FROM A CRITICAL SOCIOLINGUISTIC PERSPECTIVE

Però hem viscut per salvar-vos els mots,
per retornar-vos el nom de cada cosa.

But we lived to save the words for you
to give you back the name of each thing.

Salvador Espriu, 'Inici de càntic en el temple'

———

Chez nous c'est pas sud de France
Chez nous c'est nord de Méditerranée.

Our home is not south of France
Our home is north of the Mediterranean

Mauresca Fracàs Dub, 'Sud de France'

1.1. SAVING AUTHENTIC LANGUAGES VS. INVENTING NEW ONES

From the seventeenth century onwards, inventing new languages became a fashion-able enterprise. The nineteenth century, in turn, was keen on constructing national languages from hitherto mostly oral vernaculars. The late twentieth and early twenty-first century have expanded those interests and action upon language is now equally likely to take the form of saving disappearing languages or resuscitating long-gone ones, as numerous accounts in the media as well as in academic literature can attest. Popular books on the topic, such as the Canadian journalist Mark Abley's (2003) *Spoken here* have enjoyed considerable success. Language revival concerns not only established languages such as Catalan, Welsh, Nahuatl or even less-spoken ones such as Australian or North American indigenous languages, or Cornish. New trends also mobilise fringe movements and encompass such languages as Norn in Shetland, Devonian or Cambrian in England, or Tasmanian in Australia, through initiatives undertaken by small groups of enthusiasts. A Facebook community has recently, rather unexpectedly, reconstructed a version of Gaulish (which it calls *Galáthach hAtheviu*) and uses it on a daily basis online. In practice, revived Gaulish is not radically different from Esperanto or Volapük (in fact, according to some critics, neither is standard Breton, Occitan, etc.), but the underlying ideology is. For Gaulish, as well as for the 'endangered languages' of contemporary revival movements, legitimacy harks to a representation of the past to justify a particular projection of groupness onto the future. Esperanto, on the other hand, relied on its newness and artificiality to herald a new, brighter future for a renewed humankind. Of course scholarly work on Cornish in the nineteenth and early twentieth centuries was already an early forerunner of contemporary revival movements. But the worldwide generalisation of language as an indicator and essential component of something called 'diversity', in effect a mode of definition and management of difference, should alert us that something is at stake.

An analysis of the differences between earlier processes and contemporary ones would likely tell us much about both eras. In both cases however, issues of control over language and over meaning lie at the core of the actions involved. While invented languages might satisfy fantasies of almightiness, absolute control over speech and variation and full transparency, endangered language revivals also raise the question of who has authority to speak on behalf of a language and of the community it allegedly stands for. This is particularly the case as traditional speakers ('native speakers') die and the positions of authority conferred by their nativeness become available. This book argues that language revival, or revitalisation as it has come to be known, is primarily a matter of the attribution of authority over groups that, far from pre-existing the movement that articulates language-based claims, are invented in the process.

1.2. LANGUAGE REVITALISATION

Language revitalisation, as a form of action on language and people, is fundamentally about individuals who believe that, for one reason or another, some other people do not speak the way they should, thereby affiliating with a group to which they are not supposed to be associated with. It is, in other words, about expressing an opinion about and acting upon how people ought to speak. In contemporary movements, this deficit generally relies on a historical narrative of suppressed groupness as well as on the necessity to re-establish the criteria thought to warrant the very existence of the said group. This group 'exists' due to its historical presence or attestation (in the case of groups with no obvious or institutionally recognised historical continuity).

This book argues that an analysis of language revitalisation is crucial to an understanding of some of the cultural and social dynamics of our times, in particular those relating to so-called minority issues. This form of understanding entails a shift in the type of study we, as anthropologists or sociolinguists need to conduct. This type of comprehension of the dynamics of language-based movements does not require, as many studies propose, to assess degrees of language precarity in a gloomy context of language endangerment or disappearance. Nor should it lead us to reflect upon how languages can or should be saved: while this is a matter of great importance for language advocates around the world, understanding what is at stake requires a different type of work.

The case put forward in this book is that language revitalisation movements need to be understood in their own terms in light of their multiplication in recent years: what do they stand for? What do they use language for? Who are the people involved in them? As the linguistic anthropologist Jacqueline Urla (2012: 5) notes, '[l]anguage-revival efforts are on the rise around the globe'. Over the past two decades at least, from Europe to Latin America and Oceania, and increasingly from Asia to Africa (see Are 2015 for a recent update on Africa), people have indeed been mobilising in the name of language to articulate certain claims about the world we live in, and to voice concerns and demands. These movements, this book argues, should be understood in relation to other types of social and cultural movements. Their discursive apparatus, which tends to position language on the terrain of culture (rather than, say, politics) likens them to a number of other movements analysed by by the anthropologist Arjun Appadurai. Writing about the role of culture in late modern societies in a 2006 essay on minorities, he writes:

> The virtually complete loss of even the fiction of a national economy, which had some evidence for its existence in the eras of strong socialist states and central planning, now leaves the cultural field as the main one in which fantasies of purity, authenticity, borders and security can be enacted. (Appadurai 2006: 22–3)

Whether or not national economies are vanishing is debatable, but other commentators have also insisted on the role of 'culture' as a catalyst for action in various parts of the world – either as mobilising force for contestation or as resource to be commodified on a variety of markets (see Yúdice 2003). 'Language' has been appropriated much in the same way (see Duchêne & Heller 2011). In this context, the local, the indigenous (Clifford, 2013), the autochthonous (Ceuppens & Geschiere, 2005) and the authentic (Heller, 2014) have become staples of contemporary social demands. According to the anthropologist James Clifford (2013: 7), 'the indigenous histories of survival, struggle and renewal [...] became widely visible during the 1980s and 1990s'. Language revitalisation, in Europe in particular, does have a (partly) different genealogy; yet, the frames mobilised by indigenous movements worldwide have since the 1990s merged in part with those in European language-based movements.

What do those movements stand for? Are they really a sign of a reaction to globalising forces, in the sense that they wish to foster a return to previous conditions of living? Are they even (only) about language, or are they not processes which use language as a terrain to articulate a number of social issues, as Monica Heller (2004) suggests? 'Language and religion are arguably the two most socially and politically consequential domains of cultural difference in the modern world', Brubaker (2015: 85) contends. Could language-based claims and demands be ways of affirming a certain type of presence within the social struggles subsumed under the globalisation umbrella?

Language revitalisation sits rather uncomfortably between the social and liberation movements of the 1960s and 1970s and the cultural demands and economic logics of late capitalism, which have tended to value certain forms of multiculturalism and multilingualism as a form of regimentation, that is, of hierarchised organisation of social difference (Žižek 1997; Michaels 2006; Comaroff & Comaroff 2009).

1.3. LANGUAGE REVITALISATION IN ACADEMIC WORK

Language revitalisation and its supposed cause, language endangerment, have also been important concerns among different types of scholars over the past thirty years. While both terms have separate genealogies, in contemporary discourses on revitalisation the latter is usually presented as a consequence of the former. As I was writing this book, Google Scholar would pour references to new articles on the topic into my email inbox almost every day. Those articles referred to languages from all around the globe and were written by scholars on all continents. Although all contributed valuable information to situations I knew nothing about, dissatisfaction continued to grow as new articles piled on my desk. Most such contributions were indeed building on a discourse according to which situations should be described before it is too late, and on what could or should accordingly be done. Works drew on a number of academic discourses, from conversations on language endangerment in documentary linguistics or sociolinguistics to issues of language rights and institutional frameworks seeking to implement legal frameworks for the promotion of minority or endangered languages. The Council of Europe or UNESCO feature among such institutions.

In a characterisation of what language revitalisation means for scholars as well as for language advocates, Nancy Hornberger, a prominent figure in the sociolinguistics of education, considers the value of such an enterprise and assesses her role:

> We start from the premise that Indigenous language revitalization is worth doing, both for the sake of the speakers of the languages and for the ways of knowing and being that their languages encode and express. Our focus here is on how to achieve Indigenous language revitalization, and in particular, the role of schools in that endeavor. (Hornberger 2008: 1)

This book, on the other hand, starts from the premise that whether or not revitalisation is worth doing is none of our concern as sociolinguists or anthropologists. Of course we might have our own personal preferences as citizens. This book, however, posits that language revitalisation is, first and foremost, worth *understanding*. For although language is of course the central rallying point, the actions that we are referring to are primarily not about language but about people: people coming together to act in the world, people articulating opinions about how society should be ordered and about who should take part in that order. It is those issues that I seek to address here.

The two epigraphs quoted at the beginning of this introduction originate in the works of a contemporary Catalan poet for the first one, and from an Occitan ragamuffin band for the second one. Together they provide a forceful introduction to the motif of this book. In each case, the authors were concerned about the continued usage of a language they sought to defend. But beyond language, what they are doing is insisting that some words are better than others to describe a particular type of reality, and to do things in the world. They remind us that for many people, words are worth fighting for, not for words themselves, but for the symbolic orders they encapsulate, or are thought to encapsulate, which ultimately amounts to the same thing. In the case of language revitalisation movements, entire sets of words, as well as syntactic and phonological features, are thought to be worth fighting for. Again, not for their intrinsic value, but for what is believed to be the semiotic and material order that they express or construct. But saving words is not the only objective of the day in the quotations above. Beyond salvation, what is implied is a struggle over the classifications that words allow us to perform, and over the dominant forms of categorisation that exist in a society.

The central idea here is that language advocacy movements are really about a 'struggle over classifications' (Bourdieu 1980a). This book is therefore about what people do when they 'do language' in a particular way (Heller 2011); it is about what they seek to achieve for themselves and in the world. It is ultimately also about who gets to be involved in such practices, and who doesn't.

1.4. REVITALISING OCCITAN IN SOUTHERN FRANCE: OCCITANIA AND PROVENCE

The work involved in order to understand revitalisation, its consequences as a potentially organisational force and the struggles it proceeds from and generates is based on fieldwork contexted in the Occitan South of France.

According to most linguistic studies, Occitan or Langue d'oc is a Romance language spoken by several hundred thousand people in Southern France as well as in parts of Spain and Italy (Bec 1973; e.g. Boyer & Gardy 2001). Linguistically, it thus stands between Italian, Catalan, Spanish and French, bordering the Mediterranean as well as the Atlantic, encompassing the Northern slopes of the Pyrenees and the Western Alps. To the speaker of Standard French it is mostly unintelligible, but the same person might read Occitan fairly easily if written down. Yet Occitan and Occitania are also, and perhaps primarily, fantasies or dreams couched on a map. Occitan is an idea wrought by generations of writers and linguists who since the nineteenth century have dreamt, among other things, of tolerance and of bygone medieval days when Occitan was a language of high culture and refined poetry, a language of kings and troubadours, poets and heretics. In a preface to an anthology of twentieth century poetry in Occitan, the distinguished writer, linguist and sociolinguist Robert Lafont writes:

> [a]u début, au XIIe siècle, sur un terreau d'écriture latine cléricale, une
> floraison subite : une façon toute nouvelle de dire l'amour de l'homme

pour la femme dans une langue laïque qui n'a encore été qu'essayée dans l'expression littéraire. En trois-quarts de siècle, les troubadours auront empli l'espace entre Loire, Èbre et Arno de strophes chantées dont le ton et le sens nous ravissent encore et nous interrogent. On se demande comment, en si peu de temps et dans une langue toute verte de jeunesse, ces poètes ont pu élaborer un art si raffiné que nous ne sommes pas bien assurés d'en tenir toutes les clefs, et ouvrir les abîmes du cœur passionné comme nous les découvrons à peine aujourd'hui. L'Europe a trouvé ses guides à chanter, tellement imités, jamais égalés, et ses maîtres à énoncer l'inédit en un beau langage. Ce n'est qu'une constatation : l'Europe des poètes est née occitane.

Après quoi, des siècles sous le couvercle d'une occupation française par les armes et la langue. Mais la voix du Sud ne s'éteint jamais vraiment, l'écriture faufile le silence. Sans cesse, entre Provence et Gascogne, Limousin et Catalogne, la plume d'un fils du pays renoue selon ses moyens avec l'antique gloire.

[at] the beginning, in the twelfth century, springing from the fertile ground of Latin clerical writing, a sudden poetic explosion: a radically new way of expressing the love of a man for a woman in a secular language that had barely been tested for literary purposes. Within three quarters of a century, the troubadours would have filled the space between the Loire, the Ebre and the Arno with sung stanzas, the tone and signification of which still enchant and question us. One wonders how, in such a short lapse of time, and in a language still in its infancy those poets were able to craft an art so refined that we are still not quite certain to master all its ways, an art capable of opening the depths of impassioned hearts in a way that we barely understand today. Europe found its guides to song, so often imitated but still unrivalled, and its masters in stating the yet unspoken in poetic language. This is but an observation: the Europe of poets was born Occitan.

After this, the French kept it stifled for centuries under the cloak of occupation by way of their weapons and their language. But the voice of the South never died entirely, and writing crept in through the silence. Relentlessly, from Provence to Gascony, from Limousin to Catalonia, the quill of a son of the land would, in its own way, reach for the ancient glory. (Lafont 2004)

Provence, a term which for many people designates the Southeastern part of the Occitan domain, might on the other hand seem a more tangible reality. It is, after all, the name of an established entity from Roman times onward, and under the name Provence-Alpes-Côte d'Azur it is an administrative region of contemporary France. Yet its contours have changed so often since Roman times, its status was altered so many times, that it too lends itself well to projections and fantasies on maps. Maps are invariably situated perspectives on a given object, and I do not wish to provide such a perspective at this point. Not everyone agrees as to whether Provence should be part of Occitania either, as we shall see at a later stage. A quick search on the Internet will yield countless examples of such maps however.

In an organised (and mainly literary) form, the language-based movement in Southern France dates back to the 1850s – making it one of the earliest such movements in the world. This characteristic makes Southern France an appropriate candidate to reach a certain understanding of language revitalisation (or at least to propose one interpretation of what it consists in): not only because it is respectably ancient, but also because much documentation exists recounting and analysing its historical developments and internal jolts. This book will draw extensively on this historical material in order to historicise the contemporary movement and to understand current issues in terms of legitimacy of language use.

The term 'organised' is key to understanding the approach adopted in this book. Language revitalisation is understood as the product of the actions (real or expected) of a social movement, a collective form of action that aims at transforming the world or part of it. At the core of social movements lies conflict, that is to say a particular relation to an identified opponent (Della Porta & Diani 2006: 20). Social movements, Della Porta and Diani further argue, are also structured by dense informal networks as well as by a 'distinct collective identity'. Instead of the latter however, I suggest that social movements share a common myth, one that guides the deeds of its members collectively and individually and provides framing for action and projection of a collective self.

In this book, the reader will encounter both the terms 'Provençal' and 'Occitan' to refer to what the revitalisation movement aims at revitalising. Historically the two words (as well as other such as *langue romane*–see Gardy 1991) have been used to refer to the myriad of speech varieties used in a territory that now constitutes the southern third of the French state (as well as small portions of Piedmont in Italy and Catalonia in what is now the Spanish State), an amalgam of territories gradually annexed by the Kingdom of France during the Middle Ages. The language-based movement in Southern France has been a shaping force in the local politics since the nineteenth century, although in different forms according to time and place. In the various struggles that affected the ebbs and flows of language and political life, the naming of the language as well as its representation on paper, its orthography, have consistently been at the fore. From Gascony to Provence, from Limousin to Languedoc, language thus comes under a variety of names and forms. Depending on how it is called, the language can refer to one or several territories and it can be written according to several standards, two of which dominate the possibility of choices in particular in Provence. Yet social actors also accommodate their usage according to a wealth of local circumstances, sometimes mixing them either consciously or unconsciously. In this book, Provençal refers to the variety of Occitan spoken in Provence and both terms are used interchangeably, except when I specifically address the issue of conflict. When referring to particular usages, this volume respects the terminological and orthographic choices of the people at stake.

1.5. POSITIONING

The work I present in this volume is a socially and historically situated interpretation. By interpretation I mean that I do not believe there is a reality of language revitalisation out there waiting to be discovered and described by objective interpreters – even less so that there is a situation to be diagnosed, and to which this work would propose a remedy (see Heller 2008: 249).

This book derives (albeit loosely) from a PhD thesis I defended at the University of Grenoble in 2010. The original text comprised an analysis of two revitalisation movements aiming at promoting Occitan in Provence and Scots in Scotland. I initially viewed both situations as neatly mirroring one another. Eventually, I came to realise they did not, at least not in the way I had expected. This book is interested in what it means to revitalise a language, and for the sake of clarity focuses on one of those movements only. Publications derived from the work conducted in Scotland have nonetheless been published in various outlets (see Costa 2009, 2010, 2015a).

I first became involved in the Occitan language movement in the Marseille area (in Provence) in 2001. At the time I was teaching Welsh at the University of Rennes in Brittany on a temporary contract, following an academic trajectory in Celtic Studies at the University of Wales in Aberystwyth. I too was drawn to Occitan by the pull of a medieval mystique, by the language of poets and heretics. At that time the language movement was being deeply reorganised under the new leadership of an extremely active and charismatic figure, the journalist and founder of the Occitan weekly *La Setmana*, David Grosclaude. Grosclaude is now the Vice-President of the Aquitaine administrative region, but his work then was fundamental in rejuvenating the language movement and in imposing a new agenda in line with the more dynamic revitalisation movements in Europe – in the Basque Country, in Wales, in Frisia, etc. This was also a time when language transmission in the home was becoming more prominent within the language movement, a shift from a previous emphasis on education. In Provence the movement was also benefiting from the involvement of a retired sea captain, Jean Saubrement, whose role was instrumental in mobilising new energies around the Provençal project.

By 2003 I had moved to Provence and become a teacher of Occitan in secondary public education, as well as the editor of the local Institut d'Estudis Occitans (IEO) internal newsletter for the Marseille area. In 2004 I was sent to teach the language in four secondary schools in the Drôme region in Northern Provence, eighty miles north of Marseille. In 2006 the opportunity to work at a research centre in education in Lyon presented itself and I availed myself of it. But the three years of teaching Occitan were decisive in terms of formulating research questions: what was it that the pupils (aged ten to fifteen) who chose to learn that language on a purely voluntary basis were looking for? More generally, the question became: what are people looking for when they say they want to defend, promote or revive a language?

At that time, the conflict between mainstream language advocates who believed in the existence of one language across the entire South of France split between several dialects and another, newer group that viewed Provençal as a separate language was becoming rife. The issue was growing extremely sensitive, in particular in the field of education. To give but one example, while I was writing my PhD dissertation a teacher of Occitan in Provence was denounced to the academic authorities by the Provençal-as-a-separate-language group for displaying the (alleged) pro-independence Occitan flag on the website of his school. An atmosphere of libel and smear was developing, amidst violent discourses in the media and on the fast-growing Internet. The language issue was clearly not only language, but about defining and imposing legitimate norms and forms of knowledge. This conflict and its consequences are at the centre of this book.

1.6. CRITICAL SOCIOLINGUISTICS

> S[tudent]: [My supervisor] always says: 'Student, you need a framework'
> P[rofessor]: Maybe your supervisor is in the business of selling pictures! It's true that frames are nice for showing: gilded, white, carved, baroque, aluminum, etc. But have you ever met a painter who began his masterpiece by first choosing the frame? That would be odd, wouldn't it? (Latour 2005: 143)

What follows is not a framework *per se*. I wish first to trace the intellectual genealogy of my work, and second to introduce some of the overarching questions that have informed my investigations and some of the notions that the reader will need to understand them.

Two very different bodies of work inspired that teaching period and the early years of my doctoral research. Language endangerment was one of them; the (unconnected) critical work of Deborah Cameron, Robert Lafont and Pierre Bourdieu was another. The issue of language endangerment manifested itself through *Vanishing voices* (Nettle & Romaine, 2000), a volume that sought to draw attention to the threats to global linguistic diversity by linking those issues to questions of biodiversity endangerment. But the way an issue is constructed as a problem also constrains the answers provided to that question. The only answer that could be given to the question asked by Nettle and Romaine was: what can be done? A most unsatisfactory answer to the former teacher of languages, who knows very well what can be done: get pupils to speak the language. But my pupils would not, however much they were capable of doing so. Neither did language advocates on many occasions, even when they could. 'Language revitalisation' was clearly not just about getting people to talk in a language, it was about understanding why people were doing it, what they got out of it, and how it framed their actions.

Many of the practices that fall under the heading of language revitalisation could be characterised as 'verbal hygiene', to use a term Deborah Cameron (1995) proposed in her acclaimed eponymous book. Verbal hygiene comprises judgements on language use as well as actions to transform language for one reason or another. It 'comes into being whenever people reflect in a critical (in the sense of "evaluative") way' (Cameron 1995: 9). Language revitalisation is, consequently, about norms and values. More precisely it is about changing existing norms and replacing them with new ones. It entails defining norms of action and knowledge and the hierarchies that sustain them. Language revitalisation is therefore not so much about language as about society and the sphere of the social (Cameron 1995: 11).

Robert Lafont was an Occitan sociolinguist, who taught at the University of Montpellier. In the 1960s and 1970s, together with Valencian and Catalan sociolinguists, he developed a brand of sociolinguistics that focused on diglossia as conflict (Gardy & Lafont 1981). Lafont's work pitted itself in opposition to that of Joshua Fishman in that respect, and labelled Fishman's functional approach 'a screen hiding the actual conflict within society' (Lafont 1997: 94). Lafont was also instrumental in problematising the role of the sociolinguist in the analysis of conflicts. In order not to adhere to the dominant schema of power and consequently give dominants further weapons to sustain their action, sociolinguists should 'affirm their denouncing implication in the process' (Lafont 1997: 94). Yet their action should remain sociolinguistic (i.e. scientific), in that their analysis 'constructs and deconstructs the objectivity of the object, and concomitantly objectifies the sociolinguist as such' (Lafont 1997: 95). Lafont (1984) thus insists that the objective of sociolinguistic research is the uncovering and analysis of representations and ideologies in order to liberate condemned voices (Lafont 1971).

Bourdieu was perhaps the most influential source of all, in particular his 1980 article entitled 'Identity and representation: Elements for a critical reflection on the idea of region' (translated in Bourdieu 1991b: 220–8). The idea of a struggle over categorisations proved particularly potent to analyse the discourses and actions of language revitalisation movements. As those ideas are developed throughout the text, I expand no further here.

Overall this books finds itself at home in critical sociolinguistics. Following Monica Heller:

> [d]oing critique means discovering how [processes of categorization, selection and legitimization] work in the specific sites and specific moments we attend to. It means getting underneath why people get excited about things in order to figure out what is at stake for them, and why (whether or not they are aware of it themselves). It means identifying what resources are circulating, what resources people are competing for, as well as the conditions that make them available and valuable; it means figuring out how their distribution is organized and how it works, and how people position themselves with respect to them; and it means figuring out what the consequences of those processes are, for whom, in terms of who gets to control access to resources and who gets to assign them value. (Heller 2011: 39)

The implications of this project for language revitalisation are paramount. Such processes, I will argue, are primarily about identifying linguistic elements that will (and can) count as resources, and about regimenting their circulation and the market conditions that guarantee their sustained value. Doing critique, in the case of this study, means paying attention to how language is constructed as a resource, by whom and how this construction becomes the object of conflict. Conflict can take two different forms: against a dominant Other outwith the language movement; and as part of the struggle for hegemony within the movement. It is, however, always a component of the struggle to establish what counts as legitimate language.

Finally, and although I have sought to 'make the familiar strange, the exotic quotidian' (Clifford 1986: 2), this is not an ethnography of language revitalisation in Provence, at least not in the traditional sense of the term. There are two main reasons to this. First, due mostly to lack of funds, I was unable to spend the sufficient amount of time required for a full-scale ethnographic description after I had moved to Lyon to work on my dissertation. Second, my concern in this book is primarily with understanding the notion of language revitalisation, for which I could find no satisfactory account. The first part of the book is therefore largely a theoretical discussion. What I account for in the second and third parts of the book is the product of ten years (2002–2012) of systematic as well as unsystematic observations in 'the field', as a language advocate, as a teacher and as a scholar in order to make the theoretical observations of the first part more explicit. This work involved my participation in a wide array of language-based activities, often in all three capacities: in summer schools, evening classes (both as student and teacher), in meetings, in demonstrations, in informal conversations and in education. For the purpose of his volume I focused on two main areas: language advocacy movements, in particular the Institut d'Estudis Occitans (IEO, Institute for Occitan Studies, one of the two main historical movements), and education (as a teacher and as a researcher). While in the field as a researcher, I also conducted interviews, some of which are reproduced in the final two chapters. But I usually limited formal interviews to a minimum, bearing in mind Dell Hymes's (1981: 84) advice that 'some social research seems incredibly to assume that what there is to find out can be found out by asking'. Finally, I also heavily relied on written documentation, historical or current. I owe much of my historical documentation to the generosity of long-standing language advocates. I collected other documents at various cultural or political events (the distinction is important to language advocates) across the entire South of France.

Two more notions need defining: discourse and ideology. Although grounded in the idea that social action is paramount to social explication, this book focuses on discourse. The contradiction is only apparent, as this book treats discourse as action, as a mode of acting in and upon the world (Bourdieu 1991b). One speaks and writes not only to exchange views and ideas, but also and perhaps primarily to convince, to argue, to bring about change, to position oneself with respect to others, to classify and hierarchise the world, etc. Ideology, on the other hand, is in this text no longer the central notion it was in the original dissertation. It pervades the entire book but its use felt less necessary, perhaps because it has become so overused of late in sociolinguistics and linguistic anthropology that it has lost some of its force.

Ideologies are bodies of ideas (social constructions) that legitimise the particular institutions of a given society (Duchêne 2008). They are 'representational and collective', 'structuring and structured, 'discursive' and they 'bring out interests arising from relations of power, of domination and of economic and political issues' (Duchêne 2008: 27).

I mostly follow Bourdieu and Eagleton (1991) when he argues against the fuzziness of the term 'ideology' and in its stead substitutes such terms as 'symbolic domination'. But when the term is used in this book, it follows the definition of the sociologist and historian Benjamin Halpern. Ideologies, Halpern (1961: 136) writes, 'procure advantages for specific social positions and [...] segregate and consolidate competing groups around rival ideas'. Language ideologies thus 'represent the perception of language and discourse that is constructed in the interest of specific social or cultural groups' (Kroskrity 2000: 8).

Two main ideologies pervade the entire movement: the ideology of the standard, and what Lafont (1997: 114) calls a 'revivalist ideology of the redeeming text'. The former relates to practices that justify and maintain a certain idea of what Occitan is supposed to look and sound like; the latter to the centrality of the written word in the legitimation process of the entire movement: its reliance, in other words, on a discourse of long-standing literary tradition dating back to the Middle Ages. A good example is provided by the quotation from Robert Lafont himself above.

In this book, I am also particularly concerned with what I term, following Malinowski (1954), the charter myth of the language revitalisation movement in Provence – that is to say, the origin myth legitimising the existence and actions of the very movement and of the group that the movement acts on behalf of. Myth, in this sense, is more than just a narrative: it is 'ideology in narrative form' (Lincoln 2000: 141).

1.7. Volume outline

The following chapters are divided into three main parts. Part 1 focuses on revitalisation as a theoretical and empirical object of scholarly discussion. The main objective is to make explicit the genealogies that constrain current scholarly conversations on language revitalisation and to challenge their main tenets. Although most works on the topic tend to adopt a diagnosis/remedy approach to processes they construe as inherently problematic, in that part I argue that revitalisation needs to be problematised in such a way as to ask questions concerning what social actors are doing when they engage in such activities. Genealogies of notions of endangerment and revitalisation thus serve to show how those notions are historically situated social constructs, as much part of the legacy of colonisation and modernity as the processes they seek to describe. This approach allows re-placing language revitalisation within a wider class of social processes, identified in cultural anthropology as nativisms or revitalisation movements. Even though those have existed throughout human history, only since the eighteenth or nineteenth centuries have they taken the form of *language* revitalisation. The question then becomes: why language, and what is at stake? I define language revitalisation as primarily a struggle over classifications centred on language, thus focusing on the inherently conflictive nature of those movements.

Parts 2 and 3 focus on language revitalisation as a form of conflict – first with a group which the revitalisation movement construes as dominant, enabling itself to construct itself as a minority, thus narrating contact as conflict. I argue that the aim of revitalisation movements is to renegotiate the unequal terms of this contact, but this entails much groupness work, the constitution of who counts as a legitimate participant in the minority group. I borrow this term from the sociologist Rogers Brubaker (2002), implying that groups are never pre-constituted entities but always constructions in the making:

> By *invoking* groups, [social actors] seek to *evoke* them, summon them, call them into being. Their categories are *for doing* — designed to stir, summon, justify, mobilize, kindle and energize. (Brubaker 2002: 166, emphasis in the original)

Language is, in this respect, a terrain upon which different types of social issues are constructed and contested, and upon which positions in society are established, instituted or made irrelevant.

Second, I envisage conflict within the group, arguing against Kroskrity (2009) not only that it is probably impossible to resolve internal disputes, but also that this might not be our role as linguists or anthropologists. Part 2 is therefore about answering the questions: what is at stake in the revitalisation of Occitan, and for whom? It is also about exploring hypotheses as to why some people choose to express social concerns and anxieties through language rather than, say, religion, or political institutions. Part 3 analyses a different type of conflict, entailed by the necessity of language revitalisation movements to reshape language in a modern fashion according to ideologies of nation states. In turn this necessity (essential to address the governments from whom they seek recognition) generates changes in terms of what constitutes legitimate knowledge over language, and legitimate language. Revitalisation movements find themselves in a paradoxical situation: on the one hand they need traditional speakers and children in order to sustain their claim to legitimacy, yet language advocates find themselves at odds with both. Consequently, Part 3 seeks to answer the question: how does language revitalisation generate groupness, and how do social actors address the question of legitimate language and speaker, one which is central to the understanding of all such movements? In chapters 10 and 11 I therefore look at two necessary yet ambiguous categories of social actors: traditional speakers and children.

REVITALISING

2

LANGUAGE REVITALISATION: A GENEALOGY

> The salvage paradigm, reflecting a desire to
> rescue 'authenticity' out of destructive
> historical change, is alive and well.
>
> James Clifford (1987)

2.1. INTRODUCTION: INVESTIGATING LANGUAGE REVITALISATION

Over the course of the past twenty-five years, the term 'language revitalisation', usually in conjunction with 'language endangerment', has become ubiquitous in the academic disciplines of linguistics, sociolinguistics and linguistic anthropology. Its ambiguous nature can be inferred both from its generally poor definition and conceptualisation among those who use it, as well as in the observation that it refers as much to a type of practice among language advocates as to an object of academic attention. The recent coinage of the term and its constitution as a field of discussion and investigation throughout the world should however raise a number of questions as to what revitalisation effectively is, and what it is about. Is it not, indeed, one of those social problems smuggled into the social sciences, a preconstructed problem that has made its way (back) into our disciplines (Bourdieu & Wacquant 1992), one we fail to understand for lack of a real problematisation of what the term refers to? Following Bourdieu and Wacquant:

> to avoid becoming the object of the problems that you take as your objects, you must retrace the history of the *emergence* of these problems, of their progressive constitution, i.e., of the collective work, oftentimes accomplished through competition and struggle, that proved necessary to make such and such issues to be known and recognized […] as *legitimate problems*, problems that are avowable, publishable, public, official. (Bourdieu & Wacquant 1992: 238)

In other words, to begin our journey into so-called revitalisation processes we must understand the intellectual fields from which this and afferent notions emerged, and the positions its proponents occupied (Brubaker 2004b: 29). The term 'language revitalisation' was imposed in the 1990s, at the expense of other terms such as 'reversing language shift', proposed around the same time (Fishman 1991), 'language revival' or 'renaissance' which had been used since the nineteenth century, to give but a few examples. Since then, the literature on the topic has been plentiful, and a few classics have emerged (Grenoble & Whaley 1998a, 2006; Reyhner et al. 1999; Hinton & Hale 2001; to name but a few; Tsunoda 2006). As will become apparent in this chapter, the term as well as the problem it seeks to encapsulate was indeed smuggled into linguistics and sociolinguistics from social struggles. Although the aim of this book is not to dispute the legitimacy of those struggles, it claims, however, that this ancestry has led us to misrepresent the situations which science originally purported to describe and explain.

The genealogy of an academic category is also a way of understanding how and why, among all the potential ways to formulate an object of enquiry and action, a particular one was chosen. Indeed, when trying to ascertain whether Marxism was a science, Michel Foucault asked:

> The question or questions that have to be asked are: 'What type of knowledge are you trying to disqualify when you say that you are a science? What speaking subject, what discursive subject, what subject of experience and knowledge are you trying to minorize when you begin to say: 'I speak this discourse, I am speaking a scientific discourse, and I am a scientist?' (Foucault 2003: 10)

Similar questions need to be asked regarding language revitalisation as a scientific undertaking and field of study. The type of knowledge produced on language revivals is embedded in a discourse of loss and necessary recuperation, enshrined in a moral imperative (Cameron 2007) that to an extent prevents questioning the actions undertaken to that effect in ways other than: 'Is this an efficient way to go about things?' But to question the knowledge produced on language revitalisation movements is to avail oneself of the opportunity to ask new questions, without assuming that 'languages should be saved', or even that 'something must be done'. Perhaps language is in fact only secondary in the processes at stake, as Monica Heller (2004) suggests. It might also be so that the knowledge produced is detrimental to the groups who undertake such social actions as implied by language revitalisation, in the sense that knowledge produces positions of expertise and power that might entail unwanted consequences for various types of people (e.g. Muehlmann 2008).

A number of good introductory texts to language endangerment exist, in particular Tsunoda (2006) or Mufwene (2004). The aim of this chapter is thus to circumscribe and question the academic fields in which the conversation on 'language revitalisation' occurs, how it occurs, how it is mobilised, and how it became the dominant lens through which issues certain social processes have come to be considered and analysed. This chapter examines past and current research, and continues with a discussion of the main critiques this domain has attracted.

2.2. THE PRECURSORS: ANTIQUARIANS AND FRENCH REVOLUTIONARIES

The current discourses on revitalisation are closely associated with another set of distinct works and ideas, concerned with language death – the direct intellectual antecedent of language endangerment, in particular through the work of Nancy Dorian (1981). Although it has long been noted that so-called 'patois' or 'dialects' were fast disappearing, a state of fact oft lamented or celebrated (e.g. Dauzat 1938), the collective reformulation of this set of processes as endangerment is a relatively recent undertaking. Crucially, studies of endangerment and subsequently revitalisation are more likely to aim at redressing what they see as a moral wrong than previous documentary works on language death or attrition in linguistics or in anthropology.

The origins of our object of investigation can be traced back to the beginnings of antiquarianism, philology and dialectology in Europe, and later of anthropology in the United States. During several centuries, from the second half of the sixteenth century, antiquarians in Western Europe sought to combine nostalgia for a vanishing past and a commitment to progress (Bauman & Briggs 2003: 72). They documented what was about to become extinct, and collected fragments from the past to maintain its existence in the present. Collecting dialect words became fashionable in the second part of the eighteenth century and was part of a wider process of collecting elements from the past or the present. Vernaculars acquired newfound legitimacy, and the role of antiquarians was instrumental in this respect. In eighteenth century Wales for instance, the antiquarian Iolo Morganwg:

> was fascinated by words and he collected them wherever he went. He could not go for a stroll without jotting down unfamiliar words and phrases, and nothing interested him more than peculiarities, oddities, 'barbarisms', antiquated forms and the like. (Crowe 2005: 316)

Political powers were soon to follow suit, and the first national linguistic and social survey of language and language use can probably be traced back to the aftermath of the French Revolution when the revolutionary government, in the guise of Abbé Grégoire, commissioned a survey of the various vernaculars used in the country (Certeau et al. 1975). While the aim was to gather documentation in order to subsequently eradicate the multiplicity of languages that no longer befitted a people supposed to be one and indivisible, in effect it provided the impetus for the study and description of the various linguistic forms used in France – an encouragement emulated throughout the nineteenth and twentieth centuries by dialectologists (Bergounioux 1984, 1989, 1992; Merle 2010) who mapped dialectal variation in the entire French territory. Dialectologists were not interested in language maintenance; instead they sought to document a vanishing world.

2.3. NORTH AMERICAN SCHOLARSHIP: ANTHROPOLOGY AND SOCIOLINGUISTICS

The current academic interest in the preservation of what now gets construed as language diversity stems more directly from a more recent tradition, the long-standing project in North American anthropology to document and salvage indigenous languages – that is, writing them down and recording them for eternity, while this was still possible. Those dynamics are very much at play within the anthropological and sociolinguistic approaches to language endangerment, in at least two different ways: first to warrant the necessity for documentation and archiving, and second in the idea that language-based movements are a reaction to a threat, a form of awareness rather than, say, a way to negotiate a possible future with more powerful others.

Work on language endangerment and revitalisation continues in different ways the work of Boas and, later, of Sapir and Whorf (Fishman 1982b; Woodbury 2011) – or more generally of salvage anthropology see Gruber 1970; Clifford 1987. Although originally intended to fight the type of racism present in early twentieth-century North America, one ambiguity of the salvage paradigm also resides in how it views what it collects and assembles as essential to the future of anthropology itself, as a discipline. In a different context, in the 1970s, Lévi-Strauss (1972: 96) thus viewed the demise of traditional societies as heralding doom for the future of anthropology, another forerunner of similar discourses in contemporary linguistics.

The rationale for language description was initially motivated by the disappearance of the frontier in Western America. In early twentieth-century anthropology, as currently in several sectors of linguistics, similar dynamics were at play: they rested upon the Boasian premise that what is uniquely human is diversity and variability (Bauman & Briggs 2003 chapter 8). In the words of the American anthropologist Jacob Gruber:

> the needs of salvage then [in the early twentieth century], so readily recognized through an awareness of a savage vanishing on the disappearing frontier of an advancing civilization, set the tone and the method for much that was anthropology in the earlier years of its prosecution as a self-conscious discipline. (Gruber 1970: 1297)

The emphasis was then on recording what could still be recorded for posterity, a move initiated well before the emergence of the endangerment paradigm. For example, in *The study of man* (1898), the British biologist and anthropologist Alfred C. Haddon remarked:

> Now is the time to record. An infinitude has been irrevocably lost, a very great deal is now rapidly disappearing; thanks to colonisation, trade and missionary enterprise, the change that has come over the uttermost parts of the world during the last fifty years is almost incredible. (Haddon 1898: xxxiii)

Modernity and museification go hand in hand (Anderson 1983), embedded in a particular conception of time as a series of linear and unique occurrences of events. In the words of James Clifford (1987: 122), this particular mode of representation of time produces '[e]ndless imaginary redemptions (religious, pastoral, retro/nostalgic) [...]; archives, museums and collections preserve (construct) an authentic past'. By attempting to rescue authenticity, it also defines what can count as authentic, and what cannot. Perversely however, the creation of a past through documentation and archiving further deprives the bearers of the lives under scrutiny to produce their own representations of self:

> [w]hat's *different* about peoples [i.e. marginal groups seen as the object of salvation] seen to be moving out of 'tradition' into 'the modern world'

remains tied to inherited structures that either resist or yield to the new but cannot *produce* it. (Clifford 1987: 122)

Even though this argument might not hold with respect to European language revival movements, since after all the advocacy movements originate not outwith but within the group and among speakers or descendants of speakers, this caveat must be born in mind all the same. In a way, as Native American voices were silenced, they could finally become an object of study – as if Native American simultane-ously ceased to be dangerous through a mode of representation that portrayed them as endangered. They became travellers on the ineluctable path to modernity and could therefore be inserted into its grand narrative. In other words, the discipline of anthropology both addresses the wrongs of colonialism and progresses in its wake, illustrating Foucault's (2003) claim that the relation between knowing and silencing is at best ambiguous.

Similar concerns for language diversity and variation are found in the type of sociolinguistics also known as sociology of language, another major source in the formation of the discourse on endangerment and revitalisation. The popular historians Peter Berresford Ellis & Seumas Mac a'Ghobhainn (1971) are often cited as an early reference to the problematisation of what they term 'language revival'. Their concern was the preservation and promotion of Celtic languages, an ongo-ing preoccupation in the western fringe of Europe since the 1880s at least. The book recounts a number of language revivals throughout the world, in the Faroes, Norway, Korea and even medieval England, to provide examples that language advocates in the Celtic fringe could follow. Their ambition is however not solely based on language reclamation, but also on a social programme: 'The basis of language restoration is the reconstruction of a healthy community environment and a prime concern for the health, welfare and integrity of the individual human being' (Ellis & Mac a'Ghobhainn 1971: 7).

The sociolinguistic tradition that has enjoyed most popularity, however, grew from the work of Joshua Fishman, a sociologist of language whose main interest rested in the preservation of Yiddish in North American Jewish communities. Sociolinguistics originates, to some extent, in anthropology (Shuy 2003). It thus comes as no surprise that the discipline's most important contribution to the field of language endangerment and revitalisation, Joshua Fishman's early work on language maintenance (1964) and his later (1991, 2001) work on reversing language shift (or RLS) should be inspired by the writings of Benjamin Lee Whorf. Indeed, Whorf was himself credited by Fishman (1982b) with having given rise to works on language preservation. Fishman considers that a third type of Whorfianism (after linguistic relativity and determinism) consists in championing linguistic diversity for the benefit of all mankind. RLS is defined broadly as 'the theory and practice of assistance to speech communities whose native languages are threatened because their intergenerational continuity is proceeding negatively, with fewer and fewer users […] or uses every generation' (Fishman 1991: 1). One of Fishman's best known and most cited contribution is perhaps his eight-stage grid devised to measure endangerment and revitalisation (Fishman 1991: 395). In this perspective, RLS is never questioned: it finds its internal justification in the need some social actors might feel to engage with it as an undertaking. In this perspective identity is central. In Fishman's own words:

> The premises that Xmen[1] are not Ymen and that Xish culture (daily and life-cycle observances, distinctive artifacts, beliefs and values, exemplary literature, art, music, dance etc.) is not Yish culture must not be skipped over, no more than the premises that Xish culture is worth maintaining. (Fishman 1991: 394)

Despite its terminology, Fishman's work on RLS has now been fully integrated into the bulk of work on language revitalisation, as a quick glance at reference sections in linguistics works in the endangerment/revitalisation paradigm will attest. In more recent publications he used the term 'language revitalisation' himself (Fishman 1996). Both bodies of work are rooted in a structural functional approach to language, one that focuses on 'the functional differentiation of languages in bilingual communities' (Martin-Jones 1989: 106) rather than on the individual and on the micro-level of the interactional order. The notion of diglossia is particularly important in this tradition, and grasped at a societal level serves as an explanatory factor for status differences among languages.

Because of the focus of this volume on the Occitan language movement, it is worth noting that Fishman's earlier work on diglossia was instrumental in generating an important body of sociolinguistic work on that topic as well as one reversing diglossia in Catalonia and Occitania. However, deeming Fishman's model too consensual, the Catalan and Occitan schools of sociolinguistics (Aracil 1965; Lafont 1971) which emerged in the 1960s and 1970s insisted on the necessarily conflictive nature of language contact. This particular brand of sociolinguistics emerged at a particular historical moment when Catalonia was still under Franco's rule, and when the Occitan South of France was still largely Occitan-speaking. The sociolinguists in that school, who were trained primarily in sociology (at least in Catalonia and Valencia) point out that the only two possible outcomes of such processes where one of the languages is minorised are substitution on the one hand and normalisation on the other. Substitution (or assimilation) bears much resemblance to processes elsewhere described as language death, while normalisation entails a process of language standardisation as well as of imposition of the minorised language as the normal language of communication in all domains of public life (Boyer 1991: chapter 1). What Lafont (1984) calls *retrousser la diglossie* ('reversing diglossia') in effect bears much in common with Fishman's later RLS, save perhaps for the fact that the focus is not on language but on the structural conditions that gave rise to diglossia. The work of Catalan and Occitan sociolinguists remains little known outwith its original geographic domain, owing perhaps to its lack of translation

---

[1] Fishman calls speakers of any minority language Xmen (i.e. speakers of language X), and speakers of a dominant language (Y) Ymen.

from Catalan, Occitan or French into English. It is nevertheless worth mentioning this particular tradition for it predates the discourses of 'language endangerment' stemming from linguistics that I will analyse in the next section. It differs significantly on at least one account: its focus was indeed not so much on the language itself as on the necessity to give its speakers a voice in a public sphere (a space which is often left undefined). Robert Lafont thus wrote:

> *On signalera, pour ce qu'elle peut apporter à une psychosociologie des contacts entre langues, la visée générale de [la] reconquête [occitane] : non pas tant reconquérir l'occitanophonie pour elle-même que libérer une parole condamnée socialement.*

> Let us mention, for what it may contribute to a psychosociology of language contacts, the overall aim of [the Occitan] reconquest: not so much to reconquer Occitan speech practices for themselves as to free a socially condemned voice. (Lafont, 1971: 99)

The endangerment and revitalisation discourse, on the other hand, appears to be more centred on language and on politics of identity.

2.4. DESCRIPTIVE LINGUISTICS AND LANGUAGE ENDANGERMENT

It is indeed from linguistics that the bulk of contemporary discourses on language endangerment and revitalisation stems. The stakes for linguistics were perhaps higher than for other disciplines, in the sense that language endangerment provided it with a social outcome. Although I am not claiming that the endangerment discourse was engineered within linguistics specifically to serve a particular agenda, over the past twenty-five years issues of language endangerment and preservation have become an essential part of the discipline.

Three high-stakes areas can perhaps be identified: first, language diversity is the raw matter of descriptive of documentary linguistics (Maffi 2000). Its preservation, as emphasised by certain scholars (Krauss 1992; Crystal 2000), should be of immediate concern to the entire profession. Linguists working on such languages also emphasise the need to understand those particular situations in order to better comprehend the type of data they are working with, hence the need to classify speakers-as-informants according to fluency and the type of data they generate (Grinevald 2003; Bert & Grinevald 2010; Grinevald & Bert 2011). Second, language documentation has become (or at least became in the 2000s) an important source of funding for linguistics projects through such documentation programmes as initiated by the Volkswagen Foundation or the Hans Rausing Endangered Languages Project (HRELP). Finally, documentation (and revitalisation) are important ways of making linguistics relevant socially, and language endangerment has certainly been given more media coverage in the past years than any other aspect of linguistics work (Cameron 2007), aside perhaps from bilingualism studies. Coffee table books such as Austin (2008) or popular volumes such as Harrison (2010) also bear testimony to this trend, which in a context where academic institutions are asked to contribute to 'knowledge exchange', as dissemination has come to be called in UK institutions, is not to be overlooked.

The three main tenets of the endangerment and revitalisation discourse can in fact be summarised in the following way: language loss, death or endangerment is measurable, it is important and increasing, and it can be countered. While the latter element does not produce consensus among linguists, it remains an important focus for many linguists (see Grenoble & Whaley 2006 for an example of how linguists may contribute to such processes).

The direct antecedent of the current discourse on language revitalisation as it emerged from documentary linguistics, lies in effect in the work on language death that materialises in its present form in the mid-twentieth century with Morris Swadesh's work on language obsolescence. In a seminal (1948) paper entitled 'Sociologic Notes on Obsolescent Languages', he laid down the foundations for the problematisation of the processes leading to language death throughout history:

> In recent centuries, the conquest and colonization of new lands by European powers eventually resulted in the loss of hundreds of languages. The process is still continuing, particularly in the Americas. As a result, it is possible to observe communities whose original speech is even now in the process of disappearance, and to gain thereby an insight into the similar events that have occurred in the past. Since no serious study has yet been made of this phenomenon, the present paper attempts, by means of brief statements on a series of known cases, to indicate some of its features. (Swadesh 1948: 226)

Swadesh concluded his study by suggesting that linguistic obsolescence ought to be studied in the context of conflict, combining a linguistic and sociological approach, in particular through the collection of 'autobiographies and individual case studies' (Swadesh 1948: 234). His primary interest, however, rested in the effects of attrition on linguistic structure.

This type of work was thus initially structured around an understanding of the disappearance of languages as the result of language contact, as well as around the social conditions leading to that state of affairs. Whether the linguist ought to intervene or not was not yet an issue, and even thirty years later it remained outwith the scope of a linguist such as Nancy Dorian, whose influence was to prove decisive on the formation of the field of language endangerment. In 1981 she wrote:

> Extinction is a common enough phenomenon in the history of the world's languages [...] Linguistic extinction, or 'language death' to give it a simpler and more metaphorical name, is to be found under way currently in virtually every part of the world. (Dorian 1981: 1)

Yet Dorian, like Swadesh, soon noted that what she called 'language death' was still a poorly understood process, mostly for ideological reasons that prevented the languages at stake to be given the importance afforded to so-called full languages:

> Although extinction may be a common linguistic phenomenon, it has not
> been well studied [...] One common reason for neglect of the extinction
> process in language was the reluctance of the linguist or anthropologist to
> work with imperfect speakers of a language, who were also, by implication,
> imperfect representatives of the cultural group in question. Most
> researchers have had a natural desire to capture the most unadulterated
> picture possible of less well known cultures, and this has led to the choice
> of informants whose command of the threatened language was the fullest
> available – and to avoidance of imperfect speakers [...] My own practice
> was the same at the onset, but from 1972 I found myself seeking out
> imperfect speakers whom I had eliminated from my regular informant
> pool in 1963–70 (Dorian 1981: 3)

Dorian therefore suggested that linguistics needed to depart from its traditional concern for 'Non mobile, Older, Rural Males' (NORMS) (Chambers & Trudgill 1980) in order to describe and understand language obsolescence or attrition and language death as contact phenomena.

Dorian's pioneering work in Scotland laid the foundations for the emergence of studies on language death and obsolescence as an interdisciplinary field, and her (1989b) edited volume brings together, for the first time, studies in descriptive linguistics (e.g. Campbell & Muntzel 1989), linguistic anthropology (Gal 1989b; e.g. Hill 1989) and sociolinguistics (e.g. Romaine 1989). In this volume Dorian formalises the use of the term 'language death' but she remains conscious of its inherent limitations: 'I had published a book in a subfield [...] which had come to be known (for better of for worse) as "language death"' (Dorian 1989a: p. x), she writes about her 1981 volume. Dorian also mentions uncertainties regarding the terminology to be used in the field, including in reference to such notions as 'full fluency', 'extinction', and 'semi-speakers'. Importantly however, the contexts analysed are located in Europe as well as in the Americas, Africa and Australia. In other words, a wide variety of contexts were subsumed under the term 'obsolescence' (itself revolving around the idea of a 'tip' beyond which transmission is no longer effective), and transcended local scientific classifications as 'indigenous languages' in the Americas, 'minority languages' in Europe, etc., paving the way for the future use of the 'language endangerment' terminology worldwide. Similarly, when Robins & Uhlenbeck (1991) published a volume entitled *Endangered languages* they addressed contexts in the Americas, Australia and Asia (but the volume leaves aside Europe, the Arab world and Africa).

But the starting point of the academic debate on endangered languages as we know it now rests in Latin America. In 1991, a group of linguists working in Central America and Mexico proposed a panel at the Linguistic Society of America (LSA) annual meeting to address what they had come to view as worrying, namely the gradual disappearance of the very languages they had been studying for years. Interestingly, this panel was presented as an extra (evening) event, not during the official conference time – indicating that the LSA viewed the issue simultaneously as both timely and pressing, and as falling outside the normal scope of its activities as a scientific organisation.

The date of the panel was by no means coincidental: it took place in the run up to the celebrations of the 500 years of the so-called discovery of the Americas by Christopher Columbus, a celebration that many indigenous organisations throughout the continent had come to view with resentment. In that context, the linguists involved in the 1991 panel had been made aware of this discontent, and the concerns they voiced at the LSA meeting thus expressed both their own concerns and those of the communities where they were conducting fieldwork.[2]

The LSA panel translated into a series of short papers entitled 'Endangered languages' and published the following year in *Language* (Hale et al. 1992).[3] The term 'endangered languages' suggests leaving the realm of metaphor (language death) for one of analogy, implying that languages are comparable to living species, and should be treated on a par with them when it comes to protecting what gets to be construed as diversity, linguistic or biological. This series of papers laid the foundations for how language endangerment is viewed in the field to this day: a quantifiable process, one with clear parallels in biological diversity, and a process with moral implications and repercussions.

The idea that endangerment is quantifiable is provided in the article through a number of figures regarding the current rate of endangerment. Those figures are still used today in many academic papers and media discourses on language endangerment. Before asking what linguists should do to avert such a gloomy future, Krauss (1992: 7) writes: 'Therefore, I consider a plausible calculation that – at the rate that things are going – the coming century will see the doom of 90% of mankind's language'.

The article also introduces the biological metaphor of endangerment and loss, so often used in media discourse today:

> It is part of a much larger process of LOSS OF CULTURAL AND INTELLECTUAL DIVERSITY in which politically dominant languages and cultures simply overwhelm indigenous local languages and cultures, placing them in a condition which can only be described as embattled. The process is not unrelated to the simultaneous loss of diversity in the zoological and botanical worlds. An ecological analogy is not altogether inappropriate. (Hale 1992: 1 emphasis in the original)

---

[2] This section owes much to conversations with Colette Grinevald (then Colette Craig), one of the LSA panel organisers, for this information (see also Grinevald & Costa 2010). Note also that the LSA presentation came after several years of intense debate around the English-only movement in the United States, which threatened the already weak position of indigenous languages there, in particular in education. The importance of the descriptive paradigm within linguistics departments, and its emergence on the public scene, should also be read within the context of the debates within the field of linguistics between Chomskyans and non-Chomskyans, a task which, unfortunately lies beyond the scope of this study.

[3] The concern expressed during the LSA meeting focused on the Americas, but in Europe similar dynamics were at play when the Council of Europe adopted the European Charter for Regional or Minority Languages, which aimed at protecting Europe's linguistic diversity. Member states were subsequently invited to sign it and to ratify it, a move yet to be completed by such countries as France, Italy, Greece or Turkey.

Krauss himself assumes that the term 'language endangerment' 'is presumably drawn from biological usage' (Krauss 1992: 4), and compares at length the levels of endangerment of birds and mammals to those of languages:

> Thus 7.4% of mammals and 2.7% of birds are endangered or threatened. I should add that in both cases the majority are only 'threatened' and not 'endangered'. Interestingly, however, for political and economic reasons it is difficult to get an animal officially listed, and Alaskan biologists I've talked to concur that in view of this underlisting, especially for birds, the total of endangered or threatened mammals may be 10%, and birds 5%.
>
> Why is there so much more concern over this relatively mild threat to the world's biological diversity than over the far worse threat to its linguistic diversity, and why are we linguists so much quieter about it than biologists? (Krauss 1992: 4)

This leads him to conclude by directly comparing the demise of language with the disappearance of animal species:

> Surely, just as the extinction of any animal species diminishes our world, so does the extinction of any language. Surely we linguists know, and the general public can sense, that any language is a supreme achievement of a uniquely human collective genius, as divine and endless a mystery as a living organism. Should we mourn the loss of Eyak or Ubykh any less than the loss of the panda or California condor? (Krauss 1992: 8)

Finally, the moral wrong aspect is achieved through a comparison with abstract principles of intellectual human life:

> Like most people who have done field work for thirty years or so, I have worked on languages which are now extinct, eight of them in my case, and I have studied, and continue to study, many languages which are seriously imperiled. My experience is far from unusual, and the testimony of fieldworkers alone would amply illustrate the extent of language loss in the world of the present era.
>
> It is reasonable, I suppose, to ask what difference it makes. On the one hand, one might say, language loss has been a reality throughout history; and on the other, the loss of a language is of no great moment either for science or for human intellectual life.
>
> I think, personally, that these ideas are wrong and that language loss is a serious matter. Or, more accurately, it is part of a process which is very serious. (Hale 1992: 1)

All the ideas expressed here were to be understood as a call to arms by linguists. They were to prove particularly potent in the next decade as they translated academically into works such as Nettle & Romaine's (2000) *Vanishing voices* or Harrison's (2007)

When languages die (see in particular his diagram on page 7, comparing the endangerment rates of languages, birds and mammals).

2.5. LANGUAGE REVITALISATION AND LINGUISTICS

What linguistics did however was to turn works on language endangerment into a field, with an identifiable label, common references, and to unite scholarship from various disciplines under its flagship. As a field it is premised upon the sense of urgency that was constructed through discourses of endangerment (Heller & Duchêne 2007), and on the idea that something can and must be done. As Nancy Hornberger, who has devoted a large part of her life to her work on education in Peru, writes:

> We start from the premise that Indigenous language revitalisation is worth doing, both for the sake of the speakers of the languages and for the ways of knowing and being that their languages encode and express. (Hornberger 2008: 1)

The link between endangerment discourses and revitalisation was made from the very start. Colette Craig discussed the new Sandinista government in Nicaragua's national plan to address indigenous issues (social and cultural) in the 1992 series of papers in *Language* (Craig 1992a). She was involved in the Rama Language and Culture Project (see also Craig 1992b), 'a rescue attempt for a language at a very advanced state in the process of extinction' (Craig 1992a: 18).[4] The project itself was deemed successful by the close-knit association of community members and linguists in a favourable constitutional context. As noted before, the *Language* paper included all the elements still summoned today when arguing in favour of language revitalisation – most saliently the biological metaphor of endangerment itself and well figures and rates of endangerment. Those later led the French linguist Claude Hagège (2000) to assert that a language was being lost every fortnight, dramatising the issue further, and linguists such as Dixon (1997) to call for linguistics to focus on the documentation on as many disappearing languages as possible – even to make this a compulsory task for every self-respecting linguist.

The work of linguists was instrumental in raising awareness regarding what was over time constructed as a global issue, and linguists succeeded in creating a mythology that could be appropriated by the media: in other words linguistics not only prompted local efforts to reverse language shift, it generated interest and enthusiasm worldwide through a series of studies on the forms of human knowledge that would, according to that discourse, be lost with the death of languages (Evans 2009; see Harrison 2007). In the elaboration of an overall narrative of endangerment and revitalisation the figure of the 'last speaker' was paramount. Photos of last speakers (such as that of Ned Maddrell, the last speaker of Manx) are used for example in Nettle and

---

[4] 'Rescue' was a translation of the Spanish term 'rescate', a term used by the representatives of the Rama people (Grinevald, personal communication, 2014).

Romaine's (2000: 3–4) *Vanishing voices*. Last speakers also became the focus of media coverage, as the case of the last two speakers of Ayapaneco in Mexico testifies. That case was given much publicity in the media, attracting attention as well as, possibly, mockery from newspapers such as *The Guardian*, *The Telegraph* and even the *Daily Mail* in the United Kingdom (see also Suslak 2011).

A field, however, needs more than just advocates to count as a field: it requires enemies, that is to say significant Others who are prepared to play the same game (Bourdieu & Wacquant 1992). Those Others confer credibility upon it to the extent that they view it as worth engaging with. Such opponents were to prove plentiful from the onset (and still are), in the form of linguists, advocates of nation states and others. One of the main adversaries of initial discourses of endangerment was the linguist Peter Ladefoged. He and Nancy Dorian famously argued over the role of linguistics in the crisis that had been set out in *Language* (rather than over the fact that there was a crisis at all, note). Ladefoged thus wrote, also in *Language*:

> language preservation and maintenance is a multifaceted topic on which different opinions are possible. The views expressed in these papers are contrary to those held by many responsible linguists, and would not be appropriate in some of the African countries in which I have worked in the last few years. (Ladefoged 1992: 809)

He added that the comparisons with animal species 'are appeals to our emotions, not to our reason' (Ladefoged 1992: 810). Consequently, he argued that linguists were to keep clear from political considerations. To this, Nancy Dorian retorted that politics were equally present in both views:

> It is neither more or less political to do something 'which might seem, at least superficially, to aid in [tribalism's] preservation' (Ladefoged, 1992, p. 809) than it is to acquiesce in the efforts of an African nation-state (his instance Tanzania) to 'striv[e] for unity' (Dorian 1993: 575).

The central point here is the type of arguments deployed around one central issue: what should linguists do? The object itself is neither questioned nor disputed; as a result, the discussion of what type of intervention has become a dominant issue in the field as it was constituted, polarising the debate in terms of pros and cons. This was in fact an essential and naturalising *coup de force* in the constitution of the field of language endangerment, displacing a debate from the object to the modalities of interaction with that object. What this achieved was to draw linguistics and more importantly linguists into the spotlights, while leaving unquestioned most of the basic tenets of the newly constituted field. This would later allow other subfields to prosper, for example, 'language emancipation' (Huss & Lindgren 2011), around the idea that acting on language itself, through language policy, may alter structures of power.

Initial debates within linguistics gradually came to encompass other scholarly conversations developed in sociolinguistics or linguistic anthropology, a state of affairs reinforced with the publication of Grenoble & Whaley's (1998a) seminal volume *Endangered languages: Current issues and future prospects* and later in the *Cambridge handbook of endangered languages* (Austin & Sallabank 2011). Both indeed include contributions by anthropologists and sociolinguists alike, as well as those of descriptive linguists.

Overall, the main objectives in the field of endangered languages today can be summarised as follows:

1. linguists should attract attention on an under-documented phenomenon: language endangerment. Languages as yet undocumented should undergo that process;
2. language death needs to be better understood, and to that effect linguists should devote more attention to the study of language attrition and obsolescence in situations of contact (see Tsunoda 2006);
3. finally, linguists should pay heed to the demands of local communities undergoing language change, and assist in revitalisation efforts (e.g. Crystal 2000).

2.6. LANGUAGE DOCUMENTATION AND DESCRIPTION

Language endangerment and revitalisation was gradually constituted as an interdisciplinary field over the course of the past twenty-five years – a hugely productive one at that. It boasts its own journals such as *Language Documentation and Conservation* and *Language Documentation and Description*, its academic programmes (e.g. at the School of Oriental and African Studies in London), its annual conferences in Hawai'i or Cambridge and elsewhere, its handbooks, etc. Although this field derives in large part from descriptive linguistics, it has grown to go beyond description into documentation (with an emphasis on a greater variety of texts and documents), and also encompasses archival as well as language revitalisation (Grinevald & Bert 2014). Language documentation represents in many ways a new subfield which legitimises the entire enterprise and provides linguistics with a new sense of purpose.

Documentation has been defined as being:

> concerned with the methods, tools, and theoretical underpinnings for compiling a representative and lasting multipurpose record of a natural language or one of its varieties. It is a rapidly emerging new field in linguistics and related disciplines working with little known speech communities (Gippert et al. 2006: v).

Unlike the type of language description previously undertaken, it 'should strive to include as many and as varied records as practically feasible, covering all aspects of the set of interrelated phenomena commonly called *a language*' (Himmelmann 2006: 2).

Unlike in anthropology where concerns for diversity, variation or difference have always constituted the core business of the discipline, the concern for language endangerment is part of shaping an agenda for linguistics, a discipline that traditionally focused on universals. It places diversity, or variation (rather than universals) as the core business of linguistics, in sharp contrast to Chomskyan linguistics, and it places the responsibility to define what counts as legitimate diversity in the hands of linguists (e.g. should dialects be studied or languages? How should financial resources be allocated, according to what criteria?). In fact, by putting forth a number of languages extant in the world and by quantifying them, one could argue that the endangerment/revitalisation paradigm legitimises 'languages' (rather than, say, dialects, accents, sociolects, etc.) as the fundamental unit to describe diversity. The field of language endangerment is therefore both the product of a struggle over what counts as linguistics, and the matrix of the production of new categories of legitimate differences naturalised as diversity.

This field is currently represented in both departments of linguistics and anthropology in North America, and represents a significant part of the work conducted by members of the Society for Linguistic Anthropology. Its core vocabulary has become normalised, to the extent that in Southern France, Occitan language advocates routinely refer to their work as pertaining to the revitalisation of an endangered language, and now frame their actions in terms of preservation of global diversity. For linguistics, the focus on – and naturalisation of – 'diversity' is also consequential.

The next chapter focuses more specifically on contemporary works on language revitalisation, to understand what scholars working in that field mean when they use that term.

3

DEFINING LANGUAGE REVITALISATION

3.1. Introduction

As an object of study and inquiry, 'language revitalisation' is in many ways abstruse. While its origins lie in scholarly discourse, academic or otherwise, it now brings together work from language advocacy as well as from academic circles, and it is often inopportune to try to distinguish the former from the latter. To complicate matters further, discussing language revitalisation, even as an academic topic, remains fraught with moral issues. Academics who engage with it are more often than not sympathetic to the cause they describe, unlike those who might be content with analysing language obsolescence from a purely descriptive perspective.

This chapter focuses on definitions of revitalisation in the scholarly literature devoted to it, and on how it is problematised, that is, what debates it forms an active part of. I wish to show how much of the conversation in the field of revitalisation has concentrated on the establishment of a diagnosis/treatment framing, one that constrains the types of question that can be asked about revitalisation as a social process. I will leave aside conversations on language rights, as they pertain to a closely related yet slightly different academic conversation,[5] as pointed out by Freeland & Patrick (2004: 1). Instead I will focus more specifically on the discourses that emerged in linguistics and sociolinguistics in the 1980s and 1990s. To justify an interest in the fate of languages (and in their rescue), this type of discourse, appropriated by many language advocates in Southern France – and exemplified for example in Crystal (2000) – argues that:

- we [i.e. humankind] need diversity;

- language expresses identity;

- languages reflect collective history;

- languages are part of the total sum of knowledge of humankind; and

- languages are interesting in and for themselves.

There are, according to this argument, n languages in the world, n-x of which are likely to disappear in the next century (recall, one every fortnight) – unless something is done about it.

---

[5] See May (2013) for an up-to-date account of current works on language rights; Spolsky (1995, 2003) for a language policy perspective on language revitalisation.

What I wish to show here is that the revitalisation discourse functions as a Foucauldian regime of truth (Foucault 1988; Weir 2008), a set of discourses which one holds to be true in a particular set of social and historical conditions. Its veracity is seldom questioned for it functions as a legitimising discourse for actions that are deemed good *per se*, the salvation of languages and of the world's linguistic diversity (Cameron 2007; Costa 2013). Consequently, what this entails is the historical situatedness of discourses of revitalisation: the idea that languages can be brought back from whatever brink they find themselves in emerged in the nineteenth century, and has taken a number of forms through time. The endangerment/revitalisation discourse is one of those forms, one that superseded the types of discourses produced in the 1970s and that focused on minority languages and social inequality for example. All are modes of regimentation of social difference through a discourse on language.

3.2. DEFINING REVITALISATION

While the expression 'language revitalisation' has experienced a spectacular fortune in recent years (Fishman et al. 2006; Grenoble & Whaley 2006; Austin & Sallabank 2014; iconic and oft cited examples include Reyhner 1999; Hinton & Hale 2001; Hornberger & Coronel-Molina 2004; Huss 2008a; Meek 2010),[6] it is generally poorly defined – a point also made by Bernard Spolsky (2008: 152) about the idea of 'saving a language', which according to him is often 'sloppily presented'. I present below some of the most precise definitions or characterisations of the idea of revitalisation. They tend to focus primarily on revitalisation as a linguistic process (i.e. focused on acting upon the language itself rather than other sociocultural variables such as class status) – a few also emphasise group formation aspects. More importantly – and more problematic – those definitions tend to present revitalisation as a return to a previous stage, a form of restoration of a state in which the language was largely spoken but without the realisation that all social conditions were also different in that bygone world.

Leanne Hinton, a prominent linguist working on issues of documentation and revitalisation in California is also the main proponent in the development of what she termed the master-apprentice approach aimed at transmitting endangered languages in indigenous communities (Hinton et al. 2002). She understands revitalisation in such fashion, as the re-establishing of a language to a previous state of use:

> I use the term 'language revitalization' in a very broad sense. At its most extreme, 'language revitalization' refers to the development of programs that result in re-establishing a language which has ceased being the language of communication in the speech community and bringing it back into full use

---

[6] A number of other terms have been proposed, either to describe one process, or to distinguish between similar, related ones. Amery (2001) thus proposes to distinguish between language renewal, revitalisation and reclamation. Spolsky (2003) talks about regeneration, Fishman (1982a) about reverncularisation and (1991) reversing language shift (see chapter 1). See Tsunoda (2006: 168–9) for other terms.

in all walks of life. This is what happened with Hebrew. 'Revitalization' can also begin with a less extreme state of loss, such as that encountered in Irish or Navajo, which are both still the first language of many children, and are used in many homes as the language of communication, though both languages are losing ground. For these speech communities, revitalization would mean turning this decline around. (Hinton 2001: 5)

Another broad definition is that proposed by Leena Huss, a sociolinguist who works in the Scandinavian north. She expands Hinton's view by suggesting that 'new life and vigour' might not necessarily mean returning to a past situation:

> Revitalization is commonly understood as giving new life and vigor to a language which has been steadily decreasing in use. It can be seen as a reversal of an ongoing language shift (cf. Fishman, 1991), or it can be regarded as 'positive language shift', denoting the process of reclaiming an endangered language by its speakers. (Huss 2008a: 12)

Similar definitions were proposed by others, such as Ó Laoire (2008: 204) for example. Language revitalisation is, for him, about adding new speakers, new functions, increasing language prestige and positive action (including by way of 'strong acts of will and sacrifices' Ó Laoire 2008: 204). Language-based definitions can in fact be summarised succinctly by the American linguist Margaret Speas's (2009: 23) characterisation of revitalisation: '[w]hat you need for language revitalisation is a room and some adults speaking the language to some kids'. In other words, the language must be put at the centre of a one-way process through which new speakers of any given (endangered) language are trained to speak.

Kendall King is a sociolinguist who works in South America. Although she still focuses on language rather than people, her definition of revitalisation is more ambitious – it connects language revitalisation with status, corpus as well as acquisition planning:

> Language revitalization, as I define it, is the attempt to add new linguistic forms or social functions to an embattled minority language with the aim of increasing its uses or users. More specifically, language revitalization, as conceptualized here, encompasses efforts which might target the language structure, the uses of the language, as well as the users of the language. To use language planning terminology, language revitalization might entail corpus planning, status planning, as well as acquisition planning. (King 2001: 23)

A few lines later, however, she adheres to the renewal metaphor, leaving her reader unsure of whether the community is a thing of the past to be rekindled, or a project:

> Language revitalization is thus the process of moving towards renewed vitality of the threatened language. Somewhat similarly, although more focusedonhome-familyuseofthethreatenedlanguage,Spolsky(1995,p.178)

views language revitalization as a process of restoring vitality. (King 2001: 24)

In fact, what holds together most works on language revitalisation is not an adherence to a set of theoretical or methodological principles, or a quest for particular epistemologies, but a set of beliefs: first in the quantifiability of language and the measurability of their global demise, an idea premised on Western European ideologies of languages as bounded, finite and countable items. This amounts to a belief in the capacity of language to be separated from self and societal conditions (an idea shared in discourses on language rights – see Whiteley 2003). The second belief is in the idea that languages can be returned to previous conditions of use. The first point is widely illustrated in the literature on language endangerment and revitalisation (e.g. Crystal 2000, 2005; Bradley 2014) as well as in the media. The second point echoes what the Valencian sociolinguist Lluís Aracil has termed a *'fraseologia del "re-"'*, a phraseology of recursion (Aracil 1997: 187). With reference to the Catalan linguistic revival, he writes:

> [t]hese days the phraseology of recursion is now recited as a magical spell, compulsory in all sorts of ritual celebrations and gregarious effusions. The point always seems to be to recover, to recuperate, to re-establish, to return. As if there could be no other conceivable future than an incredible past. (Aracil 1997: 187–8, my translation)

It would be wrong, however, to view this phraseology of recursion merely as a way to hark back to 'an incredible past'. It is rather, and can only be, about selecting and interpreting certain elements of the past to project them onto an imagined future within a particular political project.

3.3. Establishing a discourse of diagnosis and remedy

The rest of this chapter examines how the academic discourse on revitalisation is constructed as a particular project, and how it functions. Characteristically, and as we saw just above, it is presented as the reverse of language death. Usually written from an advocacy perspective, scholarship within the endangerment/revitalisation paradigm falls broadly into two categories: descriptions of endangered language, and descriptions of situations of endangerment. While the first type of studies aims at describing languages as systems, sometimes with revitalisation in mind, the second category focuses on sociocultural aspects of language endangerment and revitalisation.

Understanding revitalisation as the reverse of language death channels analyses in terms of diagnosis and remedy. Much of the work on language endangerment has thus far focused on describing situations of language shift in order to construct typologies, in combination with a strong moral dimension. In this respect Deborah Cameron writes:

> no right-thinking person would entertain the proposition that 'language extinction is a good thing' [...] *Not* deploring the rapidity with which human languages are apparently being lost once the matter has been brought to your attention would be as odd as not deploring world hunger, the HIV-AIDS epidemic, the destruction of tropical rainforests or the dying out of many animal and plant species. (Cameron 2007: 270)

Such moral aspects pervade the work of linguists such as K. David Harrison (2007) – in particular with respect to comparisons he draws between endangerment levels among mammals, fish and languages. They are equally present in Nettle & Romaine's (2000) volume, especially in the comparison between biological and linguistic diversity. The entire 'ecological discourse of language survival' (Freeland & Patrick 2004: 9) relies on a moral approach to global issues and collective responsibility, not unlike modern versions of the (ecologically) Noble Savage debate (Hames 2007) – one that views the solutions to contemporary societal issues in industrialised societies as resting among wiser (indigenous) peoples (Davis 2009).

Moralistic undertones suffuse the entire discourse which frames linguistic diversity not as a historically situated contingency but as a common human heritage (consider the collective 'we' in Nettle & Romaine 2000). Note that this approach might collide with others that view the ownership of indigenous languages as resting exclusively with the indigenous community (this approach, however, also entails a strong moral dimension). Some authors will go as far as to frame the alternative to diversity in terms of linguistic equality worldwide vs. genocide (Skutnabb-Kangas 2009). Finally, moralistic undertones are discernable in the work of scholars such as Maffi (2000) when they claim that linguists must consider their duty towards the indigenous communities they work with for the advancement of linguistics.

Assessing situations is one of the core aspects of the discourse of revitalisation, and linguists and sociolinguists alike engage in it. This can involve both counting speakers (with the caveats outlined by Moore et al. 2010 – in particular the difficulty to arrive at a satisfactory definition of who counts as a speaker, or what the language is; see also, on that topic, Muehlmann 2012a). It may also entail enumerating languages – see King (2001) for an example of this type of rhetoric – as well as more qualitative evaluations of contexts of endangerment. Some form of remedy for the situations observed is however generally at stake. Such a need for assessment is present in different approaches such as Barbra Meek's (2009) ethnographic work on language revitalisation in Yukon (Canada) or such as Grenoble & Whaley's (1998b) seminal typology of endangered languages. Meek (2009: 152) writes that 'those involved in language revitalisation often consider the first step toward reversal to be the assessment of language loss' to justify her use of Fishman's (1991) graded intergenerational disruption scale (GIDS), probably the most cited tool for evaluating language endangerment. The GIDS, Darquennes (2007: 63) writes, 'offers the opportunity to classify each language minority with the help of [...] 8 stages and enables a comparison with other language minorities'. I do not reproduce it here, as it is easily accessible and its use is widespread (e.g. Blackwood 2008: 149;

Romaine 2006: 448), but suffice it to say that with an eight-stage diagnosis, ranging from a stage where the language is widely used in education, the work sphere and government to one which requires the language to be reconstructed and all forms of transmission to be re-established, this classification 'provides a sociolinguistic taxonomy for endangered languages' (Walsh 2005: 297).

Grenoble & Whaley (1998b: 23) similarly suggest that 'one of the most useful resources the scholarly community can supply is a thorough typology of endangerment situations, one which captures both the homogeneity and the heterogeneity of these situations'. Typologies are in effect a staple of any revitalisation effort, as Joshua Fishman wrote in the introduction to a sequel (2001) volume to his initial (1991) book on reversing language shift. Fishman likens endangered language communities to an ill person:

> The recent well-justified alarm that many thousands of languages (a very high proportion indeed of all those now in existence) are dying and that thousands more are destined to die out during the first half of this century, important though it is, is not the immediate issue which this book seeks to address. Prognostications foretelling disasters are not enough. What the smaller and weaker languages (and peoples and cultures) of the world need are not generalized predictions of dire or terminal illnesses but, rather, the development of therapeutic understandings and approaches that can be adjusted so as to tackle essentially the same illness patient after patient [...] Fittingly, [the 1991 volume] did not call itself a 'theory of the life and death of languages', nor an account of 'why all languages – even English itself – must die sooner or later'. Instead, it called itself *Reversing Language Shift: Theoretical and Empirical Foundations of Assistance to Threatened Languages*. (Fishman 2001: 1)

While Fishman's GIDS remains a reference in that respect (and gave rise to a more detailed version by SIL linguists Lewis and Simons 2010), many other models have been proposed since, either to classify situations of language endangerment or to propose remedies to the problems identified in those classifications. Other examples of such typologies include the aforementioned Grenoble & Whaley (1998b), but also Krauss (2007), or UNESCO's (2009) own categorisation – see also Tsunoda (2006: 9–13) for other scales. Most classifications encompass categories such as numbers of speakers (by types of speakers whenever possible), age, intergenerational transmission of the language, and functions of the minority language in the community (Tsunoda 2006: 9). Those criteria are generally quantitative, and again aim at assessing an objective situation to be remedied. UNESCO's *Interactive atlas of the world's languages in danger*[7] functions along similar principles and categorises languages as vulnerable, definitely, severely or critically endangered, and extinct. According to this classification, Provençal is 'severely endangered', but little explanation is provided as to what makes it more endangered than Gascon, another dialect of Occitan. The atlas, like most

[7] Available online: http://www.unesco.org/languages-atlas/index.php (19 December 2016).

classifications, provides little or no clue as to what political factors lead to minorisation, and depoliticises local situations by situating them on a seemingly neutral and universal scale of endangerment.

Classifications have led to the conceptualisation of models that subsequently establish correspondences between the problems they identified and potential solutions. James Bauman's (1980) report entitled *A guide to issues in Indian language retention* is an early example of this trend, and captures the diagnosis and remedy dynamics well. Bauman suggests the following diagnoses and associated remedial strategies (see Table 1).

Table 1. Language survival status and corresponding retention strategies (Bauman 1980: 6)

Language status	flourishing	enduring	declining	obsolescent	extinct
Retention strategy	prevention	expansion	fortification	restoration	revival

Similarly, and drawing on other sources among language revitalisation experts, Tsunoda (2006: 201) identifies a continuum of degrees of endangerment (ranging from healthy, weakening and moribund to extinct) and proposes a number of solutions to tackle issues of weakening and moribund languages ('maintenance') as well as extinct ones ('revival'). Reyhner (1999) also proposes a remedial grid based on Fishman's GIDS, contrasting 'Current Status of Language' and 'Suggested Interventions to Strengthen Language'. As a remedy to the situation described in Fishman's Stage 6 ('some intergenerational use of the language') for instance, Reyhner suggests to:

> [d]evelop places in community where language is encouraged, protected and used exclusively. Encourage more young parents to speak the language in home with and about their young children (Reyhner 1999: vii).

In all such models, the guiding principle propounds that language revitalisation is about fighting objective, identifiable causes of decline. In other words, constructing a discourse of decline (rather than, say, of change) is the first step towards constructing a discourse of revitalisation.

Discourses of language revitalisation are thus about metaphors of health and morality, revitalisation is a moral duty that concerns a global 'us', in order to restore health in a global being. As narratives they operate much like the shamanic cure described by Lévi-Strauss (1956), a tale designed to restore order in the world and stasis among groups and individuals – they are, in other words, myths, with their galleries of iconic characters, their priests and beliefs. They are stories for our times, and ways to conceptualise difference in a way that characterises groups and individuals symbolically and materially, that assigns bearers of tradition a place in the world – but in whose world?

3.4. CRITICAL APPROACHES TO ENDANGERMENT AND REVITALISATION

Critique of the field of language endangerment and of the involvement of academia in language revitalisation has by now acquired a respectable genealogy, in linguistics itself (Ladefoged 1992; Mufwene 2008; Perley 2012), in integrational linguistics (Orman 2013), in critical sociolinguistics (Duchêne & Heller 2007), and in linguistic anthropology (e.g. Hill 2002; Errington 2003; Muehlmann 2009). All emphasise the problematic aspects of the use of certain ecological (language-as-species) metaphors (see in particular Israel 2001; Cameron 2007), and the ambiguous ideological heritage of discourses of language preservation (Hutton 1999) – in particular with respect to German Romanticism and 1930s' Nazi politics of language. Critics point to a pervading 'exoticising or 'orientalist' strain' in discourses of endangerment and revitalisation (Cameron 2007: 281).

Others focus on the type of vocabulary used by proponents of endangerment discourses: Mufwene (2008: 233), for example, replaces issues of 'language death' within wider frameworks of language change over the past two millennia, and rejects notions of 'language wars', 'linguicide' or 'killer languages' on the grounds that 'languages have no agency at all'. Likewise, Orman (2013) questions the very possibility of language death based on the argument that languages exist on purely ideological grounds. Perley (2012), finally, critiques metaphors of language endangerment on the grounds that they frame particular types of action, and instead calls for new sets of metaphors to be used in order to serve community needs better.

In this section I focus more specifically on the type of critique that discourses of endangerment have received in the social sciences, in order to build upon them in the next chapter. Compared to endangerment, revitalisation itself has received relatively little attention in critical studies – perhaps because language revitalisation efforts in North America in particular are particularly fraught with political tensions. This might also be so because a critique of language revitalisation may be read as an encouragement to anti-minority language policies, which are still rife in many parts of the globe.

Discourses of endangerment, to use the title chosen by Duchêne and Heller for their (2007) volume, have received critique from a number of angles. The volume editors recast discourses of endangerment within a wider framework, a type of moral panic caused by the presence of an Other that threatens the entire social order (Heller & Duchêne 2007: 4–5). The moral panic, they argue, is in part about the management of diversity and minorities. Language revitalisation represents, in that framework, 'an investment in a social order in which a specific form of diversity remains stable' (Heller & Duchêne 2007: 4). Duchêne & Heller (2007: 5) correlate their remark that current universalising discourses of endangerment have superseded previous discourses placing greater emphasis on political and conflicting aspects of the societies at stake with the 'consolidation of a globalised economy based on services and information (in which, of course, language is central)' – that is to say, with new discursive regimes of language. In other words, they insist on the historically situated nature of discourses of endangerment, and the conditions that underlie them in late capitalist societies.

Walter Benn Michaels (1992, 2006) argues similarly that those discourses are in many ways correlated with neoliberal regimes' love affair with 'diversity'. To summarise his argument, diversity is a particular mode of management of difference that serves to evacuate concerns for social equality, one that culturalises and sanctifies differences as a way to justify and legitimise social inequality. In a way, Michaels points to an apparent contradiction of discourses of endangerment: on the one hand, they need universalist arguments, and on the other hand they sanctify differences – or at least certain types of differences.

This in turn raises the question of 'legitimate diversity': how is a particular feature selected as legitimately diverse, by whom, and how does it affect or transform that feature and its bearers or non-bearers? This point is illustrated by Shaylih Muehl-mann's work among the Cucapá in Mexico (see in particular Muehlmann 2008), where access to certain subsidies, rendered necessary by water politics in the nearby United States that make fishing a more difficult task, is premised upon certain criteria of indigenousness, including linguistic ones – or at least on the ability to perform language on certain occasions.

The issues raised above underscore the necessity to question the apparently universal values of discourses of endangerment: who effectively voices them, and to what effect? Who speaks, to whom, and on whose behalf? See in that respect before Cameron's (2007) withering critique of endangerment as voicing anxieties about globalisation and homogenisation, and more specifically about where those discourses originate:

> [s]o, when we represent other people's cultures and languages as being 'destroyed' by contact with the modern, globalised world, are we defending the real, self-defined interests, or are we objectifying their 'traditions' and 'diversity' to serve our own? (Cameron 2007: 283).

Indeed, who does 'universal ownership' ultimately represent and serve, as Jane Hill (2002) asks? Deborah Cameron further remarks that media representations of academic discourses, if not those discourses themselves, 'refer to 'culture(s)', 'language(s)', 'heritage', 'traditions' and 'communities', but 'people' and 'speakers' are conspicuously absent' (Cameron 2007: 276), instead giving way to talk about 'our rich human landscape' – rich, but people-less.

Importantly for this study however, what the arguments above suggest is that language revitalisation is first and foremost a discourse of contact, and a way to act upon this contact through discourse and the recategorisation of perceived reality.

3.5. CONCLUSION

This chapter sought to present some a short genealogy of the notion of language revitalisation, and to show how entangled it is with ideas about endangerment. Revitalisation is viewed as proceeding from endangerment, allowing for a discourse of 'conscientisation': endangerment is a quantifiable empirical fact, which people can be made aware of for the greater good of humankind. Revitalisation builds on this awareness to propose a remedy to the diagnosis offered by linguists and sociolinguists. Although this summary oversimplifies, perhaps, contemporary works on language revitalisation, and although more complexity has been introduced by scholars who approach revitalisation from an ethnographic angle (Meek, 2010: Granadillo & Orcutt-Gachiri, 2011) or by those who draw on languages ideologies (e.g. Kroskrity & Field 2009) the same fundamental dynamics are at play. For example, Loether (2009) argues in favour of ideology manipulation once the ideologies that stand in the way of revitalisation among indigenous communities have been identified through 'prior ideological clarification' – a notion borrowed from Fishman (1991) and Richard and Nora Dauenhauer (1998). What the critiques of endangerment and revitalisation suggest, however, is that those are processes of social contact and that the resulting narratives of contact deserve to be studied as such and not necessarily as problems that should be assessed and remedied. This is the object of the next chapter.

4

REVITALISATION AS RECATEGORISATION

*To take seriously the current resurgence of
native, tribal or aboriginal societies we need
to avoid both romantic celebrations
and knowing critique.*

James Clifford (2013: 13)

4.1. Introduction

As the previous chapter made clear, works on language revitalisation as well as language revitalisation movements generally understand their actions as contributing to a form of empowerment, based on the awareness that a local language is at risk of disappearing. The academic as well as the advocacy approach combine a seemingly simple framework that associates a conceptualisation of language as culture and identity rooted in European modernity with a quantitative approach inherited from nineteenth century linguistics and anthropology (languages and speakers can be counted, classified, etc.). Both approaches rely on the necessity to combine diagnosis (assessment) and remedy.

This chapter seeks to reproblematise language revitalisation as one type of cultural revitalisation among others, raising the possibility of the question: Why language? Building on a framework initially proposed by the American anthropologist Anthony Wallace (1923–2015) in the 1950s to account for Native American religious revitalisation movements, I propose an approach to language revitalisation first as a struggle over classifications (Bourdieu 1980a), as textual moments of group formation; and second as inherently part of social movements that invest language with particular meaning in order to construct minority and majority groups and to provide a framework to problematise, interpret and accordingly alter collective experience.

Consequently the hypothesis this book puts forward is that language revitalisation movements address not only the minority group, as is usually assumed in particular in media discourses that frame such movements as inward-looking, but also the majority group, and the very terms of contact between them in order to renegotiate them. Language revitalisation is, according to that approach, a matter of representation of a projected self (i.e. resulting from a social project as well as from a projection) to a particular Other (Clifford 2013). For that a reason it is a primarily political issue.

The rhetorics of language endangerment (particularly that of academic circles) have been widely discussed and critiqued elsewhere (Hill 2002, Errington 2003; Duchêne & Heller 2007; see also chapter 3). Consequently, such an endeavour is not the aim of this chapter.

Whether we disapprove of it or not, language revitalisation has become of late an increasingly mobilising force worldwide, in particular in the Americas, in Oceania, and in Europe. Many individuals and groups engage in such practices under various names, drawing on similar models and references, communicating about them and exchanging experiences. They usually draw on vitalistic metaphors and refer to them as revitalisation, revival, renewal, reawakening, etc. The traditional model of revitalisation in academic literature ascribes this global movement to the awareness of a global trend of loss (of language, of identity, of culture) on the part of existing groups, and deems it a direct consequence of globalisation. On the other hand, a critical model has yet to account for why so many people seek to organise discourses of claims and demands, of self and others, around speech-as-language (rather than, say, race, ethnicity, religion, gender politics or political institutions). How, and why, does language become a salient criterion in the recategorisation process we call here revitalisation, and for whom? Whose interest does this serve, if anyone's? Is it merely that language remains one of few non-controversial categories to be mobilised for action? Or does it tell us something about language in general in the late modern period?

More generally, most works on language revitalisation treat this process as if it were primarily a question of language. Yet Heller (2004: 285) contends, provocatively perhaps, that 'struggles over language actually are not centrally about language at all'. If so, what, then, is it about? Each movement calls for specific sets of questions and answers, but this chapter aims at suggesting some overarching questions to address those issues.

4.2. RETHINKING REVITALISATION AS A SOCIAL MOVEMENT

In order to be understood as a social process, language revitalisation needs to be looked at from a different perspective. In this section I propose to apprehend it by revisiting a model defined by social anthropologists in the 1940s and 1950s, in order to shift our gaze onto the types of processes at play.

To summarise this shift, let it be said that language revitalisation can be understood as one form, among many other possible forms, of a wider category of processes identified by Anthony Wallace (1956) as 'revitalisation movements'. In that perspective, language revitalisation is not only considered as the result of social movements, it also finds a place alongside other types of revitalisation processes: cultural, religious, political, etc. In fact, Wallace argues that such movements are extremely common in history.

A Canadian-American anthropologist working on Iroquois historical sources, Wallace sought to understand a nineteenth century religious revival among the Seneca of the State of New York, led by a prophet called Ganiodaio, also known as Handsome Lake (see also Wallace 1952, 1970). Indeed, social movements seeking to reform society through arguments based on religious claims abound throughout history – Christianity and Islam themselves belong to that category. But the rise of such movements based on language appears to be recent. No examples seem to exist before the nineteenth century. Concerns for disappearing customs and words did exist in the eighteenth century – a conspicuous example is the Scottish poet Andrew Shirref's (1790: xxiv) 'Address in Scotch on the decay of that language'. In Europe at least, poets have been worried about the status of language for centuries, generally out of political, religious or moral concerns. Yet those were not organised social movement based on linguistic claims, it appears. Consequently, considering language revitalisation as part of a broader class of processes allows for many new questions to be asked – not least 'Why language?' and 'Under what historical and ideological conditions can such movements occur?'

Wallace addresses revitalisation primarily as a social movement: instead of focusing on the religious properties of the revival, he describes the process through the actions of the social actors involved. His work builds on Ralph Linton's (1943: 230)[8] earlier work on nativistic movements, 'any conscious, organised attempt on the part of a society's members to revive or perpetuate selected aspects of its culture'.

Linton further distinguished between revivalist and perpetuative nativisms, characterising the revivalist sort as focusing on the selection of certain elements current in the culture undergoing change yet derived from an idealised past (he cites the Celtic revival in Ireland as an example of this). Intriguingly, according to Linton:

[t]he avowed purpose of a nativistic movement may be either to revive the past culture or to perpetuate the current one, but it never really attempts to do either. Any attempt to revive a past phase of culture in its entirety is immediately blocked by the recognition that this phase was, in certain respects, inferior to the present one and by the incompatibility of certain past culture patterns with current conditions. [...] What really happens in all nativistic movements is that certain current or remembered elements of culture are selected for emphasis and given symbolic value. The more distinctive such elements are with respect to other cultures with which the society is in contact, the greater their potential value as symbols of the society's unique character. (Linton 1943: 231)

Finally, Linton argues that in some cases dominant societies may wish to assimilate with societies they conquered (Goths in Italy for example). Such societies might develop nativistic movements when assimilation is frustrated or when its dominant social position is threatened (Linton 1943).

Much of Linton's work finds its way into Wallace's own work on revitalisation movements, in particular with respect to their conscious and organised character. But while Wallace sought to develop a theoretical model to understand the movement initiated by Handsome Lake going beyond a simple biographical account, the move-

[8] Ralph Linton (1893–1953) was an American anthropologist who worked on Native American issues and later in Madagascar. He was for a long period of time Curator of North American materials at the Field Museum in Chicago, and later replaced Franz Boas at Columbia University, against the general consensus among Boasians — who favoured Ruth Benedict. His work took place largely outwith the sphere of influence of Boas, then the most prestigious figure in North American anthropology (see Darnell 1998).

ment he was uncovering proved more complex than what Linton as well as Franz Boas had described. Reflecting upon his enterprise many decades later, he wrote:

> the older Boasian tradition of longtime perspective and reconstruction of unadulterated precontact culture patterns, and the evolutionary schemata before it, had obstructed attention to the microdynamics of culture change. (Wallace 2003: 4)

In his 1956 paper, Wallace thus sought to uncover structures common to various types of religious and political movements, including cargo cults, charismatic movements, utopian communities, social movements and revolutions. He distinguished between nativistic movements (whose aim is to eliminate foreign elements), revivalist movements (focused on the restoration of past customs, institutions, etc.), vitalist movements (based on the import of foreign elements in a cultural system) and millenarian movements (those that emphasise radical transformations in the context of an apocalyptic vision in which supernatural forces play an important part). All, however, are 'characterised by a uniform process, for which [he proposes] the term "revitalisation"' (Wallace 1956: 264). All movements are also responses to new sets of conditions generated from outwith the communities where they occur. In the next sections, I review Wallace's model, before subsequently pointing out its implications and limitations.

4.3. REVITALISATION AS A CONSCIOUS EFFORT TO IMPLEMENT SOCIAL CHANGE

Wallace's sociological model characterises societies as inherently stable. Revitalisation is therefore a conscious attempt to restore stability (or 'gestalt', in his own words) after disruption has been introduced from outwith a given community. A revitalisation movement is thus, in Wallace's terms:

> a deliberate, organized, conscious effort by members of a society to construct a more satisfying culture. Revitalization is thus, from a cultural standpoint, a special kind of culture change phenomenon: the persons involved in the process of revitalization must perceive their culture, or some major areas of it, as a system (whether accurately or not); they must feel that this cultural system is unsatisfactory; and they must innovate not merely discrete items, but a new cultural system, specifying new relationships as well as, in some cases, new traits. The classic processes of culture change (evolution, drift, diffusion, historical change, acculturation) all produce changes in cultures as systems; however, they do not depend on deliberate intent by members of a society, but rather on a gradual chain-reaction effect: introducing A induces change in B; changing B affects C; when C shifts, A is modified; this involves D ... and so on ad infinitum [...]. In revitalization movements, however, A, B, C, D, E ... N are shifted into a new Gestalt abruptly and simultaneously in intent; and frequently within a few years the new plan is put into effect by participants in the movement. (Wallace 1956: 265)

The most important feature of this definition is the discursive component it entails. A revitalisation movement needs to express what changes it seeks to implement, and consequently it requires a discourse on the situation current at the time it occurs. Revitalisation is therefore a proposition, based on a particular retelling of a society's past and present. Importantly, revitalisation movements need to define the object they strive to revitalise, and to define conditions of participation in the movement – who will be allowed to take part, and who will not, according to what criteria?

For Wallace, the opposition between natural (and slow) change on the one hand and artificial (abrupt) change is the result of outside interference. Revitalisation is thus a consequence of contact, which Wallace identifies as individual stress (as opposed to a prior stable state). Individual stress in turn generates a period of cultural distortion, which leads to a collective process – revitalisation – through which a new steady state is reached (Wallace 1956: 268). The whole process can thus be represented in the following way in Figure 1:

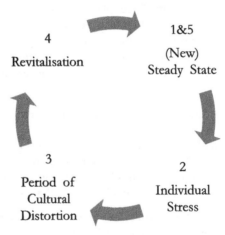

Figure 1. Revitalisation according to Wallace (1956)

In this model, the steady state typically predates contact or stress – in Wallace's case, colonial contact. The stress period is one of change: demographic, environmental, climatic, contact-induced etc. In the nineteenth century Iroquois case, new agricultural techniques had led to a population increase, causing violence within the group (Wallace 1970). Given time, this violence had come to cause severe societal disruptions, and the increasing violence was interfering with ordinary cultural and economic practices, leading to a decline of the agricultural production. In the Iroquois case, revitalisation came after such a prolonged period of 'distortion' in order to put an end to it:

> This process of deterioration can, if not checked, lead to the death of the society. Population may fall even to the point of extinction as a result of increasing death rates and decreasing birth rates; the society may be defeated in war, invaded, its population dispersed and its customs suppressed; factional disputes may nibble away areas and segments of

the population. But these dire events are not infrequently fore-stalled, or at least postponed, by a revitalization movement. (Wallace 1956: 270) Eventually, the religious movement led by Handsome Lake resulted in the prohibition of in-group fights. Although the model is unlikely to actually represent what happens during revitalisation, it does, however, depict very well how language revitalisation movements describe the past events that led to their creation. In that sense, the model represents a rationalisation of experience in the form of a narrative that sustains and supports the enterprise.

Two elements are worth mentioning at this point. First, revitalisation movements are about interpreting collectively what may otherwise be perceived as a collection of individual perceptions about an unsatisfactory situation. Whether Wallace's argument is strictly logical or actually historically founded, it is worth bearing in mind the connection between individual and collective experience. Second, revitalisation is rarely about what it appears to be concerned with – a point also made by Linton about nativisms (see above). The aim of such movements rests in the elaboration of a new steady state, which does not necessarily reproduce the old one. In the case of nativistic movements, this steady state may nevertheless be construed as the restoration of the old order.

The actual revitalisation movement takes place in six steps, and places the individual at its centre — more specifically, it places an individual acting as prophet at the centre of the revitalisation stage. In Wallace's model, revitalisation movements need to perform at least six major tasks (Wallace 1956: 270): mazeway[9] reformulation, communication, organisation, adaptation, cultural transformation, routinisation. They are synthesised below:

Mazeway reformulation	Involves and depends on the restructuring of elements already present in the society. The old way of life is recognised as dead, paving the way to a new one, and a new equilibrium. Often, this may take the form of a dream experienced by a single individual who then becomes a prophet advocating the necessary changes.
Communication	The prophet tells the target society of their dreams or revelations. The aim is to gather disciples.
Organisation	The movement becomes (at least partly) political, and becomes organised in three orders, the prophet, disciples and followers.
Adaptation	In this phase, the movement has to deal with some degree of resistance, generated either from within by powerful members of society or from the outside by agents of another group. The initial doctrine can be subject to negotiations, change or be imposed by force to counteract opposition.
Cultural transformation	This phase presupposes that the revitalisation movement becomes successful and incorporates a large proportion of a population, or at least of its elites. Various cultural changes occur as a result.
Routinisation	The movement's doctrine and programme become established in social, economic and political institutions. It loses its initial grip on society as the level of individual stress is reduced and desirable changes are implemented. In the Iroquois case, the ethnic confederation became a political one (Wallace 2003).

[9] In Wallace's framework, mazeways are 'mental images of a given society and its culture' (Wallace 1956: 266).

The process implied in Wallace's work gradually subsumes individual concerns under a general narrative which provides an explanation for the stress people experience on a personal level, as well as a possible solution to it through adhesion to the nascent movement. Consequently, in this framework revitalisation movements are essentially discursive movements, in which discourse is the central and most important form of action in the sense that they reinterpret reality and have the potential to transform social structures.

4.4. REVITALISATION AND CULTURE CHANGE IN LATER DEBATES

The main preoccupation of Linton, Wallace and theorists working within the revitalisation framework was to account for acculturation processes and social change, a domain of investigation only recently endorsed by the American Anthropological Association[10] (Wallace 2003). One of the most interesting and perhaps thought-provoking uses of the framework was proposed by the anthropologist Margaret Sanford (1974) in a paper entitled 'Revitalisation movements as indicators of completed acculturation'. Sanford's agenda was not particularly sympathetic to revitalisation processes. She viewed acculturation as positive, and argued that revitalisation was not, as some believed, 'a retrogression, a backward step in acculturation of a subordinate society to the customs and values of another' (Sanford 1974: 504). In fact, working among the Garifuna in Nicaragua, she sought to demonstrate that the existence of revitalisation indicates completed or nearly completed acculturation. According to her, revitalisation occurs when the elite of the dominated group, having achieved partial integration within the dominant group, finds itself barred from further assimilation and is maintained in a subordinate position. She writes:

> Carib groups, American Indian groups, Black American groups, having absorbed the values and orientations of the dominant society, waiting and willing to be brought into the main stream of the society, are met with impassable barriers to their entrance. This is where revitalization movements enter the picture. They spring up at times when acculturation is complete but the people are still not accepted as equal. Revitalization movements can be seen as implicit recognition that in order to raise the status of the people to a satisfactory level it is necessary to restructure the situation where people meet – the cutting edge of culture contact. (Sanford 1974: 513)

Revitalisation occurs, then, when boundaries between groups are both fuzzy and reaffirmed by the dominant group, and the very terms of contact between the two groups need renegotiating. One of the strategies resorted to by the dominated group

---

[10] Wallace writes that the possibility to devote attention to this topic had been obscured by 'the older Boasian tradition of long-time perspective and reconstruction of unadulterated pre-contact culture patterns' (Wallace 2003: 4).

is to appeal to a more prestigious time, a golden age to which one can return to re-establish pride – and to (re)assert the authority of the dominated elite.

Irrespective of Sanford's developments, Anthony Wallace's work can be critiqued on many accounts. On a general level, it is rooted in a combination of structural functionalism, modernisation theory and psychological approaches which viewed societies as stable or dysfunctional (Shoemaker 1991). It used the notion of revitalisation movements to account for instabilities and their necessary resolution for the purposes of what was deemed essential for any given group's continuing existence. The model also drew on attempts in the 1950s to design interdisciplinary work, and concepts such as 'stress' and 'equilibrium' as well as organismic metaphors (Wallace 1956: 256) were used widely to unite research in biology, psychology and social sciences (Wallace 2004). Although Wallace himself later (2004) argued that his work was continued primarily by historians, there appears to be 'little empirical support for Wallace's contention that the Seneca family transformed itself so completely and so fast' (Shoemaker 1991: 329). Wallace's approach was also criticised (including by himself) for taking a holistic take on social change, and for proposing too general a model (Wallace 2003; Harkin 2004a) that fails to account for the singularities of human experience (Wallace 2004). A number of questions also remain: can an approach in terms of revitalisation account for situations other than colonial or postcolonial ones? And also, importantly for this study, can it apply to issues of language?

Nevertheless, despite the limitations and caveats of the revitalisation approach owing to their inscription in now largely outdated research frames, recent works have made use of Wallace's approach (although in small numbers – see Liebmann 2008). In recent years, the most influential volume making use of the revitalisation movement approach has undoubtedly been Michael Harkin's (2004b) edited volume. Although it does focus on religious and political movements, many of the insights it offers also apply to language-based movements. According to Harkin (2004a: xxvii), all such movements originate and 'are defined in the dialogic space between culture', which makes contact an essential condition for revitalisation to occur. In line with Wallace's original work, Harkin also identifies two fundamental dimensions of revitalisation movements, a temporal dimension and a social one.

The tension between experienced rupture and desired stability renders the temporal dimension crucial. All revitalisation movements idealise a golden age in which a number of key elements (health, demography, morals, the economy) are thought to have yielded better conditions of life. The social dimension, on the other hand, is made central by the very processes called for by the creation of a new group identity, and, it might be argued, of a new group.[11] Revitalisation movements are thus arguably in a constant tension between the necessary summoning of 'group' as they interpret it in the present and the new group which they seek to establish based on new criteria. In order for this to be possible, discontinuities in the past and between a certain past and the present need to be identified and named, and continuities need to be established

---

[11] Harkin mentions nineteenth century Oregon revitalisation movements, which needed to accommodate US government policies that forced several unrelated indigenous groups to occupy jointly a new territorial structure.

imposed through the invention, for instance, of ancestors (archaeology, for instance, has been a way to do this in many contexts).

In sum, Harkin (2004a: xxxiv) considers revitalisation movements 'as simply one of the [...] mechanisms by which groups attempt to articulate with the outside world'. In the same volume Ann McMullen (2004) makes a similar claim by associating Wallace's approach to revitalisation with approaches in terms of invention of tradition.

4.5. The study of language revitalisation movements

Despite the caveats outlined above, recent works in sociocultural anthropology have shown that the revitalisation movement approach could both provide a valid theoretical framework to interpret a very common set of processes worldwide and to ask a number of pertinent questions to study the said processes. At the very least, Wallace's approach seems particularly relevant to ask new or different questions than those traditionally asked in linguistics or sociolinguistics. What, then, does the approach outlined above allow us to question? First and foremost perhaps, if the so-called language revitalisation movements of the endangered languages paradigm are in fact but instances of wider types of phenomena, this calls for the question: why language? – and not, say, religion, political institutions, or other cultural practices? What makes language particularly attractive, and under what conditions? Those first thoughts question the direct connection between endangerment and revitalisation as the consequence of a process of conscientisation, and instead asks what makes 'languages' so appealing, to whom, and how. In other words, what is questioned here is the very idea that the emergence of numerous language revitalisation movements worldwide results directly from the assessment of linguistic diversity as being at risk. The language revitalisation paradigm therefore depends not on putative facts ('x numbers of languages will disappear before the close of the century') but on the selection of certain observations and on their construction as facts: languages are dying at an alarming rate.

The narrative underlying the activities of many language revitalisation groups certainly seems to fit the structure outlined in his study of the Handsome Lake revitalisation movement. Whether revitalisation movements actually follow that pattern is in fact of little relevance. More significant is the rationalisation of discourse and practice along those lines in the elaboration of a supporting myth which functions as an authorising and authoritative account of the movement. The resulting narrative is indeed a fundamental piece of the puzzle put together in revitalisation movements: it is not a dead piece of text, but rather it is an active element of the movement, one subject to debate and contestation over the legitimate ancestors of the group (founding fathers, illustrious figures of the past, etc.), group membership and modalities of participation, and legitimising elements. In other words, the revitalisation narrative includes the elements described by Wallace in order to allow participants to bring into being the facts that it purports to describe, in particular the group it is meant to support and sustain.

What Wallace's framework does is therefore raise the possibility of new research questions. Instead of focusing on the conditions of accomplishment of revitalisation or on what makes such movements successful or not, considering language revitalisation as one type of revitalisation movement among others opens up the very possibility to analyse what is at stake and for whom. This situates language revitalisation movements as one type of instantiation of a series of social movements that seem to transcend boundaries of time and space (Harkin 2004a), and obversely raises the question of why language has been used so little – if at all – as a focus of revitalisation before the eighteenth or nineteenth centuries. This approach focuses on the conditions of possibility of language revitalisation movements: what makes them possible, where, for whom, and under what ideological conditions? In turn, this series of interrogations paves the way for an understanding of the current multiplication of such movements based on language across the globe. It would, of course, be naïve to ascribe all movements to the same cause or to one cause only (e.g. contact), and each needs to be considered separately, but they all also rely on similar discourses and similar ideological preconceptions. In the next sections, I outline the questions that the approach developed above generates as working hypotheses to be tested in the next chapters.

4.5.1. *Proposition 1: language revitalisation, as a social movement, is about groupness*

The term 'groupness' is borrowed from Brubaker (2002) in order to emphasise the processual nature of revitalisation. A group is 'a variable, not a constant; it cannot be presupposed', Brubaker (2004a: 4) writes. Groupness is thus constantly at play, and implies that revitalisation is not, and cannot be, about regenerating pre-existing groups (as Wallace or Sanford implied). It is, instead, about inventing new ones on new terms, based on this case on particular views on language. In that respect language revitalisation is about groupness, rather than groups. The study of revitalisation thus requires the close examination of practices as a starting point: not, crucially, languages or groups. In fact, following Brubaker (2002: 165), those categories are 'part of what we want to explain, not what we want to explain things *with*; [they belong] to our empirical data, not our analytical toolkit'. Language is one of the elements through which the constitution of groups is played out. It is a *terrain* for conversation and contestation, a set of resources put to various uses: to discuss land issues connected with nationalism, or to articulate a discourse on globalisation and on one's place within those processes, as exemplified by Brennan (2013) in the case of Irish in Ireland for example. To that end, language must undergo naturalisation work in order to be presented as a given in need to be restored to its original condition of integrity and use.

Revitalisation, then, is not an individual process. It is born of a collective construction, and as such it forms a type of social movement. Social movements, according to the sociologists Snow, Soule and Kriesi:

> can be thought of as collectivities acting with some degree of organization and continuity outside of institutional or organizational channels for

the purpose of challenging or defending extant authority, whether it is institutionally or culturally based, in the group, organization, society, culture, or world order of which they are a part. (Snow et al. 2004: 11)

Considering language revitalisation in terms of social movements and groupness generates a problematisation of revitalisation in terms of 'practical categories, situated actions, cultural idioms, cognitive schemas, discursive frames, organisational routines, institutional forms, political projects, and contingent events' (Brubaker 2004a: 11). The group upon which a revitalisation process is premised is, in that sense, only called into being 'for doing' (Brubaker 2004a: 10). Part of that 'doing' is to 'contribute to producing what [discourses of revitalisation] apparently describe or designate' (Bourdieu 1991a: 220). Language, in this respect, is a potential basis for group-formation, a category that can be seized upon at specific historical moments by certain types of social actors to act in and upon the world and upon others. Bearing this in mind is crucial for, as Brubaker also reminds us, doing things as groups with categories 'includes limiting access to scarce resources of particular domains of activity by excluding categorically distinguished outsiders' (Brubaker 2004a: 13). The notion of groupness thus draws our attention to a conceptualisation of language not as a system in need of being promoted, but as a set of more or less widely available resources undergoing a process to re-evaluate them on specific markets, for specific people, under specific conditions. It calls, then, for an approach to revitalisation in terms of political economy (Gal 1989a; Irvine 1989; Del Percio et al. forthcoming).

4.5.2. *Proposition 2: language revitalisation as the consequence of social contact*

Language revitalisation movements should be considered as born of an event or series of events interpreted by some individuals as a form of contact giving rise to a crisis. It is in the dialogic spaces between cultures or societies that the very elements, which then form the basis of the LR movement, are selected and receive their value. Such spaces function as symbolic markets in which various elements acquire value. How and what elements are selected to prompt a revitalisation movement is thus not random. This construction originates in that very dialog between what gets constructed as different cultures (as Harkin 2004a would say) or groups. This in turn raises a number of questions: what sort of entities are those groups, and who gets to be part of them – or not? And whose elements get to be assigned the necessary authority to be taken up on a larger scale in the interstitial spaces generated by contact?

An analysis of revitalisation in terms of contact allows us to shift our gaze from the group that the language movement apparently addresses to analyse the interstices it generates. Revitalisation movements construct groups as dominant and dominated, majority and minority, and define the type of relationship between them. So while the literature on the language revitalisation movement focuses on the minority groups, who, we should ask, are those movements actually addressing? The minority group it purports to serve, or the majority group in whose hands power rests, or is thought to rest? Revitalisation can be thought of as being about renegotiating the very terms of contact between emergent majorities and minorities, of addressing the question of the instertices, thus addressing the majority group as much as, if not more than, the minority one – the opposite of the inward-looking characteristics associated with those movements.

Such a renegotiation of terms of contact means primarily reshaping the dominant narrative of the encounter, or its negation (as in the Occitan case where France is usually constructed as a quasi-natural entity in the dominant narrative, and issues of peripheral integration into France are generally ignored). Through this process, language advocates seek to secure control over this story, in what can be read as a struggle to establish a monopoly over the production of a dominant narrative. The elements it will seek to gain control over will therefore include the establishment of the existence of a group ('the Occitans') and of the conditions of belonging, a particular vision of its past, its territorial claims, and its minority status.

If, then, revitalisation movements address the majority group as much as the minority one, the choice of the variable at its origin might lie within the former rather than with the latter group. In other words, languages might become important at certain moments in time not because 'they are vanishing at an alarming rate' (Abrams & Strogatz 2003), but because of the historical form and importance taken by language among the hegemonic form of groupness in Western societies – that is to say, nation states. In effect, language has, in the modern era, become a privileged terrain on which to articulate and contest ideas of belonging and rootedness, tradition and territoriality, political affiliation as well as patterns of distinction (Bauman & Briggs 2003).

While in some instances the construction of minority and majority groups can perhaps be a fairly straightforward undertaking, as in instances of colonial contact, in Europe this is much more complicated. In the twenty-first century South of France for instance, are 'the Occitans' really a minority, or even a minority-language group, in the same way that they could be thought of in that way until the 1970s? Language advocates often relate to middle-class socio-professional groups (civil servants, teachers, etc.) yet the language-based narrative allows them to dichotomise the world according to a majority vs. minority fault line, and to construct Occitan as a subordinate language and 'the Occitans' as alienated. This in turn raises a number of other questions, for example relating to the sector of society in which revitalisation movements emerge.

4.5.3. *Proposition 3: language revitalisation is fundamentally a struggle over classifications*

The question of the origin of a revitalisation movement and of the selection of a variable which will act as its central motivation (religion, language etc.), as well as the reliance on a founding narrative point to the importance of conflict and of recategorisation of the world as fundamental to those movements. Bourdieu defined (initially 1980a) struggles over classifications as:

> struggles over the monopoly of the power to make people see and believe, to get them to know and recognise, to impose the legitimate definition of the divisions of the social world and, thereby, to make and unmake groups. (Bourdieu 1991b: 221)

What, then gets selected to form what categories, by whom, how, and with what consequences?

The legitimate divisions of the social world include not only the characteristics of the group as imagined by the revitalisation movement (such as its ancestors and purported ethnocultural characteristics), but also the definition of time (how old is the group, when was it founded? What constitutes its past, and when was its golden age?), and the space it occupies (what territory does it – did it use to – own?). Such elements need to be consciously selected from a number of potential sources of knowledge formation (historical, folkloric, etc.), organised and presented in a coherent narrative. In turn, this narrative presents a collective account, explanation, and subsequently remedy for the individual hardships thought to originate in the situation of conflict, through an act of social magic that naturalises and institutionalises the new categories or the new definitions of existing categories. As Bourdieu put it:

> the activist's work consists precisely in transforming the personal, individual misfortune ('I've been made redundant') into a particular case of a more general social relation ('you've been made redundant because …'). (Bourdieu 1993: 38)

The power to impose new categories or to redefine existing ones generates positions of power, linked to new forms of knowledge, linguistic or otherwise, which the language movement seeks to impose. Knowledge is invariably one of the causes for contestation and further struggle, an important dimension of revitalisation movements worldwide: not only struggles against a dominant group, but internal struggles over legitimate forms of knowledge and authority (manifested for example through debates over orthography, neologisms, lexicon and also over the geographic boundaries of the language). A logical implication of this is the necessity to pay attention to internal struggles not in view to provide a solution through ideological clarification as Kroskrity (2009) suggests,[12] but in order to understand what is at stake – and consequently to share the resulting situated accounts with the people engaged in language revitalisation. It should perhaps be clear at this point that the aim of such a line of questioning is not to ultimately legitimise inaction and the continued domination of hegemonic groups, but to provide accounts that could serve the political purpose of emancipation, rather than the languages in and for themselves.

---

[12] Kroskrity (2009: 171) writes: 'Treating language renewal activities as "sites" [...] for ideological struggles and as stages upon which differences in language beliefs and practices are often dramatically displayed, I focus on the necessity of recognizing and resolving ideological conflict that would impede local efforts at linguistic revitalization'.

In that respect, linguistic anthropological or sociolinguistic work on language revitalisation cannot be about success of failure, or about assistance or neutrality. That enterprise is *de facto* nullified as there can be no success or failure, only the interplay between competing imagined groupnesses to impose new categories or redefine old ones in order to achieve new aims in the world: define new groups, establish or impose new positions of power, erase other types of social actors or other social processes. It is, in other words, a constant *rapport de forces* or power struggle. Language revitalisation should consequently be analysed as a Bourdieusian field (Bourdieu 1993), one in which the different and unequal positions occupied by the various social actors involved need to be examined in relation to one another.

4.5.4. *Language revitalisation is ultimately not about language or even about past linguistic hierarchies*

Movements organised around language seek to invent new futures based on the construction of speech as language on the model of dominant European languages, but language is used as a proxy to articulate a wealth of possible other types of claims about the world (Linton 1943; Heller 2004). What claims and positions, therefore, does the terrain of 'language' allow people to voice and articulate that other fields do not, at least in the current historical conditions?

Consequently, in a linguistic anthropological perspective, language revitalisation is perhaps best analysed as a form of groupness production through collective action based on the mobilisation of language as a foundational category. By doing so, and by recategorising reality, revitalisation movements present a societal project – on what the group they seek to bring into being is and is not, and on what the resulting outcome ought to be in terms of hierarchisation of knowledge, groups and individuals. Such movements attempt to implement that project through various forms of social action, including through putting forth a legitimising narrative, narratives of continuity where discontinuity had otherwise been the dominant view. They are thus about inventing groups through a majority/minority frame, rather than about the representation of existing groups.

In the next chapters, based on an analysis of language revitalisation in the Occitan South of France, I will thus propose answers to the following questions:

1. How are language revitalisation movements brought about, by whom, and through the mobilisation of what categories? What narrative is constructed, and what elements does it seek to gain control over? How is this achieved?

2. What do conflicts within revitalisation movements tell us about them?

3. How is groupness shaped? How are legitimate participants selected and validated as as members of the group defined through revitalisation?

4.6. CONCLUSION

In this chapter I proposed an approach to the study of language revitalisation that relies on the repoliticisation of the processes at stake, by considering them primarily as social movements in which language plays a central part. This entails studying social actors who mobilise linguistic arguments to make claims about societies and about the world, rather than focusing on actual languages. Such a take calls for more individual studies, and implies renouncing claims that languages are dying worldwide, and that 'our common heritage' is at risk. Every situation, then, should be seen as different in that it constructs language as a terrain for particular local issues – yet concomitantly we need to pay attention to why so many such movements are being created and brought to the fore worldwide – and why now. What brings them together, and who are they addressing?

Consequently perhaps, the perspective described in this chapter requires us to cease thinking about language revitalisation 'as the emancipation of minorities and their cultures on their own terms rather than on the terms of the larger society as has long been the case', as Leena Huss (2008b: 133) put it. On the contrary, language-based social movements emerge as a response to challenges identified as resulting from social contact. They formulate responses that are audible by a group construed as dominant – and that, therefore, are dictated by that very group, rather than by the agenda of the minority.

Both local factors and global dynamics naturally need to be taken into account. In effect what is becoming increasingly obvious is the circulation of a type of rhetoric based on 'discourses of endangerment', to paraphrase the title of Duchêne and Heller's (2007) oft cited volume. But rather than a universal awareness that languages are dying, what this indicates is the currency of those discourses, and their value on certain national and transnational markets.

CONFLICT IN THE OCCITAN SOUTH OF FRANCE

5

DOES CONTEXT STINK?

> History is not simply something
> that happens to people, but something
> they make – within, of course,
> the very powerful constraints of the
> system within which they are operating.
>
> Sherry Ortner (1984: 159)

5.1. Introduction

Thus far, this book has mainly been concerned with theoretical issues and with circumscribing its object and the questions that arise from our definition of an object of inquiry. This chapter examines how we can come to know our object –'language revitalisation' – how it is accessible and which of its aspects we can expect to focus upon.

The previous chapter proposed that language revitalisation movements function primarily through the creation and promotion of a general narrative serving to sustain a recategorisation enterprise in order to engage in a struggle over the legitimate definition of the group it seeks to represent. The narrative provides a rationalised account of contact, to impose particular views on the conditions in which it took place, and to promote the aims of the language movement. In Western societies at least, the narrative contains three main components relating to the definition of: (1) group membership (or groupness); (2) time (i.e. history); and (3) place. All three are areas over which a struggle is necessary: between minority and majority, but also within the newly defined minority group.

The next chapters are devoted to understanding first what dominant narrative the revitalisation movement in Southern France found itself confronted with in the nineteenth century (chapter 6), one which constrained how that language movement would expand – or not. Second, chapter 7 analyses the narrative, or founding myth of the language movement in Southern France. Third, chapter 8 seeks to understand how the struggle over categorisations taking place among minority and majority is fractally reproduced within the minority group itself, thus creating once more new categories of majority and minority. But first, in this chapter, I wish to reflect upon the idea of contextualisation: what constitutes context, and how should context be presented in a study on language revitalisation?

5.2. THE PREDICAMENT OF CONTEXTUALISING: DOES CONTEXT STINK?

Analysing any narrative of change and recategorisation raises a number of methodological issues, in particular in terms of what contextual evidence is needed. What (if anything) counts as context outwith the narrative itself? In many European sociolinguistic texts in particular, contextual data is all too often presented as a given, a background or precondition for the unfolding of a study which only begins when contextual trivialities have been dealt with. Many sociolinguistic studies assume that 'the focal event cannot be properly understood, interpreted appropriately, or described in a relevant fashion, unless one looks beyond the event itself to other phenomena [...] within which the event is embedded' (Goodwin & Duranti 1992: 3), to quote from a simple definition of 'context'. The assumption is therefore, implicitly, that context surrounds the object, which can in turn be extracted and abstracted from it: context can thus be made external to the object. The problem this approach leads to resides in the choice of events or elements that we, as researchers, include as context: what counts as a relevant event or a useful element, on what basis, and to what effect?

Context, in studies of language revitalisation, is more often than not thought to include some elements of history and geography. Both are problematic in that such contextualisations often merely reproduce the narratives offered by language revitalisation movements, thereby contributing to reproducing the narrative itself rather than to its analysis. Instead, given that the next chapters endeavour to explore how the Occitan movement crafts its own narrative, I must try to show what elements are selected in view of creating a unified narrative transcending ruptures and creating continuities through time, space and belonging. This chapter thus proposes to view context as the description of a set of interrelated fields, that is to say 'network[s], or [...] configuration[s], of objective relations between positions' (Bourdieu & Wacquant 1992: 97; see also Bourdieu 1976). A field is also characterised by the existence of stakes, something that social actors involved in that field compete for (see Bourdieu's 2013: 32 EPHE notes from his seminar on the concept of field). While what is at stake is ostentatiously language, it is narratives of place, historical time and groupness that are the product and the matrix of the types of relationships that structure the field of language revitalisation at a particular moment in time. In turn, such narratives are indicators of the conversations taking place inside the field, and of whom those conversations are directed to.

The narratives crafted by revitalisation movements to justify their claims and project their existence into the future are in that sense very similar in form and usage to what the British anthropologist Bronislaw Malinowski (1954) called 'charter myths'. Yet, importantly, those narratives are part of what must be explained, rather than a source of contextualisation, that is to say, something that explains a language movement. Charter myths are narratives that 'convey, expresses and strengthen the fundamental facts of local unity and of the kinship unity of the group of people' (Malinowski 1954: 116). They are origin myths, ones that 'literally contains the legal charter of the community' (Malinowski 1954: 116), often taking the form of an authoritative historical narrative. Lucien Lévy-Bruhl (1999: 349) adds that charter myths 'most directly express the sense of the social group's relationship, whether it be with its legendary members and those no longer living, or with the groups that surround it'. A charter myth therefore constructs continuity beyond the lived experience of individuals. Much in the same vein, the linguistic anthropologist Kathryn Woolard (2004: 58) described how 'representations of the history of languages often function as Malinowskian charter myths, projecting from the present to an originary past a legitimation of contemporary power relations and interested positions'.

When the subject of a study is, in fact, that narrative itself, what should be included as context? Context, Felski (2011) tells us, is ubiquitous. It is also 'an endlessly contested concept, subject to often rancorous rehashing and occasional bursts of sectarian sniper fire' (Felski 2011: 573). Context, according to Bruno Latour (2005: 148), 'is simply a way of stopping the description when you are tired or too lazy to go on'. It other words, Latour continues, quoting the Dutch architect Rem Koolhaas: it stinks.

The charter myths that the next chapters are concerned with function largely as texts. The point of this book is not to debunk any myths, but to explain how myths constitute revitalisation movements, how they are shaped by historical and social forces, how they guide action, in particular in terms of legitimation of who may or may not make use of them – and, in actual fact, how they being about new worlds. Context, in this book, will therefore be ubiquitous throughout the next chapters (rather than being exposed in one preliminary chapter). It will consist in subjectively explaining who the social actors involved are, and how revitalisation was constructed as a way to reframe dominant categories. For that reason, this book involves telling not only the story of the language movement, but also the story of the dominant group against which it needs to pit itself. It will, effectively, consider that context is not something that happens to people, to paraphrase Sherry Ortner's words quoted at the opening of this chapter, but something they make. Context only stinks if it is dead – that is to say, if it does not inform the analysis.

The question of which story to tell is central, since it forms part of any process of analysis and interpretation. Let me give one example: in a recent book on language policy in an endangered language community (which shall remain anonymous, for many works function on that model), the author provides 'extra-linguistic' (the author's own terms) information for the reader to understand the book's argument. This includes political information on the legal status of the region studied, as well as geographic elements (to justify the rise of tourism during the twentieth century) and some historical elements. History, here, mostly means who the land belonged to, and who its rulers swore allegiance to – how they negotiated the position of that particular piece of land with neighbouring rulers. In other words, context and history are in that case restricted to (broad) political rather than social history. What, indeed, does it imply for a territory to have enjoyed a particular status for the past few hundred years? How is this relevant to the analysis of the current language movement? How does this feed into the narrative of that movement? Some elements of that story may well be mobilised by language advocates, but should they be treated in a positivist manner and provided as background facts, or should they be presented as signs that have been made available through a number of social processes and are now currently reentextualised by the language movement to serve new purposes?

A similar approach to historical context in the Occitan South of France would closely resemble the following account given by Wardhaugh (1987: 104–5):[13]

> The major linguistic division within France is undoubtedly that which is associated with the north-south division between the *langue d'oil* of the north and the *langue d'oc* of the south. [...]
>
> The south has been part of France since the thirteenth century when it lost its independence in the Albigensian Crusade. Before then the Occitans had flourished with an independent but never unified civilization of considerable culture. When they lost their independence they felt themselves swallowed up by an inferior people, the French, a process that has continued to this day. French has long been promoted as the language of the area and Occitan, in spite of its literary tradition, has been downgraded to a patois. As we have just noted, it was not until the end of the 19th century that the French met with any great success in francicizing the south but their progress in so doing has been rapid ever since.
>
> The first deliberate attempt to resist this move to eliminate Occitan came in he nineteenth century with the movement known as the *Félibrige* led by the poet Mistral. This movement had as its goals the standardization and unifying of the language of the south of France and some measure of cultural and political autonomy for Occitania. The movement was not successful in many of its goals.

To this, writing in 2015, one could add that the language revival movement was given a new impetus in the 1960s and 1970s, met another sharp decline in the 1980s and a new impulse in the first decade of the twenty-first century, thanks possibly to a worldwide context in which 'language diversity' and issues of belonging and identity have become fashionable. We would then proceed on to the actual study. But what does such an account contribute to the understanding of the analysis in the next chapters, and what it is indeed telling us? Regarding the understanding of the present situation, it seems to imply that this is a generally accepted truth (if perhaps a subversive one with regard to the other, 'official' historical truth), one that should be taken out of the way to allow us to concentrate on our issues. What this perspective fails to tell us however, is who this account is important to (or for), how its various components were selected, by whom, and to what (intended) effect: how, in other words, it came to be, and why. What it does give us, however, is the basic charter myth of the Occitan language movement, one which functions with a limited number of units: a golden age, a unified threat from the outside, resistance and hopes of subsequent victory achieved through the adhesion of many to the ideas of the revitalisation movement.

[13] See Wright (2007: 218–21) for a similar – albeit more recent – account in English.

5.3. Language revitalisation in the South of France: who are we talking about?

In 2010 the Institut d'Estudis Occitans (IEO), one of the main organised branches of the Occitan movement, claimed to have around 2,000 members (information from field notes and interviews with IEO employees). Their distribution across the Occitan South of France was fairly uneven. For example, at that same moment, the Alpes-Maritimes branch of the IEO (centred around the town of Nice, a town near the Italian border with a population of around 350,000 inhabitants) claimed around 160 of those members, while the Bouches-du-Rhône branch (the Marseille département, an area that numbers well over one million inhabitants) counted just under 100 members – many of them connected directly or indirectly to the French communist party or some form of political engagement on the left side of the spectrum. Among them, those whom I was in touch with on a regular basis were often civil servants or teachers (in activity or retired). In 2014, the bilingual Provençal monthly *Aquò d'Aquí*, closely connected to the IEO through its editor (paid on a part-time basis) and voluntary contributors, had a circulation of about 200, down from around 400 in 2010. Its online version has 1,200 subscribers (subscription is free) and an estimated total of 40,000 visitors in 2014 (its second year of existence), up from 25,000 in 2013 (Michel Neumuller, chief editor of the newspaper and website, private communication, 13 September 2014).

While it is important to ascertain whence the revitalisation charter myth originates and where it circulates, it remains impossible, nevertheless, to determine who counts (or who would count themselves) as a 'language advocate' based only on those figures, and probably on any figure. The music band Massilia Sound System has been composing Ragamuffin music since the early 1980s and has drawn thousands of visitors to its concerts, well beyond the usual crowd of language advocates. The group members do not claim to be language advocates themselves (despite releasing an album called *Occitanista*, that is, a member of the Occitan language movement, in 2002) and hold that they are mainly drawn to the subversive potential of Occitan as a language of creation to sing about Marseille as a cosmopolitan and Mediterranean vibrant city (Chabaud 2013). Another example: the journalist and well-known language advocate Glaudi Barsotti, then in his 70s, told me of groups of workers in the Gardanne mining industry near Aix-en-Provence who, in the 1980s and 1990s, would read the Occitan weekly supplement[14] to the communist daily *La Marseillaise* as they ended their day's work. However, they did not necessarily affiliate to a language movement.

Those elements do not aim at painting a detailed sociological analysis of the Occitan movement, merely to provide a picture of those people whom I interacted with from 2003 until 2013 as I was involved with the Occitan linguistic movement. The types of activities they organised were in many ways similar to what other language-based social movements do (See Jaffe 1999 and Urla 2012 for examples from Corsica and the Basque Country). They proposed language classes, summer courses,

---

[14] The *Pagina de Mesclum* ('Mesclum page') has been published in *La Marseillaise* each Thursday since 1985.

culture-based classes (e.g. Provençal cuisine), they got involved in secondary education, took part in institutional life (through participation in institutionalised meetings about the presence of Provençal in education for example or regarding television programmes in the language). They also published books, which, together with public funding and individual memberships (€30 in 2015, or €12 concessions) constituted the main source of income for all the associations involved in the defence of Provençal. Not all members were originally from Provence, and very few of them had been brought up speaking Provençal. Many, if not most, were retired.

Since the middle of the 2000s, the sociological fabric of the Occitan movement has been considerably altered: while traditionally much of the activities depended on voluntary work, several associations have, over the years between 2005 and 2013, been hiring professional staff to manage their work – perhaps as a result of managerial changes in the IEO after the election of David Grosclaude, a journalist, as president of the national IEO organisation in 2001. This also came as a result of more funding being made available in regional institutions as a consequence of increased political power of the Occitan political movement (mainly through agreements with the Green party, itself often in alliances with the Socialist Party). These changes met a growing population of students graduating in Occitan studies from universities in Montpellier and Toulouse in search of jobs outwith the traditional area of education (see also Milhé 2008: 245).

The association structure is in many ways central to the organisation of collective life in France, and is regulated by a law dating back to 1901. As far as Occitan language revitalisation is concerned, the Felibrige and the Institut d'Estudis Occitans (IEO) are the two main components of that movement in terms of membership as well as of historical importance, and we will encounter both movements later in this book. Both rely on powerful origin myths: the Felibrige was, so (its own) legend has it, founded in 1854 by a group of seven Provençal poets; the IEO in 1945 after the end of the Second World War by a group of former *Résistance* members. But central to my point here is that the distinction between 'language advocates' and/or 'language activists' is by no means a clear-cut one. And certainly, the various versions of the Occitan charter myth are known and reproduced well beyond the traditional circles of those who belong to some of the language organisations in the South of France. Well outwith, in fact, the reach of all language associations in Provence, namely, the Felibrige, the IEO, Parlaren ('we will speak'), the Unioun Prouvençalo ('the Provençal Union') or the Collectif Prouvènço (the Provence Collective).

Revitalisation movements are organised around a number of types of social actors who are all connected by relations of dependence, alliances or conflict. In the sense that they only exist as networks of relations between individuals, they constitute fields in Bourdieu's sense of the term. The sociological composition of those who recognise the Occitan narrative as a source of authority and a motivation for action, or to whom it is meaningful in some way, has changed since the Felibrige was formed but overall positions of power have remained fairly fixed, save for the birth of new organisations that replicate the hierarchical structure of the

Felibrige (see chapter 7), and for the professionalisation of the movement. However, different groups of people have used the charter myth developed in the nineteenth century in different ways to do different things – without, however, modifying its principles in a significant way.

The particular field of language advocacy relies on its own symbolic and material rewards, and also intersects with a number of other fields, including the academic field. Broadly speaking, three main types of social actors have some form of direct agency within that field. That is to say, people who are legitimate to voice a discourse of authority about the language they promote: experts (academics, writers, amateur philologists), language advocates with no particular claim to expertise, and traditional speakers. To those central categories should also be added policy makers, actors in the field of education (teachers, pupils, inspectors, parents) and the media. They are, nevertheless, secondary figures in the sense that their voices can only be considered legitimate or authoritative in the field of revitalisation in as far as they are also language experts or advocates or traditional speakers (although that latter figure is also ambiguous, see chapter 9).

5.3.1. *Experts: legitimising knowledge and revitalisation*

The relationship between experts and non-expert advocates is a complex one. On the one hand, the definition of the expert, of their legitimacy and of the extent of their authority is itself an object of debate and contestation among experts and non-experts. On the other hand, both experts and advocates rely on each other for data and ideas to sustain arguments, recognition and the attribution of symbolic benefits (e.g. invitations to participate in language advocacy public events, reputation, prestige, literary prizes, etc.). In fact, each category of social actors legitimises the other.

Experts play a particularly fundamental role in the definition (and the reproduction) of the spatial and temporal framework in which revitalisation practices can be inscribed. The figure of the expert itself has changed over time: during the nineteenth century, it was represented primarily by writers and later by philologists (Zantedeschi 2013). Over the course of the twentieth century, the figure of the linguist became increasingly important. More recently other figures such as that of the psycholinguist (e.g. Professor Jean Petit, a psycholinguist at the Universities of Reims in France and Constance in Germany) have risen in public discourse, particularly in that of language advocates. The figure of the psycholinguist projects an unquestionable scientific persona in order to provide some elements of justification for bilingual education: in one case I analysed elsewhere (Costa, 2012), a discourse derived from psycholinguistics enables language advocates to reframe language loss in terms of psychological damage, providing elements for the emergence of a medicalised discourse on language loss, and consequently of further rationales for language revitalisation. Linguists do, however, retain a certain amount of authority when it comes to generating neologism: in 2015, a rivalry between several linguistic authoritative bodies could be read as a sign that linguistic knowledge still carries weight.

5.3.2. *Language advocates: disseminating the revitalisation narrative*

Language advocates are essential agents in the reproduction and diffusion of the charter myth and in the recruitment of new advocates. Their practices also translate elements of the revitalisation narratives into everyday actions, such as the act of speaking Occitan to their children (or not), the creation of immersion schools, the scriptural use of the language in various settings, the diffusion of one particular way of writing and spelling, cultural references, etc.

There are at least three constant elements in the sociological composition of the Occitan movement. First, its association with some segments of the middle classes (Touraine et al. 1981; Martel 1997), that is, not with the main economic and cultural elites who switched to French during the eighteenth and early nineteenth centuries – soon followed by large swathes of the middle classes (Martel 1997). Of course, the very notion of 'middle class' is problematic, but in this case, those are groups of people who do not have direct, unmediated access, to economic (and to some extent institutional) power. Also, although the Felibrige has, at times, been a meeting point for some of the political elites of Southern France, no particular policies resulted from this on either a national or a regional level. Second characteristic: across the roughly 160 years covered by Occitan language movements, active language advocates are recruited mostly in urban areas, rather than in the rural parts where Occitan speakers were most numerous (Martel 2010b). Third significant element: the most convinced language advocates were and still are found among those who have been educated in French (in the nineteenth century) or whose main or only medium of communication is French (in the twentieth century). That is to say, language advocates are found among those who have the least to fear in terms of being called illegitimate with respect to their mastery of or participation in the dominant cultural and linguistic markets (see also Bourdieu 1991b: 69) – although their accent might still mark them as Southerners.

5.3.3. *Traditional and new speakers*

The term 'traditional speakers' is used among language advocates to refer to those people who have acquired (some) Occitan during their formative years (childhood or adolescence), and yet often have no particular interest or stake in defending or promoting it. Their importance lies primarily in their numerical strength, since that element alone provides language advocates with elements of justification for their own discourse in terms of equality with regard to other speakers of French. For instance, language advocates often claim that Occitan is the only European language with over one million speakers not to have access to a public television service. The status of traditional speakers within the revitalisation movement is ambiguous: they are the authentic repositories of the language and of its authenticity, the *raison d'être* of the language movement in many ways. Yet, simultaneously, they are often viewed as those not passing on the language and as using linguistic forms (lexis in particular) influenced by French.

Another central-yet-ambiguous group is that of school children who attend bilingual or immersion schools in Occitan, or who follow some Occitan language classes at school. Increasingly called new speakers (O'Rourke & Pujolar 2015; see also chapter 10) rather than, say, learners, they can be viewed both as the future of the language, and as the representatives and agents of its demise. They are thus both idealised and scrutinised, in particular with respect to how their accent is thought to be influenced by French – and therefore to lack authenticity (see Hornsby 2005, 2015 for a similar discussion in Brittany).

Both traditional speakers and school children as learners of Occitan as a second language are interesting in that they reveal how groupness is at work in the revitalisation movement and challenges the widely circulating idea that all those living in the Occitan area are legitimate Occitans, and potential legitimate speakers of the language. Their speech is indeed very often an object of debate among both experts and advocates.

5.4. CONCLUSION

It should be clear that the categories outlined above are both derived from observation and heuristic. The frontiers that separate them are often blurred in reality. What makes them important is their significance to social actors who take part in language revitalisation, in the sense that they represent a categorisation of the world as language advocates see it. Nevertheless an expert can also be a traditional speaker and a staunch language advocate, as in the case of the distinguished Occitan sociolinguist Robert Lafont. Some people may call their speech 'patois' in certain instances, in family gatherings for instance, and yet banish it from others (in language advocacy groups for example). To give another example: how should Lafitte & Pepin's (2009) book, devoted to a discussion of whether there is one or several oc languages, be categorised? Its authors both put forward academic credentials on the back cover, yet the book develops a scientific line of reasoning to demonstrate what they themselves view as a language advocacy statement, namely that Gascon should be viewed as an autonomous language rather than as a dialect of Occitan. To give another example, an authoritative Provençal dictionary (Coupier et al. 1995) is the product of amateur philological work, but it also benefited from the help of numerous anonymous informants as well as from the endorsement of Philippe Blanchet, a well-known sociolinguist, a specialist of Provençal and an advocate of the position that Provençal is an autonomous language rather than a dialect of Occitan.

There are therefore no clear-cut distinctions. Yet the categories used in this book remain valid as voices, standpoints in a field from which claims are made and discourses articulated rather than as fixed positions assigned to discrete individuals.

6

WHAT THE OCCITAN LANGUAGE MOVEMENT IS UP AGAINST: THE FRENCH NATIONALIST AND LINGUISTIC PROJECT

> At the risk of unwittingly assuming responsibility for the acts of constitution of whose logic and necessity they are unaware, the social sciences must take as their object of study the social operation of naming and the rites of institution through which they are accomplished.
>
> Pierre Bourdieu (1991b: 105)

6.1. Introduction

Understanding language revitalisation movements as a way to renegotiate terms of contact between minority and majority and to recategorise dominant classifications implies that those movements do not get to choose what terrain the battle is fought on. In the case of language, this entails that language can only become a terrain upon which other societal issues are played out if language issues have already been invested with meaning by another, dominant group. This observation has several implications. First, as stated above, and contrary to what Huss (2008a: 133) writes, revitalisation cannot 'be seen as the emancipation of minorities and their cultures on their own terms rather than on the terms of the larger society as has long been the case'. Quite the opposite in fact: language revitalisation movements are not inward-looking movements: they strive to construct and position a minority group they contribute to defining along lines defined outwith that group – here language. Second, and consequently, it is indispensable to understand how language has become important in the project defined in the group viewed as dominant, for this will determine how the response was articulated. In France this entails understanding how language issues became the object of social and political projects, thus paving the way for minority language movements to emerge as viable undertakings. The promotion of French against Latin under the (pre-revolutionary) *Ancien Régime*, and its gradual integration into a hegemonic cultural and political project after the French Revolution in the late eighteenth century, is indeed not unlike contemporary language revitalisation movements.

6.2. Narratives of Frenchness

The Occitan charter myth stems from the historically situated need to contest the traditional institutional categorisations in social and geographic terms of the people it aimed at representing. In this section I review the general ways in which Northern and Southern France and their inhabitants were construed before the formalisation of the language movement in 1854 with the creation of the Felibrige in Provence – the very discourses and projects the revitalisation movement was meant to oppose. In fact, the Occitan movement was born, or rather formalised at a moment in time, the nineteenth century, when various types of experts, in particular historians and linguists (see Bergounioux 1989) were putting the finishing touches to the charter myth of the French nation. They were rooting language and nation (both consubstantial with one another) into time and place and entrenching language in a more than respectable pedigree – an enterprise which had begun in the 1550s (Cerquiglini 2007).

At that crucial time for nation building, the southern part of the country remained a problem to many, especially in the North: it was still a foreign place. Jules Michelet, one of France's most prominent nineteenth century historians, famously wrote: *'Le Dauphiné appartient déjà à la vraie France, la France du Nord'* ('Dauphiné is already part of real France, Northern France' – Dauphiné, roughly, is the region between Lyon and Provence, encompassing the Drôme, the Grenoble region and parts of the Alps) (Michelet 1840: 183). The main institutional way to describe otherness through language in France at the onset of the modern era was produced both by monarchic authorities as well as by established linguistic authorities such as writers or the *Académie française* (established in 1635). This process took place alongside the construction of French as a language in the modern sense of the term, as a discrete, describable and bounded object connected with spheres of power and, later, territory and peoplehood (Bauman & Briggs 2003). It took multiple forms, for instance the lack of acknowledgement and naming of any linguistic reality other than French – as was the case in most legislative texts pertaining to issues of language (Courouau, 2012) – or through the distribution of speech as 'languages' on the one hand and *patois*, that is to say 'non-language', on the other (Gardy 1990; Laurendea, 1994; Boyer 2005b).

In this section, and in order to understand the conditions that led to the emergence of the Occitan language movement, I analyse three key historical moments during which the modern narrative to account for linguistic difference in France was elaborated. I begin with the Ordinance of Villers-Cotterêts in 1539, before looking at the revolutionary period in the eighteenth century. Finally I highlight some of the debates that took place in nineteenth century dialectology. All three moments are paramount not only for the construction of a discourse of linguistic otherness and for the categorisation of groups and individuals along linguistic lines, but also for determining forms of authoritative knowledge from which ideas about legitimate language are still derived. Over time, the French language narrative developed authoritative ways of discussing not only issues of language, but also of official, legitimate versions of historical time, place and groupness in France. I do not contend that the steps described below were planned to happen the way they did in the order in which they took place. I merely historicise the dominant narrative against which the Occitan movement positioned itself, and how language came to be an object worthy of struggle as well as a terrain upon which other struggles could be played out.

6.3 ERASING LINGUISTIC OTHERNESS IN THE SIXTEENTH CENTURY

The first step in the process of constructing language as a key category in French political life was erasure (or murder, as Gardy, 1990 puts it) – erasure of all other linguistic categories, ensuring that French only in official documents. But importantly, the North-South divide did not yet feature as one of the important axes of differentiation in sixteenth century France. The sixteenth century is central in the sense that it sees various types of social actors (institutional and from the field of literature) constructing vernacular languages as terrains upon which struggles could potentially be conducted – French, certainly, but also some vernaculars in Southern France became objects of attention. I turn to the institutional domain here, as the construction of French as the sole language of administrative life led to its later monopoly in public life as a bourgeois public sphere emerged several centuries later (Habermas 1991).

Erasure is particularly manifest in the oft-commented Ordinance of Villers-Cotterêts (1539), the first piece of linguistic legislation in France enacted under King Francis I and defining the king's language as the only judicial language of the kingdom (Lodge 1993). Whether it instituted French as the judicial language or merely confirmed what was already a common state of affairs is still a matter for debate (Merlin-Kajman 2011; Courouau 2012), but the important element for now is how languages other than French are referred to. Article 111 of the original text states:

> *tous arrestz ensemble toutes aultres procedures, soit des cours souveraines ou aultres subalternes et inferieures, soit de registres, enquetes, contrats, commissions, sentences, testaments ou aultres quelquonques actes ou exploits de justice ou qui en dependent [...] soient prononcez enregistrez et deliverez aux parties* en langage maternel françoys, et non aultrement.

> all legal decisions and all procedures pertaining either to the highest courts or to the lower or inferior ones, whether they concern records, inquests, contracts, commissions, wills or whatever other legal acts or instruments or whatever is dependent thereon [...] should be pronounced, registered and delivered to the litigants *in the French mother tongue and in no other way*. (quoted in and translated by Lodge 1993: 126 – emphasis mine, I also substituted 'mother tongue', closer to the original French text, for Lodge's original 'vernacular language')

The mention of French amounts to an act of social magic (Bourdieu 1980a) that not only ratifies a more or less already prevailing situation (French as the administrative language of the kingdom), but also imposes (the idea of) French as the sole authoritative language of power, thereby making all other linguistic forms invisible. The attack was possibly initially launched against Latin, but there have been many debates over the hypothesis that this new legislation also targeted the various forms of Occitan still in administrative use in parts of the southern regions of the kingdom. Conversely, did *langage maternel françoys et non autrement* only refer to French (thus excluding the other administrative languages) or to all vernaculars spoken at the time?

Whether or not southern vernacular linguistic practices were under attack or not is of little importance to the argument here. Indeed, Courouau (2012: 35) shows on the one hand that the use of the vernaculars in administrative acts was already a minority practice by the end of the 1530s, and on the other hand that these practices survived despite the Ordinance into the 1600s in parts of Provence, Rouergue or Languedoc. This lends credit to the hypothesis that, at least in the Occitan case, and if indeed vernacular practices were targeted, the ordinance was ratifying common practice rather than strictly enforcing new rules (Laurent 1989; Martel 2001a; Courouau 2012). While prohibiting written vernacular uses other than those in French was unlikely to alienate a large proportion of the population, the prohibition of Latin, on the other hand, was more consequential: Latin was the preserve of the Church, Academia, and the Law professions, all powerful bodies which conflicted with the authority of the king (Cavaillé 2008). The ordinance did indeed turn language into a central political concern, but as noted above linguistic Frenchification was already under way, in various domains such as administration but also literature (Lafont & Anatole 1970: 277).

It is worth considering this debate in contrast with a similar piece of legislation passed in England in 1535, only a few years before the Ordinance of Villers-Cotterêts, in relation to justice in Wales. According to the Occitan historian Philippe Martel (personal communication, July 2011), this text might very well have provided the impetus or the inspiration for the French Ordinance. Courouau (2006: 258) is more cautious and notes that the historical proximity of the English and French texts should not come as a surprise: the linguistic question emerged at a key moment in time, as both English and French monarchs sought to reinforce their authority. Language was construed as a symbolic issue at a time when the languages of king and subjects were different, a time also when royal power entered a consolidating phase.

Whatever the connection between those two documents, Section XX of the Laws in Wales Act (1535) clearly juxtaposed – and through that process, named – English and Welsh:

> Also be it enacted by the Authority aforesaid, That all Justices Commissioners Sheriffs Coroners Escheators Stewards and their Lieutenants, and all other Officers and Ministers of the Law, shall proclaim and keep the Sessions Courts Hundreds Leets, Sheriffs Courts, and all other Courts

in the *English* Tongue; and all Oaths of Officers, Juries and Inquests, and all other Affidavits, Verdicts and Wager of Law, to be given and done in the *English* Tongue; and also that from henceforth no Person or Persons that use the *Welch* Speech or Language, shall have or enjoy any manner Office or Fees within this Realm of *England*, *Wales*, or other the King's Dominion, upon Pain of forfeiting the same Offices or Fees, unless he or they use and exercise the *English* Speech or Language. (reproduced by Raithby 1811: 252; emphasis in 1811 version)

If nothing else, this text suggests the emergence of new forms of language policy at the time in Western Europe. But it also points to the fact that outwith France different types of narratives of linguistic otherness existed, suggesting either that language was not as important an issue in Britain, or that strategies to address otherness were different (and indeed the history of contact between the English and the Welsh is rather uncomparable to that of the contact of French and Bretons, say). What this also suggests, however, is the connection between language and groupness in England and Wales, a move that does not obtain in France (or that is concealed).

What, then, does this episode tell us about the construction of place, time and otherness in France, and the selection of terrains for subsequent struggles? First, it points to a very hierarchical model, calqued on the structure of power in France: the language of the king is to become the language of law and governance throughout the kingdom, a process well under way already in 1539. Language and place are also explicitly dissociated: French is not to prevail where it is spoken (if indeed French was *spoken* anywhere at all) but it is to become the language of all functions in official spheres everywhere. Note that it is not the language of a people that is banned, but explicit usages in specific fields.

Importantly for later language-based revivals in France, this narrative left no space for the construction of minority peoplehoods, which had to be carved out entirely in the nineteenth century. It creates no explicitly oppressed part of the realm based on linguistic reasons. The North-South divide as we know it in fact made little sense then – it only emerged later in the nineteenth century. In this respect, the historian Jean-Pierre Cavaillé wrote that:

> Le problème est que, à ma connaissance, personne n'écrit au XVe et au XVIe siècle que la civilisation et la culture du nord sont supérieures à celles du Midi. Cette représentation même de deux entités séparées et formant des blocs homogènes, France du Nord et Midi, l'une tirant et éclairant l'autre, lui indiquant le sens du progrès et la faisant participer aux trésors de culture dont cette autre serait évidemment dépourvue, est celle d'un historien de la première moitié du XXe siècle, non celle des hommes de la Renaissance.[15]

---

[15] Jean-Pierre Cavaillé, 'Villers-Cotterêts et la langue qui n'avait pas de nom' ('Villers-Cotterêt and the nameless language'): http://taban.canalblog.com/archives/2008/12/17/11786374.html (15 August 2016). My translation.

The trouble is that, as far as I know, nobody from the 15th or the 16th centuries wrote that northern civilisation or culture was superior to that of the south. This very representation of two separate entities consisting in two homogenous blocs, Northern France and the Midi, the one pulling and bringing light to the other, showing it the way to progress, and allowing it to take part in cultural treasures which it would obviously lack belongs to early 20th century history, not to the Renaissance.

The main Other in *Ancien Régime* France is not a geographic other, but a social one: the people, as opposed to the ruling elites, the poor as opposed to the wealthy. This is also valid in the field of philology: writing about the seventeenth century, Lodge (1993: 169) states that '[w]hen the grammarians got to work on codifying good usage (the *surnorme*), one of their major concerns (if not *the* major concern) appears to have been to differentiate the speech of the ruling elite from that of the *peuple*'.[16] Groupness based on the construction of particular geographic areas is thus not the prime intention of the linguistic politics of the time, yet the linguistic focus generated the conditions for a provincial literature to emerge after the 1650s and to lay political claims in linguistic terms.

In this context, it can also be inferred from the use of French in official settings (at least) and from the nobility's gradual relinquishing of local vernaculars in favour of French that geographical categorisations were less important in the dominant account of groupness than the social aspect. The vernaculars were mostly the preserve of the common people, whose history was also thought to be different: the aristocracy narrated itself as descended from Frankish aristocracy, while the people were thought to descend from the Gaulish tribes they had subdued (e.g. Naudet 1827: 402). Two different groups, with different inherited rights, privileges or duties, were thus said to share the same place (the Kingdom of France), imagined in a radically different way from the one we know now, a much wider place where transportation between cities was a much more adventurous undertaking than it would become in the late eighteenth century and nineteenth century (see Hobsbawm 1996: 9–10). On the other hand, they did not share the same genealogies, and referred to different foundation myths.

Whether or not southern vernacular administrative practices were at stake in the French case, it remains that the mechanism through which other languages remain unnamed was apparently so successful that it continued until the 1951 Loi Deixonne named the regional languages that would be taught in schools, under certain restrictive conditions. In France, the historical erasure of any other potentially recognisable linguistic entities ensured that the only named and nameable

---

[16] This dual opposition was an enduring one, and might remain the main axis of differentiation in late capitalist societies, echoing Benjamin Disraeli's words in 1845. Speaking of England, he wrote of two groups 'between whom there is no intercourse and no sympathy; who are as ignorant of each other's habits, thoughts, and feelings, as if they were dwellers in different zones, or inhabitants of different planets; who are formed by a different breeding, are fed by a different food, and ordered by different manners, and are not governed by the same laws ... the rich and the poor' (quoted by Colley 1986: 97).

linguistic reality was French. Naming confers reality upon an object, and in France constituted a first challenge for anyone wishing to use any vernacular as the basis of particular claims. The overall importance of the Ordinance of Villers-Cotterêts lies more in its central place in the French national mythology (Boulard 1999: 45; Citron 2008: 240) than in what it concretely achieved. An example of this is the influential historian of the French language Ferdinand Bruno's (1947, quoted by Boulard 1999: 47) rephrasing of the passage concerning the *langage maternel françoys* as *français*, that is, simply French: 'Elle [l'ordonnance] stipulait, dans ses articles 110 et 111, que tous les actes et operations de justice se feraient désormais en français' ('in its Articles 110 and 111, it [the ordinance] stipulated that all judicial acts and operations would henceforth be conducted in French'). The distinctions operated in the sixteenth century were of paramount importance for the formation of new narratives of peoplehood and for new discourses of equality in post-revolutionary France, the topic of the next section.

6.4. PATOIS AND THE CONSTRUCTION OF CITIZENSHIP

Following the erasure process that had taken place in the previous centuries, the main stage in the construction of a French narrative of language was the redefinition of anything that was not French as 'non-language', and the construction of a new type of link between language and territory. The linguistic history of France during and after the revolutionary period in the late eighteenth century is well known and needs not be summarised at length.[17] This section is concerned with the process through which the regime of erasure as implemented after the Ordinance of Villers-Cotterêts led to the partitioning of speech in the Kingdom of France into categories of 'language' on the one hand and 'non-language' on the other, with consequences in terms of how linguistic Others were gradually constructed in terms of time, place, and groups. With French occupying the role as the language *par excellence*, the 'non-language' gradually came to be referred to as 'patois' (Laurendeau 1994; Gardy 2001; Boyer 2005b), a categorisation that survives widely to the present day. Note that, unlike in Britain, the term 'dialect' was not used for spoken languages other than French, for it remained confined to the study of Greek. It did not form part of the French regime of language at the time, a situation which has changed very little since (Bergounioux 1989: 24).

    Regrettably, no study of the political economy of the term 'patois' exists as yet. Its genealogy was nevertheless comprehensively traced by Laurendeau (1994) as the meaning of the term shifted from 'epilinguistic' to metalinguistic during the seventeenth and eighteenth centuries. Epilinguistic (or 'logonym' in Laurendeau's 1994 terminology) refers to derogative categorisations of non-normative speech –

---

[17] For Occitan during the revolutionary period, see in particular the *Dictionnaire des usages socio-politiques (1770-1815)*, Fascicule 5: Langue, occitan, usages Equipe (1991), Merle (1990), Boyer and Gardy (2001), Garabato (1999) as well as Martel (1998).

for instance slang, argot, cant, jargon – whereas metalinguistic describes situations where social actors seek to pass a more or less objective judgement on forms of speech (e.g. language, dialect etc; Boyer 2005b: 74–5). In other words, 'patois' first characterised certain (stigmatised) ways of speaking or of doing language, including in certain cases foreign languages deemed incomprehensible such as German (Laurendeau 1994: 148). Gradually the term came to categorise all forms of speech in France other than French in a hierarchical way: first came 'languages', then 'patois'. According to Boyer (2005b: 76), Diderot and D'Alembert's *Encyclopédie* (1765) article on 'patois' illustrates this shift particularly well:

> *PATOIS, (Gramm.) langage corrompu tel qu'il se parle presque dans toutes les provinces: chacune a son patois; ainsi nous avons le patois bourguignon, le patois normand, le patois champenois, le patois gascon, le patois provençal, &c. On ne parle la langue que dans la capitale. Je ne doute point qu'il n'en soit ainsi de toutes les langues vivantes, & qu'il n'en fût ainsi de toutes les langues mortes. Qu'est-ce que les différens dialectes de la langue greque, sinon les patois des différentes contrées de la Grece?*

> PATOIS, (Gramm.) corrupt language as spoken in almost all the provinces: each has its own *patois*; thus we have the Bourguignon *patois*, the Normand *patois*, the Champenois *patois*, the Gascon *patois*, the Provençal *patois*, &c. The language is only spoken in the capital. I have no doubt that it is thus for all living languages, & that such was the case for all dead languages. What are the different dialects of the Greek language, other than the *patois* of the different parts of Greece? (Diderot and D'Alembert 1765: 174, volume 12; emphasis in the original. My translation)

According to this definition, in the eighteenth century, the term patois was not only derogatory, as it was already in the seventeenth century; the definition also reflects the ongoing hierarchisation of certain forms of speech as subordinate to others, and constructs 'patois' as (illegitimate) subparts of 'language'.

The final stage of the shift towards the contemporary regime occurred in the last decade of the eighteenth century. 'Patois' became a depreciated and deprecated glossonym substitute: one spoke 'patois' in the same way that one would speak 'French' (Boyer 2005b: 77). While languages such as French, English or German were being constituted as languages in the modern sense of the term – as discrete, bounded and describable objects – those linguistic forms were rejected into the realm of non-language, corrupt and rule-less speech forms to be progressively stamped out. A patois is also a non-language in the sense that it renders impossible the associations between language, people and territory that modernity construes as constitutive of real languages. The indistinctiveness of 'patois' makes it difficult to associate it with either territory (there is no such place as *Patoisie*) or people: the 'patoisants' are not the inhabitants of Patoisie, but the mass of illiterate speakers of patois, those who are supposed to access full political consciousness and participation in the public sphere after the French Revolution by acquiring the national language.

The role of language during the Revolution is not as clear-cut as is usually affirmed among minority language advocates in France. The revolutionary narrative was not one of 'centre against margins', or one seeking to eradicate provinces because they were provinces. In fact, nationalism, linguistic or otherwise, was not even part of the initial revolutionary project, according to the British historian Eric Hobsbawm (1990: 18–23). The project was a unitary one, constructing the nation and the people as one under a single state. The monarchic past of France was (initially) abolished, and months were also given new names as a sign that the new order was founded upon reason. But nation, being tied with people and state, was also no longer associated with localised, concrete origin and instead could be linked with territory-as-abstraction.

It is well known that after the mid-1790s and the Reign of Terror, the French national project became tied up to a monolingual ideal. As a social construct, patois was increasingly viewed by the new ruling elites, the bourgeoisie, as an index of obscurantism and pre-Enlightenment times, and deemed unfit for the new times. While the monarchic ideal had no plans to turn all subjects into speakers of French or even to make them all alike, the revolutionary project wished to make the people French (Weber 1976), building on centuries of Royal language policy and using language as one of the terrains on which this was played out. What is less known is the impetus given to the very possibility of counter-narratives by central actors of the Revolution, in particular Abbé Grégoire, the commissioner of a nationwide survey of the use of patois, in view of documenting them and eradicating their practice (Certeau et al. 1975). By so doing, Martel argues,[18] Grégoire named the enemy (a practice the legislator had always kept clear of, remember), thus generating interest and debates on the subject and giving linguistic otherness a form of existence. Grégoire, according to Martel, thus unwittingly acted as one of the founding fathers of the Occitan renaissance movement. It could also be argued that the type of work Grégoire commissioned also contributed to anchoring the patois in the new regimes of knowledge and of representation of knowledge developed at the time, based on corpora, lists of words and dictionaries.

The elements outlined above have a number of implications for the type of linguistic narrative developed at the time. While the monarchic project implied the division of subjects into different orders according to rank and privilege, and wasn't concerned with associating peoplehood, culture and territory, the revolutionary project anchored the only legitimate group, that of citizens, into a territorial project – but that territory was to be unique, and previous divisions were to be made invisible. The form this took was the division of the national territory into

---

[18] Online comment a blog post on the historian Jean-Pierre Cavaillé's blog, 9 February 2014. http://taban.canalblog.com/archives/2014/02/09/29159432.html (15 February 2015).

départements, new administrative units that generally disregarded the limits of former provinces. This project was soon to be associated with one of the revolutionaries' most prized loot, the language of the king. In the historian of the French language Renée Balibar's (1985: 195) words:

> *[à] aucun moment de l'histoire de la langue royale il n'avait pu être question de faire pratiquer le français par les masses. Dès les débuts de la Révolution de 1789 au contraire, l'avènement de la souveraineté populaire change le statut de tous les langages.*

> [at] no moment in the history of the royal language had it been envisaged to make it the language of the masses. From the onset of the 1789 Revolution, on the contrary, the advent of popular sovereignty changed the status of all forms of speech.

Crucially, this particular project built on the previous work of erasure initiated under the monarchy, seemingly making impossible projects of groupness in terms of languages other than French in particular by emphasising the idea that the various patois differed so much from village to village that communication was severely hampered (Branca-Rosoff 1998).

Thus, the French national project rejected the patois into a non-time and a non-space, into indeterminacy. By making 'language' the only possible way to conceptualise legitimate speech, and by claiming that category for French alone, it ensured that French became entrenched as ultimately desirable for all citizens. However, by dividing the realm of speech into 'language' and 'non-language' (patois), this particular project simultaneously turned 'language' into a legitimate terrain on which to articulate other societal claims (such as territorial imbalance), and on the other hand it made it impossible to enter the terrain of speech without conceptualising speech in terms of language, lest one be barred from entering. In other words, it made it impossible for the patois to exist as patois if they were to be used politically – people wishing to mobilise the linguistic terrain to voice particular societal claim would have to go the whole 'language way'.

6.5. DIALECTOLOGY AND THE LINGUISTIC MAKING OF FRANCE

By the beginning of the nineteenth century the main elements of the French national narrative were in place. Otherness had been dealt with in the previous centuries and decades; linguistic otherness in particular had been denied the process of nomination that conferred authority to French alone. The patois nevertheless remained, and raised a number of questions regarding the origins and genealogy of the French language (Cerquiglini 2007). Importantly, the nineteenth century consecrated the idea that patois and village corresponded, impeding the association of language with groups or geographic areas beyond the microlocal.

The Revolutionary project in France was soon succeeded by a nationalist project during the course of the nineteenth century, one according to which nation and state were meant to coincide (Hobsbawm 1990). It too envisaged groupness in terms of belonging to one territorially bounded nation under one state. In this section I outline how language became a strategic terrain for the discussion of groupness, time and place in nineteenth century France, as the ideas that led to the creation of the language movement were also debated in Southern France.

The making of language as a terrain to articulate a nationalist ideology is exemplified in Bertrand Barère's oft quoted 1794 *Rapport du Comité de salut public sur les idiomes* to the revolutionary National Convention, which explicitly associated language with national loyalties: French to France, and other idioms to enemies of the Revolution. In this report, French is characterised as beautiful and indexically tied to what would now be termed human rights. French is, in that sense, a language previously confiscated by the ruling classes that was to be spread among the people – for democratic purposes (the control over institutions), as well as in order to control the said people. In the aftermath of the revolutionary wars, languages other than French were, on the other hand, treated as a tool for collusion between anti-revolutionary forces in France and enemies outside France.

Throughout the nineteenth century, it became essential for French nationalists to entrench the idea that there could be only one community, the national one, fundamentally linked to time and place. France was to be presented as a project that had unfolded through time, a virtual reality in the making, only to be finally realised in the nineteenth century (Citron 2008). All nationalist projects place history and geography at the centre of their narrative (Anderson 1983): whose history and territory is of course a matter for debate. In the case of France, the southern literary heritage of the Troubadours was in fact incorporated in the national historical narrative, but it was soon excluded. That heritage became superfluous as more French language medieval manuscripts were uncovered (Martel 2010b, see also infra).

One interesting debate involving language took place in the 1870s, that is, after the creation of the Felibrige (the first Provençal linguistic and literary association) and in the aftermath of France's 1870 military defeat to Prussia, but it illustrates the types of tensions the period was giving rise to. It involved the very definition of France as linguistically one or multiple, and it focused both on the existence of France's linguistic bipartition (*Oc* in the South and *Oïl* in the North), and on the existence of a third Romance language type in France, Francoprovençal. According to Gaston Paris and Paul Meyer, two dialectologists who dominated French linguistics at the time, and against the then dominant philological view in the late 1860s, there could be no dialects in the contemporary Gallo-Romance linguistic domain – that notion was reserved for the Middle Ages (or Ancient Greece). In the journal they founded, *Romania*, Paris and Meyer defended a view according to which the village was the unit upon which dialectology should focus. They promoted a view according to which the speech of each village gradually faded into the variety of the next locality (Bergounioux 1989). In linguistic terms, France was linguistically one, a mosaic of idioms merging into one another. The various patois were viewed as remnants of bygone times, to be studied and collected before they vanished forever (Dauzat 1938) – but not to be promoted. They belonged to France's past.

Paris and Meyer's view derived directly from the dominant perspective on language in nineteenth century France, one that viewed the state as the source of (legitimate) language (Branca-Rosoff 1998) – barring the consideration of all the patois as revelant in any way. The patois were part of French, testimonies of its past, and should serve no other purpose than documenting this. The linguistic market was far from unified, but the ideological market certainly was increasingly so: becoming a language was the only way to ensure that provincial linguistic capital could ever be valorised. In France, this entailed the certain demise of all vernaculars, the price of progress.

The question of the limits of the southern vernacular, or of the very possibility of limits to it and hence of its existence as a language was the object of a debate in the early 1870s between Paris, Meyer and an Italian dialectologist, Graziadio Isaia Ascoli. The controversy was prompted by the Ascoli's hypothesis that a third language existed between Oc and Oïl, a hypothesis resting on the indeterminacy of a number of patois in the Lyon area of France, in eastern Switzerland and in north-eastern Italy (Merle 2010). Those forms resisted the usual classification of Gallo-Romance into Oïl and Oc, and gave Meyer and Paris the opportunity to voice their opinion that France was a tapestry of linguistic forms, out of which no languages (other than French, the unifying force) could be carved. According to this view, France's ideal unity was thus maintained. On the other side, the Montpellier philological school, based in Languedoc and organised around the *Revue d'Études Romanes* (see Zantedeschi 2013), promoted Ascoli's views, and the Société d'Études Romanes in Montpellier awarded him its gold medal for his research. This debate eventually led to the definition of a north-eastern linguistic limit for Occitan (see also Bert & Costa 2014) as well as to the institutionalisation (among linguists at least) of a third Romance language in France, then called Franco-Provençal (Ascoli 1878; Lodge 2005; Pivot 2014). The gradual acceptance of Francoprovençal (as it is now spelt), or Arpitan (as language advocacy movements increasingly call it), did lead to the consolidation of the bipartition of France hypothesis – albeit at a time when it no longer really mattered.

Yet, and despite those debates, the principle according to which languages other than French should not be named in official discourse and legislation persisted, and the 1880s' Ferry laws on education specified: *Le Français sera seul en usage dans l'école* ('French only shall be used in the schools') (Martel 2007). No idioms were officially banned: they were merely treated as inexistent.

6.6. THE FRENCH NATIONALIST PROJECT AND THE MARGINALISATION OF THE SOUTH

The dominant frame through which France was linguistically constituted went from monarchic to republican and then to nationalist, each broad period casting its own ideological agenda onto debates of place, time and groupness. It does not necessarily mean, however, that the argument was straightforward at every stage, and involved no debate; nor does it signify that the erasure of linguistic otherness in different social projects, aristocratic, republican or nationalist prevented othering the *Méridional* or Southerner in ways other than linguistic.

France's South – including its literary and to some extent linguistic heritage – was, for a few decades in the eighteenth and nineteenth centuries integrated into the national narrative in order to serve it (Martel 2010b). At the beginning of the nineteenth century, the Troubadours became the object of a number of publications and are integrated into works on the origins of literature in France and Europe, taking the role of founding fathers (Lafont 1982; Martel 2010b: 56) for all subsequent literary achievements. They thus became suitable candidates for inclusion in the national narrative and could contribute to the prestige of the nation as a whole. This period was soon to come to an end, however, as the ideological demands of the intellectual elites changed. The Troubadours were useful as long as they could be conceptualised as the ancestors of French and its literature. They became cumbersome once their speech began to be viewed as the unlucky brother of French (Martel 2010b: 65). From the 1840s onward, the Troubadours were recategorised as minor poets without an intellectual succession. Of the Troubadours, the historian Jules Michelet, one of the main conceptualisers of the French national narrative under the third Republic wrote:

> *Gracieuse, légère et immorale littérature, qui n'a pas connu d'autre idéal que l'amour, l'amour de la femme, qui ne s'est jamais élevée à la beauté éternelle. Parfum stérile, fleur éphémère qui avait cru sur le roc et qui se fanait d'elle-même quand la lourde main des hommes du Nord vint de poser dessus pour l'écraser.*

> Graceful, flimsy and immoral literature, that has known no ideal other than love, the love of woman, that never rose to eternal beauty. Fruitless perfume, fleeting flower that had grown on the rock, already withering when the heavy hand of the men of the North landed upon it to crush it (Michelet, 1833, Histoire de France, quoted by Martel 2010b: 57. My translation)

The discovery in 1837 of the Oxford manuscript of the *Chanson de Roland* completed this narrative by providing a new, more acceptable ancestor to French literature.

During the same period, Southerners were also being othered in different ways, in a manner that originated in the eighteenth century – in Montesquieu's climate theory for instance (Bourdieu 1980b). According to those ideas, the opposition between a cold, strong and courageous (i.e. male) North, and a warm, passionate, weak and lazy (i.e. female) South structured perceptions of space. This logic was meant to apply to the entire world as it was then known, but it also functioned for France as contacts between North and South were becoming more frequent.[19] Life in the South was deemed easier than in the North, the thinking of Southerners scarcer,

---

[19] See Christian Philibert's (2005) documentary film, *Le complexe du santon* for a thorough examination of the process of othering of Southerners throughout the nineteenth century.

their reason overtaken by passions. Above all, what characterised Southerners was their liveliness, which easily led to violence. The celebrated French novelist Stendhal, for instance, wrote:

> *Que deviendraient ces malheureux paysans du Midi si quelqu'un ne leur parlait pas morale ? Ils seraient des bêtes brutes, et avec leurs passions ardentes ils appliqueraient sans remord la loi de Linch (Etats-Unis) (sic) à tous ceux qui leur déplairaient.*

> What would become of those poor peasants of the Midi [i.e. South] if no one told them about morals? They would be but brutal beasts, and their burning passions would make them apply Lynch's law (United States) remorselessly to all who displease them. (Stendhal, Voyages en France, 1837, quoted by Martel 2010b: 47. My translation)

6.7. CONCLUSION: A NEW WORLD READY FOR LANGUAGE REVIVALS TO HAPPEN

As the language issue unfolded in the 1850s, all the elements necessary for the emergence of revitalisation movements based on language: first, a contact situation between Northern and Southern France which the development of new means of transportation had rendered more acute, and which could be thought of in terms of a North/South divide. Second, the principle that all people living in France were one people, accompanying the idea that Southerners were also different (and seen from afar, united in their differences) – and could only really be French on Northern French terms. Third, the idea (and availability) of a potential golden age, located in the Middle Ages at the time of Troubadours – one excluded from the French narrative after the mid-nineteenth century. The final element was the gradual development of a mass education system, which created the possibility of a large readership throughout the southern part of France, allowing for new types of knowledge and new models of knowledge dissemination to emerge.

7

REVIVING OCCITAN

Dis Aup i Pirenèu e la man dins la man,
Troubaire, aubouren dounc lou viei parla rouman.

From the Alps to the Pyrenees, and hand in hand
Poets, let us raise the old Romance language

Frédéric Mistral, 'I troubaïre catalan'
(Ode to the Catalan poets), 1861

7.1. INTRODUCTION

In the previous chapter I traced the development of the dominant discourse on language, place and time that any language revitalisation movement in France would have to counter through its own charter myth. There was in fact little room for manoeuvre for an educated elite in the South to use language as a way to assert its position in Southern France and at the same time define a terrain upon which it would address the Northern French cultural elite on equal terms. Bear in mind also that most of the South's cultural, political and cultural elites, those who remained, had already switched to French in the previous centuries.

This chapter concerns itself with the elaboration of the Occitan[20] charter myth in the nineteenth century. It still forms the basis for the justification of the language movement to this day. The main question I ask, then, is: what is the Occitan narrative, what elements were selected, by whom, and to what effect? I first look at previous attempts to craft early forms of discourses of endangerment in Southern France, in order to highlight what was missing for a social movement to arise, before turning to the language movement as we know now and to its historical foundation in the 1850s. I focus specifically on the narrative as it reframes the categories determined above – place, time (or history) and groupness. My aim is to understand how the language movement attempts to create minority and majority groups, how it frames contact between them and how it seeks to renegotiate the very terms of this contact.

7.2. THE FIRST 'OCCITAN' REVIVALS?

Before looking at the modern language movement, and in order to understand what makes it a product of the nineteenth and twentieth centuries, I ask why it was impossible

---

[20] I use the term 'Occitan' as the adjective pertaining to 'Oc', as used by Frédéric Mistral in his *Tresor dóu Felibrige*, or Provençal-French dictionary (Mistral, 1879).

for similar movements to emerge before. Early traces of discourses of endangerment can be found in literature in Gascony, Languedoc and Provence from the sixteenth century onwards. Yet those discourses never resulted in a social movement, and certainly not a unified one across the South of France.

Whether this was a consequence of ideological debates which had led to the passing of the ordinance of Villers-Cotterêts in 1539, or an indirect consequence of the ordinance itself, or perhaps an echo to the publication of Joachim Du Bellay's major *Deffence et Illustration de la Langue Françoyse* (1549),[21] is unknown. Yet, in the second half of the sixteenth century, a number of literary publications engaged with linguistic themes in Gascony, Languedoc and Provence – apparently independently from one another (Lafont & Anatole, 1970; Courouau, 1999, 2001a, 2001b, 2003). Some of those texts take language as a terrain to debate and to express forms of early patriotism (Courouau 2001b). In fact, in some cases, they go as far as to represent, in the theatrical sense, a form of linguistic conflict and produce a legitimising discourse based on an idealised past, to be found in antiquity for the Gascon poet Pey de Garros, or in the medieval era for Robert Ruffi in Provence.

Ruffi, born in Marseille in 1542, was a notary. His linguistic argument, based on the antiquity of his Provençal was possibly inspired by another poet of the Provençal literary revival and author of a study on the medieval Troubadours, Jean de Nostredame (the brother of Michel de Nostredame, also known as Nostradamus). The following verses by Ruffi (1611) are often quoted in anthologies and described as an act of defence of Provençal:

Lou provensau, baudoment,	Provençal, boldly,
A lou drech de premier agi	Has the right of first age
D'aver tant antiquoment	For having so antiquely
Rimat en vulgar ramagi;	Rhymed in vulgar song
Apres venguet lo Tuscan,	Then came Tuscan,
Coumo dioun Danto e Petrarquo,	As Dante and Petrarch say,
Puis pron d'autres, l'on remarquo,	Then others, we remark,
An seguit de man en man.	Followed hand in hand.

("Ode à Pierre Paul", reproduced by Teissier 1894: 30)

What he meant by Provençal, incidentally, is unclear: he could very well refer to the entire area now included in Southern France, most of which give rise to troubadour-esque poetry.

Similar texts can be found elsewhere around the same period in the southern parts of the kingdom. The following text is by Pierre Goudouli (or Pèire Godolin in the modern Occitan spelling). It is part of a collection of poems, the *Ramelet Moundi* ('Toulousain bouquet', after the town of Toulouse), published in several

---

[21] Joachim Du Bellay's text is usually considered to be the first literary manifest in French, and extols the merits and advantages of French for literary works with respect to Latin and Greek. This publication itself appears to be modelled on Cicero's defence of Latin against Greek's hegemony (Courouau 2004: 37).

instalments between 1617 and 1648. Addressed to 'all' (i.e. readers), it praised the local vernacular:

A touts
[...] Nouirigat de Toulouso, me play de manteni soun lengatge bel é
capable de derrambulha touto sorto de councepcius, é per aco digne de
se carra d'amb'un plumachou de préts é d'estimo. Aqueste reprochi ly
poden manda, que debés qualque mout se taing é s'encadeno dan le Lati :
amour, cel, terro, mar, tabés au fa le blous Francés, l'Italien é l'Espagnol,
que dignomen se banton de touca le pu naut escalou de la perfecciu.

To all
[...] An infant of Toulouse, I am glad to maintain its beautiful language, capable of untangling all sorts of concepts and for that reason to fare in the world with a panache of worth and esteem. One may rebuke it for being close and related to Latin: amour, cel, terro, mar. But so too do pure French and Italian and Spanish, that in a dignified way brag about reaching the highest level of perfection. (quoted in Doujat 1811: XLVI)

On the surface, the contents of those texts are fairly similar to the type of works published during the nineteenth century. Yet they did not result in or accompany any social movements based on language, either locally or on a wider scale. According to Courouau (2001b), the debates in which these texts were partaking in were concerned mainly with authenticity on a literary level. The southern vernaculars were valuable because they were closer to nature than French (viewed as too artificial), and because they conveyed pleasure and enjoyment – an element eventually leading to Occitan's indexical associations with the grotesque (Courouau 2001b: 24).

So while the themes that would emerge in later movements were all in place at the time of the Renaissance (associations with nature, conviviality, expressiveness, as well as language hierarchisation and the extolling of the minority language), the ideological conditions were never met for a social movement to structure itself around language. Those works must be situated in a wider European context in which elites were engaging in a competition over the antiquity of their origins and languages (Courouau 2004: 37), as part of a struggle over the hierarchisation of language and people (Courouau, 2003). They were not, in the Southern French case, connected to national projects (Courouau 2001b: 23), or to groups conceptualised in terms of language. Although languages could compete in poetic terms, and although there are embryos of work that begin to try to define time and place, and perhaps to challenge other, more dominant categorisations, there is no narrative of groups transcending social classes and competing over issues of language. It might be that what appears to prevent a revitalisation movement from developing then is the possibility of the idea of groups transcending social boundaries, an ideological construct strongly connected with nationalism which, as a set of ideas and practices, would only be widely available in the nineteenth century. The next section examines the emergence of the language movement in that period.

7.3. THE CONTEMPORARY LANGUAGE MOVEMENT IN SOUTHERN FRANCE: FROM
THE FELIBRIGE TO THE INSTITUT D'ESTUDIS OCCITANS

This section analyses the ideological context that makes possible the emergence
of such a language advocacy movement as the Occitan one. Remember that the
nineteenth century was a time of change for the South of France, in particular as
regards migration patterns, a consequence of the industrial revolution: 'integrated
into the national market as it was being constituted, [the South] witnesses a number
of changes with regard to its traditional social patterns and its previous dynamic'
(Martel 1997: 3518).

The language movement in Southern France, one of the oldest in Europe, developed
in the footsteps of European Romanticism and the so-called awakening of Nation-
alities – like other revival movements initially based on language and literature in
Catalonia, Galicia, or Finland for example (Martel 1982a). Although the Provençal
movement never experienced the same developments as its counterpart in Catalonia,
both nevertheless share many traits, particularly concerning the processes of eth-
nogenesis they develop. The Felibrige was the first organised attempt to defend and
promote the language of the South of France. Amongst its objectives, the 'promotion
of the revival of the Langue d'oc, instrument of expression of the people of the South
of France' feature as an central element (Martel 1997: 3515). The Felibrige did so, and
still does, by focusing primarily on the one hand on the rehabilitation of a 'despised
language' and the other hand on the invention of a glorious and mythologised past
linked with a distinct people (within France, however).

Social change in the nineteenth century was a consequence of a number of events,
which were to shape the historical context in which the language revival would be
launched. As the railway network slowly connected the Rhone Valley to Paris, Northern
France became an increasingly common destination for inhabitants of rural areas of
the South, replacing traditional migration patterns towards southern cities or even
Spain. As Michel Foucault (2000: 353) wrote:

> Europe was immediately sensitive to the changes in behaviour that the
> railroads entailed. What was going to happen, for example, if it was
> possible to get married between Bordeaux and Nantes? [...] In France,
> a theory developed that the railroads would increase familiarity among
> people, and that the new forms of human universality made possible
> would render war impossible.

At that same time, the political regime in place after the restoration of the monarchy
(1814–1830) had also implemented a period of intellectual censorship. Developing a
discourse on the Middle Ages became a way to bypass this state of affairs: 'medieval
history provided the ideal pretext for cautious but clear attacks against the regime. And
from this perspective the fate of the civilised Midi crushed by Ultramontanes[22] with

---

[22] Or people adhering to a branch of the Catholic Church which places emphasis on the Pope's
authority on the spiritual and political worlds.

the help of plundering barons thus enjoyed a frank success' (Martel 1982a: 51). Finally, the language revival 'took place within an ideological space, within a gap created by the national science itself' (Martel 2010b: 84). This space was a consequence of the interest that the Gascon poet Jacques Jasmin (Jacques Boé, known in Occitan as *Jansemin*), a wigmaker in Agen (a town between Bordeaux and Toulouse), enjoyed in Paris. His success allowed the literature in the southern vernacular to exist in the eyes of the Paris literati – the aspects of Jasmin that were valued were his craftsmanship and his simple singing of his homeland in those troubled post-revolutionary times. It should also be borne in mind that at the same moment a discourse on the death of Provençal was emerging, exemplified by the Marseille poet Victor Gelu, who, in the foreword to the first edition of his *Chansons Provençales* (1840), lamented the passing of the language: '*L'idiome provençal se meurt*' ('The Provençal idiom is waning') (Gelu 1856: 5 – foreword reproduced in the second editon). In the second (1856) edition of his works, Gelu added that the situation had worsened.

Provençal was undoubtedly still largely spoken then, but contacts with the North of France had intensified, and with them the market of available ideas had widened. It wasn't only new ideas that Provençals were being exposed to, but also new worlds, and new words. Gelu (1856: 18) could thus write: 'the honers of Gallicisms have burst into the national sanctuary from which they have outdriven the aboriginal bards'.

The organised language revival movement as we know it originated in 1854 when a group of seven young poets congregated, so the legend has it, in Font Ségugne near Avignon to form an organisation they called Felibrige (or *Félibrige* in French), a name for which there is to this day no satisfactory explanation (Martel 2010b: 87). There are many accounts of the birth of that movement, which grew from seven to several thousand members over the second half of the nineteenth century, and eventually included members of parliament and ministers (Lafont & Anatole 1970; Jouveau 1984; Zaretsky 2004; Martel 2010b). What is important here is to situate that movement in the debates of its time, and to look at its legacy in terms of what categories it sought to impose. Whether they really were seven at the foundation of the movement is doubtful, but the number itself is important in that it allowed for identification with the seven poets of the French Renaissance Pléïade movement, or with the Toulouse medieval Gay Saber Academy.

Who were those poets? Joseph Roumanille, the oldest member of the group, was a publisher. So was Théodore Aubanel. Frédéric Mistral and Anselme Matieu came from families of small landowners. Paul Giera was a pious notary, Alphonse Tavan an annuitant and Jean Brunet a painter (Martel 2010b: 87–8) – a disparate group, in Martel's words, which also displayed heterogeneity in social terms. Giera and Aubanel were of a much higher extraction than the other members of the group, and in political terms Roumanille, Aubanel and Giera are situated on the right side of the political spectrum whereas Mistral and the others were more left leaning. All, however, knew French. Even though they struggled for recognition from France's cultural centres in Paris, none of them can be said to have belonged to the type of social groups they purported to represent, if only through literature.

The Felibrige never came to be the popular movement its founders had hoped. Not only was the population of Provence eager to acquire French, and not prepared to invest in the terrain of language, but the conditions of admission into the language movement made its access available to few. To become a *Felibre* (a member of the Felibrige), one had to be co-opted, and the dues were high – a way to implement selection. Felibres were also relatively few. The organisation was presided over by the *Capoulié*, the *Baile* (the vice-Capoulié), fifty *Majourau*, and 228 *manteneire* (basic members) in 1877, 471 in 1887, and 928 in 1914. To those figures one should also add members of the local branches of the organisation, the *escolo*, or schools (Martel 2010b: 100). Members were overwhelmingly educated, urban men: 'the Felibrige did not recruit in the remote countryside, where most Occitan speakers lived […]. [Members] lived in the cities of the South-East' (Martel 2010b: 108). Even though membership became more affordable over time, in 1877 as in 1914 most members were from the (liberal) professions and the civil service (15% to 20% each). There were close to no factory workers among its members, and only 4.5% of farmers in 1914 (Martel 2010b: 111). Despite being the movement of a certain intellectual elite, the Felibrige was, however, not the product of a bourgeoisie prepared to create its own national market, as was the case in Catalonia. In fact, even if one considers that opportunities to create a national movement existed, for example during the 1907 riots lead by wine-makers in Languedoc, those elites never took advantage of them.

The Felibrige's work drew heavily on the idea that Provençal was both disappearing, and the preserve of the Provençal *volk*. See for example the opening lines from Mistral's (1859) Masterpiece, *Mirèio*, a long epic poem that recounts the love of two teenagers and its unhappy ending:

Cante uno chato de Prouvènço.	Emai soun front noun lusiguèsse
Dins lis amour de sa jouvènço,	Que de jouinesso ; emai [n'aguèsse
A travès de la Crau, vers la mar, dins li bla,	Ni diademo d'or ni mantèu de Damas,
Umble escoulan dóu grand Oumèro,	Vole qu'en glòri fugue aussado
Iéu la vòle segui. Coumo èro	Coumo uno rèino, e caressado
Rèn qu'uno chato de la terro,	Pèr nosto lengo mespresado,
En foro de la Crau se n'es gaire parla.	Car cantan que pèr vautre, o pastre
	e gènt [di mas.
	(Frédéric Mistral 1859: 2)

A Provence maid I sing,	What though youth's halo only decked her [brow!
Whom through the love-tale of her youth, the corn,	What though she wore
Across La Crau, far as the sea,	No diadem of gold or damask cloak!
I mean to follow, as an humble pupil	I'll have her raised to glory like a Queen,

Of great Homer. Being but a daughter
Of the soil she, beyond La Crau,
Was little known.

And honored in our own despisëd
[tongue;
For 'tis for you we sing,
O shepherds and mas-dwelling folk.

(Frédéric Mistral 1867: 1, translated by C.H. Grant)

This text draws on themes common to all nineteenth century national literary revivals, but who was it addressing? This text speaks both to the Parisian cultural elites (it was published bilingually, and dedicated to the French Romantic poet Lamartine, a tremendous literary figure at the time who also wrote an extensive foreword to *Mirèio*) (Lafont 1954: 80–7) and 'the simple folk of Provence'. But Mistral was not only arguing that an imagined and sublimed people should find renewed pride in its language. He was also simultaneously addressing the more local elites who were then still switching to French and pushing forward new criteria for the establishment of cultural authority in the South of France, one based on the mastery of Provençal. Against contempt, and through an analysis of the language situation and its denunciation, the Felibrige purported to offer a way to a renewed pride in Provençalness. Mistral was thus able to take the posture of the prophet guiding the people to and through the restoration of its true language, one foot in mythicised Provençal scenery, and the other in a vision of a no less mythicised and prestigious history steeped in troubarouresque origins.

Among the Felibres, Mistral's work was central to the establishment of a revitalisation mythology. In his memoirs, he recalled (or reinvented, over half a century later) the initial impetus that had led him to dream the Provençal revival, steeped in the type of eternity that his native Provençal scenery summons:

> *E aqui meme, – d'aquelo ouro aviéu vinto-un-an, – lou pèd sus lou lindau de moun mas peirenau emé lis iue vers lis Aupiho, entre iéu e d'esper-iéu prenguère la resoulucioun: proumieramen, de releva, de reviéuda 'n Prouvènço lou sentimen de raço, que vesiéu s'avali souto l'educacioun contro naturo e fausso de tóuti lis escolo; segoundamen, d'esmòure aquelo respelido pèr la restauracioun de la lengo naturalo dóu païs – que tóuti lis escolo ié fan uno guerro à mort; tresencamen, de rèndre la vogo au prouvençau pèr l'aflat e la flamo de la divino pouësìo.*

And then and there – at that time I was one and twenty – with my foot on the threshold of the paternal home, and my eyes looking towards the Alpilles, I formed the resolution, first, to raise and revivify in Provence the sentiment of race that I saw being annihilated by the false and unnatural education of all the schools; secondly, to promote that resurrection by the restoration of the native and historic language of the country, against which the schools waged war to the death; and lastly, to make that language popular by illuminating it with the divine flame of poetry. (Frédéric Mistral 1907: 166, translated by C. E. Maud)

Mistral was describing his revival project featuring himself as a prophet possessed by a vision. His dream is rooted in his people ('race'), place (the Alpilles, a range of hills in Southern Provence) and time, the divine flame of poetry recalling the golden age of the Troubadours' poetry, and perhaps Dante's *Divine Comedy*. But importantly, Mistral also mentions the project against which his own enterprise is directed: beyond the schools and their war against Provençal, he brings in France's centralising narrative.

From the very start, the Provençal revival movement was anchored in myth: the seven poets, and an enterprise placed under the aegis of the Sun, the first god in the Mistralian pantheon according to Robert Lafont (1954: 137). The movement's hierarchy itself was calqued on that of the Catholic Church. Although the Felibrige was later reorganised several times, it must be credited with the invention (or perhaps, rather, the synthesis) of a collective narrative based on a particular reading of history, and acting as a charter myth for the entire Occitan movement from the nineteenth century until the present. This myth placed an emphasis on a group of people defined primarily in language terms and geographic provenance, a group that transcended dialectal barriers and that, although initially centred in Western Provence, came to encompass all of the territory of the Langue d'oc. The Felibrige approached groupness by inventing a certain historical and geographic context it defined through mythmaking.

The foundation of the Felibrige thus constitutes the first step of the language revival in Southern France (Lafont 1991). The linguistic revival movement was to experience a second breath or moment after the 1920s with the elaboration of a new type of discourse on language, in particular in terms of emancipation from the French language as a point of reference. The most important achievement of that period is probably the definition and implementation of a new orthographic norm based on the medieval administrative script as used in various parts of the Occitan linguistic domain as defined by revivalists until the fifteenth century (see Lodge 1993: 123 for a cartographic representation of the spread of French orthographic conventions in the southern parts of the Kingdom). The Occitanist movement emerged gradually throughout the first half of the twentieth century, originally from within the Felibrige (Abrate 2001). This move eventually gave rise, in 1945, to the creation of a new association, the Institut d'Estudis Occitans (IEO, Institute of Occitan Studies) modelled on the Institut d'Estudis Catalans (Institute of Catalan Studies), an organisation focusing on the development and implementation of a stable norm for Catalan. The main charter myth remained unchanged, but crucially the linguistic renaissance's centre of gravity gradually moved from Provence to Languedoc (Martel 2012). The following sections analyse how space and time are woven together into this narrative.

7.4. THE PRIMACY OF PLACE, OR THE IDENTIFICATION OF LANGUAGE AND TERRITORY

Some language-based revitalisation movements emphasise historical aspects to justify their claims to legitimate existence (e.g. the Scots language movement in

Scotland, see Costa 2009). To the question 'What is Occitan?', however, the answer is likely to be framed in geographic or territorial terms. This section describes how this characterisation functions, and links this particular development with ideologies of French nationalism. The documents used are taken from language advocate or academic sources – both being in many ways interrelated.

Occitan is a language inscribed in a particular space only then filled with place-ness, that is, cultural references (historical, ethnographic, gastronomic) that bring Occitania into being and give it substance. The initial empty space of Occitan is often summarised as consisting of thirty-two French *départements*, twelve Italian valleys and one Catalan *comarca* or valley in Spain, constructing a unified and coherent space. This space is also often described as reaching from the Mediterranean to the Atlantic, or from the Alps to the Pyrenees.

Linguistically, that space is also filled with six main dialects broadly associated with historically defined provinces: Gascon, Limousin, Lengadocian, Auvergnat, Provençal and Vivaro-Alpine. The dialects begin to give the territory some substance, and their juxtaposition in nineteenth century philological work contributed to creating a sense of a common language, in the modern sense of the term, in Southern France. An early example of this is provided by Mistral's (1879) *Tresor dóu Felibrige* choice to represent a number of pronunciations for each word he documents and to associate them with their dialectal geographic provenance (Figure 2). The figure below, taken from the *Tresor*, shows various versions of the word for 'a small street', *carreireto*, or *carriereto* in the provençal of the Avignon area, *carrierouno* in Languedoc, *carrereto* in Béarn, *carreiroto* in Gascony.

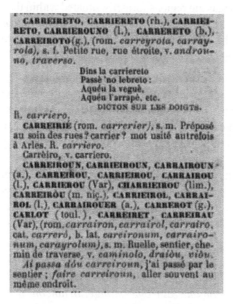

Figure 2. Extract from Mistral's (1879: 477) Provençal-French dictionary, 'embracing the various dialects of contemporary Langue d'oc'

The Occitan sociolinguist René Merle provides a more recent and more compelling example of the importance of space in his (2002) novel *Le couteau sur la langue* ('*The knife on the tongue*'). In this murder mystery, a number of unexplained murders begin to make sense once the detective realises that the bodies are placed at precise locations which, taken together, draw the northern limit of Occitania.

Consider also the following description of Occitan by the sociolinguist Robert Lafont in the introduction to a short book on the principles of Occitan orthography applied to the Provençal dialect. While linking history and geography, Lafont reduces the historical divisions of the linguistic domain to historical contingencies:

> *Sota lo nom de provençau plaçam primier lei parlars de Provènça istorica, valènt-a-dire tant de l'ancian Marquesat, terra de Sant-Gèli, vengut puèi Comtat de Venissa, coma dau Comtat, terra catalana, puèi angevina, puèi província francesa d'Ancian Regim [...]. Son aquò de rasons simplament istoricas. Pèr de rasons inversas, consideram, còntra l'apartenéncia istorica au Lengadòc, lei parlars bas-rodanencs de la riba drecha (entre Ròse e Vidorle) coma « provençaus ».*

Under the name 'Provençal' we include first the varieties of historical Provence, i.e. from the former Marquisate owned by the Saint-Giles and later known as the Comtat Venaissin, as well as from the County, formerly placed under the rule of Catalan counts and later of the House of Anjou, later to become the French Ancien Régime province. [follows a description of other Provençal-speaking regions formerly situated within the county] [...]. Those are mere historical reasons. For opposite reasons we consider the varieties spoken on the right bank of the Lower Rhône valley to be 'Provençal' in speech despite their historical ties with Languedoc. (Lafont 1972: 1)

Lafont's text also connects linguistic and territorial projects. The logic deployed by Lafont is indeed a typological one: he states what he will consider to the way to define territory according to a set of predefined (linguistic and historical) categories, rather than to ethnographically constructed categories. In that sense, the project consists just as much in an internal reorganisation of the Occitan territory as in its definition with respect to external boundaries.

The next text is much more recent, and shows permanence in terms of identification strategies. It was published in a special issue on Occitan of a dissemination bulletin edited by the *Délégation générale à la langue française et aux langues de France*, a language-planning institution placed under the authority of the Ministry for Culture:

> *On appelle langue d'oc, ou occitan, une langue romane parlée dans le Sud de la France (Roussillon et Pays basque non compris) jusqu'à une ligne passant quelques kilomètres au nord de Libourne, Confolens, Guéret, Montluçon, Tain-L'hermitage, Briançon. Il est également parlé dans douze vallées alpines d'Italie et, sous sa forme gasconne, dans le Val d'Aran en Espagne.*

We call Langue d'oc, or Occitan, a Romance language spoken in the
South of France (except in Roussillon and the Basque Country) up to a
line running north of Libourne, Confolens, Guéret, Montluçon, Tain-
L'hermitage, and Briançon. It is also spoken in twelve Alpine valleys in
Italy and, in its Gascon variety, in the Val d'Aran in Spain. (Sibille 2007: 2)

Another way of representing Occitan as a primarily spatial object is through maps
of a space given the attributes of place. Such maps, although always representing the
same territory,[23] can be said to represent either a linguistic entity (see Sumien 2009a for
a number of examples) or a political one called Occitania. Maps featuring the linguistic
domain of Occitan in one way or another are the direct heirs of nineteenth century
dialectological maps: their northern limits are still those established through linguistic
surveys at that time (e.g. Tourtoulon & Bringuier 1876) and documented throughout
the twentieth century before the last traditional speakers died (Brun-Trigaud 1990; Bert
2001). Such maps now represent an idealised homogenous linguistic map, one now
presented as the traditional domain of the language rather than as its current domain.
In other words while the territory was initially based on the mapping of language
practices it did not evolve to follow its own logic and instead developed a discourse of
geographic continuity as the actual continuity of speech receded.

Figure 3, taken from the Occitan language Wikipedia page, represents Occitania
as a political space and marks the main Occitan dialects. This suggests the strength of
the link between language and territory as a place imagined on the basis of language
but invested with other political and symbolic elements.

Figure 3. 'Map of Occitania', designed by Lu Collectiu Arri!/arrilemosin.fr, CC licence

[23] One exception to this rule consists in representing together Occitan and Catalan-speaking
territories, as in the various instances found in Lafont's (2003) European history of Occitania.

The documents presented above propose and reproduce a particular representation of space and classification of speech as consisting of dialects forming a language. They are both descriptive and performative, and in a struggle over the right to impose certain categorisations of the social space strive to impose a particular view – that of the Occitan revitalisation movement. History inhabits this space; better still, it instils a dramatic element into it. In Lafont's text above, history is present through the evocation of Catalonia, often construed as the successful cousin of Occitania and the ally of the County of Toulouse, Occitania's mythological forebear, during the Albigensian Crusade (in Lafont 1991, he compares the destinies of both linguitic and political entities, and contrasts the success of Catalonia with the shortcomings of Occitania). Through the invocation of the name of Saint-Giles, a name associated with the Counts of Toulouse, Lafont again convokes the Albigensian crusade.

Nevertheless, the primacy of space for the definition of an Occitan domain is a consequence both of the elaboration of a notion of space based on language and a dialectological take on language, and, perhaps more significantly, of the prominence of geography in the French national discourse. To use the terms of Ernest Renan (1882: 7), France needed to forget. Lacking in cultural unity, with no clear geographic boundaries, it required its existence as a nation and as a Republic to be legitimised. Among the first steps taken after the French Revolution was the dissolution of provinces and their replacement by new administrative entities, the *départements* (22 December 1789). The emphasis on geography and on the naturalness of France's borders was heightened after the 1870 defeat of France against Prussia and the subsequent loss of Alsace and Lorraine. Under the Third Republic, born of this defeat, the exaltation of French geography is a way to extol France's grandeur and superiority (Thiesse 2001: 11). One frequently given example is the publication in 1877 of the book aimed at children entitled *Le tour de la France par deux enfants* (Fouillée, 1877), recounting the escape from Lorraine of two young orphans and their journey through the various parts of France. In this respect, the Occitan revival movement's emphasis on space not only mirrors the ideological construction of France as a nation state, but also disputes these claims in the very terms it imposes. While the French narrative uses geography to construct a type of national unity transcending geographic and climatic differenced, the Occitan narrative establishes separate entities within France and lays the ground for its linguistic claims.

The Occitan movement is effectively a consequence of a politics of space: Abbé Grégoire's revolutionary endeavour was born of the need to map the territory, and to map it in a way that erased former provinces and would lead to the erasure of linguistic difference. Dialectological surveys throughout the nineteenth and twentieth centuries were instrumental in defining the language itself, and in making it a unified one. The definition of that territory was not initially fixed, and some nineteenth century maps include the Francoprovençal domain within the Occitan domain (Pivot 2014). Overall, after Mistral established the limits of the language he purports to describe in his (1879) Provençal dictionary, the outer limits of the linguistic domain remain remarkably stable throughout the twentieth century – see

Sumien (2009a) for the main classificatory maps of internal limits. External limits are never subject to contestation among linguists.

Ultimately however, for all the weight of geography in the crafting of the revitalisation narrative, a discourse on history remains essential. Bourdieu, drawing on the linguist Emile Benveniste's work on Indo-European institutions, underlines not only the act of classification, but also the authority that those who perform it can muster:

> *Regere fines*, the act which consists in 'tracing out the limits by straight lines', in delimiting 'the interior and the exterior, the realm of the sacred and the realm of the profane, the national territory and foreign territory', is a *religious* act performed by the person invested with the highest authority. The *rex*, whose responsibility it is to *regere sacra*, to fix the rules which bring into existence what they decree, to speak with authority, to pre-dict in the sense of calling into being, by an enforceable saying, what one says, of making the future that one utters come into being. The *regio* and its frontiers (*fines*) are merely the dead trace of the act of authority which consists in circumscribing the country, the territory […]. (Bourdieu 1991b: 221–2)

The strength of myth lies in its capacity to be disseminated and to attract new converts. And this power of persuasion ultimately derives from the ideological weight conveyed by those for whom its implementation is important. It is necessary for those who seek to perform an ideological *coup de force* to impose not only one's categories as legitimate, but also certain figures of authority, to call them into being. To be authoritative, such figures need first to be legitimate in the language which conveys authority and legitimate discourse in the eyes of those who can determine what counts as legitimate, that is, Standard French. Second, they must be able to mobilise forms of action within the political and cultural fields generally accepted to command authority. In the Occitan South, this figure was initially the writer, thought to mobilise the authority of the written word, and the historical narrative the next section dwells upon serves to establish and impose this figure – to the detriment of perhaps more perennial ones.

7.5. HISTORY: IMAGINING THE PAST AND CALLING THE FUTURE INTO BEING

In this section, I address first how the revitalisation narrative imagined its past from the second half of the nineteenth century onward, and second what ancestors it selected for itself. In appearance, history and geography provide a backdrop to the central preoccupations of the language movement, one against which language itself is set. In reality, the struggle for the legitimate representation of history and geography lies at the very core of the revitalisation narrative. Language revitalisation, viewed as a struggle over the legitimate definition of authoritative categories, entails the attempt to control those categories to impose new legitimate divisions of the social world and to bring them into existence materially and symbolically. It is a struggle over the authority to do so, and over the sources of knowledge that legitimise this authority.

This is realised through a number of acts of institution, of which, when successful, frontiers and limits are the dead traces (Bourdieu 1991b: 222).

This myth is rarely available as a single bloc. Rather its is more often than not distilled in the publications of language advocates in more or less complete forms, in language learning material, textbooks, and more recently in local institutional publications. Its backbone consists in a relatively simple narrative, featuring a golden age, a fall, and a subsequent return to the golden age through the action of language advocacy movements. Figure 4, taken from a dissemination book on Occitan literature by Jean Rouquette, a.k.a. Jean Larzac, a famous Occitan writer, provides its simplest yet most coherent form. Rouquette belongs to the intellectual current that led to the second moment of the revival, the Occitanist moment. The essential element is the connection of time and space through the invocation of writers and, implicitly, a common written medium:

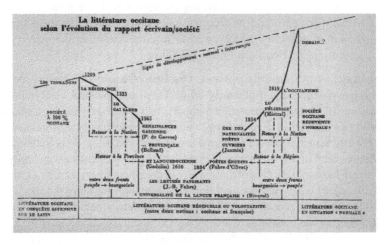

Figure 4. 'Occitan literature according to the evolution of the writer/society relation'
(Rouquette 1980: 12)

Continuity throughout the ages is ensured through the figure of the writer, and through the presence of a written language, exemplifying the leading force driving the Occitan revitalisation movement: the central importance of the written medium. From its very beginning, the entire movement finds its legitimation in the written word, or what Lafont (1984, reproduced in Lafont 1997: 114) calls an *'idéologie renaissantiste du texte rédempteur'*, a 'revivalist ideology of the redemptive text': the people's salvation originates in the written text.

What readers are provided with in this instance is a unique example of a graphic representation of an ideal discourse of revitalisation that closely matches Wallace's (1956) own representation of such movements (see chapter 2). To the four main phases (stable state, stress, revitalisation and new stable state) correspond a *'Société à 100% occitane'* ('100% Occitan society'), the Albigensian crusade after 1209, the subsequent linguistic fall from greatness (the Troubadours) into the state of patois represented by the '*lettrés patoisants*' ('patois literati'), and finally the hope to reach a '*société occitane redevenue "normale"* ('an Occitan society returned to its "normal" state'). A line of '*ligne de développement "normal" interrompu*' ('uninterrupted normal development') unites the golden age with the return to a normal situation that the revitalisation movement is to achieve.

The diagram, in which Occitan appears as French's inverted and shameful double,[24] further presents literature as inextricably linked to the political evolution of what was to become the southern part of France, segmenting that evolution into a movement from nation to province, and subsequently from province to region and to nation again. Historical continuities are introduced (the connection between various resistances from the Middle Ages to the contemporary era), as well as geographical ones (e.g. the linking of the Provençal, Gascon and Lengadocian sixteenth century literary revivals). A narrative unity is thus conferred upon the general Occitan myth in order to connect past and future golden ages, making way for claims to be made for the entire southern part of France despite no actual common institutional past. This strategy triggers a *rapport de force* between two large and seemingly equal sections of the French territory.

One detail should nevertheless capture our attention: the treatment of the 1854 revival and the representation of the Felibrige. It is of particular significance for it singles out one central dimension of revitalisation movements and of their charter myths: the struggle over the definition of legitimate and acceptable ancestors. The creation of the Felibrige – like that of the Occitanist movement – is conceptualised as only one moment among many others. This, again, confers historicity upon the movement, but it also marks who the real ancestors are: the Troubadours, not the Felibres, a move that can be understood as a way to neutralise the quasi-prophetic figure of Mistral (who died in 1914).

The ancestors that the architects of the revitalisation movement selected for themselves are first and foremost writers – rather than, say, political leaders. This trend continues to this day: studies in Occitan literature abound (see for instance Parayre 2015 for a survey of studies published in 2013), and studies of Mistral's work are innumerable (e.g. Mauron, 1993; Casanova, 2004). Ancestors can thus be selected among a wealth of different figures, who can subsequently be used and adapted to fit different ideological purposes: Dante (alleged to have first identified the Occitan domain and to have given it its name [*lingua di oco*, Langue d'oc], see for example Sibille 2002, 2007), the Troubadours, the Félibres, the pre-Felibrean Marseille writers, etc. Of all the possible choice, only sixteenth and seventeenth century authors seem not to have been subjected to any particular ideological work.

This choice provided two distinct advantages: first, it allowed the revitalisation claims to be framed in purely cultural terms, rather than in political ones – a par-

---

[24] This is reminiscent of Cerquignlini's (2007) characterisation of Occitan as the language 'in the Iron Mask', a reference to the famous seventeenth century prisoner at the Castle of If in Marseille, believed by some (including the novelist Alexandre Dumas) to be Louis XIV's identical twin. Occitan is, in this configuration, French's shameful twin.

ticular sensitive issue throughout the nineteenth and twentieth centuries given the force of French nationalism. Despite accusations of separatism launched against the language movement from its onset (Martel 2004), the bulk of the Occitan movement has consistently adhered to the project of the French state, albeit in critical ways. Second, it anchored the revival in the seriousness of the written medium, allowing the movement to dispute the prestige of French letters, and to exist in the eyes of French academic and intellectual circles.

Throughout the nineteenth and twentieth centuries, the various actors of the Occitan revitalisation movements invested much energy into the field of culture defined in a way that equated it with the literary field. This has been challenged since the 1970s, in particular within the musical field (see Mazerolles 2008; Chabaud 2013; Martel 2013) which was particularly instrumental in promoting the internal colonialism thesis according to which Occitania found itself in a similar situation, culturally and economically, to that of French overseas colonies (Drott 2011).

The overall investment in the writer as a figure of authority subjected the movement to the fluctuations of the value of culture defined in relation to traditional figures of authority. In the words of one language advocate working in the Toulouse area, Occitan has never had as many writers as it has at present, and so few readers, actual or potential.

7.6. CONCLUSION

In this chapter, I have shown that language revitalisation involves primarily the discursive construction of a narrative able to synthesise a collective project as a response to another project, conceptualised as hegemonic or dominant. This narrative performs the tasks of a charter myth, fuelling the language promotion discourse and rationalising action, claims and discourses linked to the revitalisation process. The aim of this charter myth is both to construct the legitimacy of the revival and to establish new forms of authority based on the definition of new types of authoritative knowledge, primarily linguistic in this case. Finally, the focus on language is a way for certain people to speak in the name of a wider group which it defines through the charter myth in a way that permits the rationalisation of individual hardship as a collective experience.

The charter myth laid out by the Occitan revitalisation movement in the nineteenth century and subsequently elaborated upon but never radically modified articulated its story and claims through a particular emphasis first on language as a unified system, and second on language framed through time and space as ways of generating groupness. In doing so, it adopted the framework set out by the French narrative since the sixteenth century, and in that way can be interpreted as a response to it. In other words, revitalisation emerges from a semiotisation of contact, resulting in the invention of two groups of unequal power as minority and majority groups founded on a particular element. Revitalisation movements address not only the group they claim to represent, but also the group they wish to oppose or gain recognition from, and in order to do this they need to borrow the ideological frames to which that group is responsive. In this case, language, and a particular way to frame language as describable, homogenous, whole, bounded, and steeped in time and place. In the Occitan case, the language movement was therefore never a backward movement, as its opponents have claimed since its inception, but one fully embedded in its time, one which engaged with society at large on that society's own terms. In other words, if language became an issue in nineteenth century Provence, it is primarily because language was a meaningful element for the French state and intellectual elite, one which any contestant needed to engage and grapple with to obtain if not recognition, at least consideration and acknowledgment of existence.

8

INTERNAL STRUGGLES

8.1. Introduction: language revitalisation as a terrain for language ideological debates

In the previous chapters, I redefined language revitalisation as a struggle over categorisations, and as a way to redefine the very terms of contact between groups that come to be understood as majority and minority as they are shaped. Language is, in other words, a possible terrain among an array of others that are historically and ideologically formed. Thus far I have analysed the meaning of such movements in light of historical contact between different groups. This chapter analyses internal debates within language movements, and asks what interests are at stake in internal struggles over categorisations. In the same way that time, space and groupness are central issues in the inter-group struggle over legitimate categorisations, those categories remain paramount within the minority group. This chapter does not present an exhaustive panorama of all the struggles within the revival movements, as this would amount to writing a full history of the language revitalisation process. Instead, I focus on two key moments during which central ideological issues were at stake, in the mid-nineteenth century first and in the early twenty-first century. In other words, I ask how language can serve as a terrain to articulate different societal projects within language-based social movements. What, if anything, is at stake through the control over the definition of what counts as the language to be revitalised?

Let us begin with a brief illustration of what I mean by language debates by providing an example that involves orthography – always, it seems, the most obvious terrain. There are two generally accepted orthographic standards in Provence, the first one originating in the Felibrige and the second in the Occitan movement but based on the medieval tradition (see Figure 5). One main fault line is the representation of the feminine markers in nouns, spelt <-o> in the former tradition vs. <-a> in the latter. I took the following picture of the Orange municipality entry sign in 2008. Beyond its apparent normality it provides an interesting way into the types of debates that have marked the Occitan South of France for the past 150 years or so.

The value of this sign is more connotational than denotational. Its purpose is not to inform monolingual (or even bilingual) speakers of Occitan or Provençal that they are entering the town of *Aurenjo*; it is meant to let them know that the Town Council has taken a stance on the local language. It also informs non-locals that they are in a place that is *other*, whatever different social actors might choose to put behind this term. Yet this road sign, written in one of the possible Provençal standards, the one developed by Frédéric Mistral in the nineteenth century, also points to a more

Figure 5: Bilingual road sign in Orange (photo: author)

interesting story. It was put up before 1995, but it originally bore a different form of the town's name in the local language. The cover up is apparent on the following close-up picture of the last letter (Figure 6):

The sticker with the letter <o> covers an <a>, the feminine in the Occitan standard. <Aurenjo> thus replaced <Aurenja>, on the grounds (I was told by the mayor) that the former is more authentically Provençal than the latter – a disputable assertion since the local pronunciation has [a]. The change, the mayor told me in 2008, occurred in 1995 just after he was elected. He was responding favourably to the demands of one of the language groups in Orange. The story is complicated, however, by the fact that the mayor, Jacques Bompard, was elected under the Front

Figure 6: Close-up of the sign shown above (photo: JC)

National (extreme right) label, and the change from <a> to <o> was also an attack on the previous municipal administration, an alliance between the Socialist Party and the Occitan Party. This type of debate, well represented across the world in other contexts (e.g. Schieffelin & Doucet, 1994; Flor, 2011) illustrates the types of debates that might be fought on the terrain of language within the language movement itself, or among the different language movements – depending on whether one considers that revitalisation movements are unitary or inherently heterogeneous in form. The divide between those in favour of the spelling conventions adopted by the Felibrige (<o>, in this case) and those advocating a more etymological approach (<a>) largely structures the linguistic debate in Southern France throughout the twentieth century (see Blanchet 1992; Kremnitz 2007; Costa & Gasquet-Cyrus 2012; Martel 2012).

The argument of this chapter is that the societal issues at stake in language revitalisation movements are best studied through the numerous debates that run through any such movement – and certainly the Occitan movement is no exception. Such debates are approached as 'language ideological debates', to use the term coined by Blommaert (1999a), and which he defines as:

> moments of textual formation and transformation, in which minority views can be transformed into majority views and vice versa, in which group-specific discourses can be incorporated into a master text, in which a variety of discursive means are mobilized and deployed (styles, genres, arguments, claims to authority), and in which sociopolitical alliances are shaped or altered in discourse. (Blommaert 1999b: 10)

Such debates are ideological in the sense that they shape what becomes natural, and what can subsequently count as the naturalised version of a particular truth. In that respect, the ideology that underlies the idea of language standards as the correct version of a language is the outcome of a series of debates that took place in Europe during the seventeenth, eighteenth and nineteenth centuries. In the case of the promotion of minority languages, such debates have taken place throughout the nineteenth and twentieth centuries, but in many cases, and this is certainly so in France, no single version of the idea that minority languages were in fact languages at all ever became naturalised. Those ideas are constantly challenged through new sets of debates.

Language ideological debates do not, nevertheless, only take place between proponents of different 'languages', but also within the ideological space that individual 'languages' come to constitute through their progressive constitution, or grammatisation (to use Auroux's 1995 term). Internal debates as to what constitutes 'the language', what its boundaries are, how it should be represented, by whom, with reference to whom, and for what purposes, is a constant of all minority language movements (see for instance Flor 2011 on the particularly emblematic Catalan/Valencian case).

Internal debates are often viewed among language advocates as well as in the scholarly literature on revitalisation as a hindrance to language programmes. For instance, in a paper drawing on fieldwork among Western Mono and Tewa communities in

California and Arizona, Kroskrity (2009) acknowledges the existence of such debates and calls for ideological clarification in order to overcome the type of dispute they lead to. He writes:

> Treating language renewal activities as 'sites' (Silverstein 1998) for ideological struggles and as stages upon which differences in language beliefs and practices are often dramatically displayed, I focus on the necessity of recognizing and resolving ideological conflict that would impede local efforts at linguistic revitalization. (Kroskrity 2009: 71)

Kroskrity (2009: 73) subsequently suggests that some of those conflicts originate outwith the community itself and implies that ideological clarification should allow for the separation of native and outsider issues in order to 'successfully engage in language maintenance and renewal'. The implications are that revitalisation is important in and of itself, and that any impediment standing in its way can be overcome through clarification. In my experience of the Occitan movement however, this is not the case. The debates are in fact constitutive of the movement, and no entity – language or group – can be said to be more important than the ideas expressed through those debates. In fact, some social actors in the various sectors of the language movements in Southern France have told me they would rather see the language disappear than have the version promoted by an adversary group imposed onto them. In those conditions, can language revitalisation ever be about 'the language', in a context where 'the language' is always 'a language', somebody's language, embodying particular views on language, on the community and individuals that should speak it, and on how it should be spoken?

Language revitalisation is therefore, this chapter argues, also a struggle over what legitimately counts as the language at the centre of the revitalisation effort, and ultimately what counts as legitimate language. Consequently, this chapter argues that critical studies of language revitalisation movements cannot, in any meaningful sense, aim at ideological clarification in view of facilitating revitalisation processes. Instead, they can only aim at providing social actors with situated interpretations of revitalisation as a form of struggle in a way so as to make salient the issues they are grappling with.

Analysing a number of such ideological debates from the nineteenth down to the twenty-first centuries, this chapter argues that no amount of ideological clarification will solve any such debate. They cannot be solved – any such attempt would merely displace the terms of the debate, much in the same way that modifying borders to suit nationalistic agendas does not provide long-term peace (Brubaker 1998). Rather, they are more productively analysed in terms of terrains upon which different issues are played out through time and space, entextualised and re-entextualised at will to fit different ideological and historical conditions.

The debates analysed in this chapter originated in scholarly circles and bear at their core a definition of legitimate knowledge as well as of group membership definition. They were subsequently transferred to language advocacy groups – where they are, in turn, modified, reified and used to defend or obtain positions of power. Intellectuals are often also language advocates, and many advocates seek the legitimacy conferred by academia, rending matters complicated when trying to disentangle the discursive webs through time and space.

In the following sections, I wish to historicise the debates I analyse so as to show how the initial terms of such debates can be carried over through time and space to serve very different ideological purposes. In the Occitan case, as in other cases, the main elements around which debates are organised are spelling, the naming of the language, and its historical/geographic boundaries. In other words, debates occur around issues of representation and boundaries, around issues of legitimate knowledge, authority and groupness (Brubaker 2002), and around what groups and what political projects are constructed and summoned. This chapter therefore further emphasises how language revitalisation is above all a struggle over classification not only with respect to majority and minority groups, but also within groups, fractally replicating the majority/minority divide within what apparently constitutes the minority group.

8.2. Nineteenth century linguistic ideological debates: who can speak on behalf of the South?

This section proposes a genealogy of scholarly debates on issues of language in the Occitan South, and seeks to provide a rationale for the issues they discuss. By scholarly, it is meant debates held among writers and various types of intellectuals throughout the nineteenth century. It shows how territory and history are constituted as important political resources, and how language itself became a key resource to access, influence and control the discourses that surrounded them in the nineteenth century.

8.2.1. *History as a shaping discipline*

Scholars played a major role in shaping the arguments mobilised in the debates that structured the Occitan movement throughout the nineteenth and twentieth centuries. The debates over orthographic issues in the Occitan South are ancient, and may possibly be traced to the fifteenth or sixteenth centuries, when the various southern parts of the Kingdom of France adopted spelling systems based on French (see Lodge 1993: 123).

At the turn of the nineteenth century, the Provençal vernacular was largely discredited as a language of power, making it an unlikely candidate to debate societal issues. Indeed few accorded it prestige, even when like the writer Fabre d'Olivet some sought to restore the language according to the principles of the medieval language – which was at the time slowly being unearthed by scholars such as François Marie Raynouard (the first volume of his *Choix des poésies originales des Troubadours* was published in 1816).

Marseille was an exception in this respect. René Merle (1986b) recounts an early example of debate over spelling issues between Abbé Féraud, a grammarian of the French language, and Achard, a local archivist who had composed a Provençal dictionary based on medieval conventions. At the very start of the century, Féraud attacked Achard's spelling choices on the grounds that they were too etymological – his own choices sought to distance Provençal from Latin and make it closer to Spanish and Italian in its spelling principles. Achard died in 1807, and this debate seems not to have generated any sequel. Merle (1986b: 20) notes however that the stakes were high – none less than the mastery of the written word, a question which remained constant for as long as Provençal was massively practised among the population. Nevertheless, the terms of the debate remain constant to this day: should Occitan/ Provençal be written etymologically, or according to a more phonological system? Should it remain faithful to its medieval origins, or should it be made to resemble French, or Italian, or Spanish? The issue was paramount, particularly at a time when few could read, and when they could, would only read French. The question was then both ideological and pragmatic: who should the audience of written texts be – those who could read, or those who should be able to read? And ultimately, whose representation of the Occitan South should prevail, and in whose hands should authority over representation ultimately rest?

By the middle of the century, the language question had become important enough to generate much tension among writers, philologists and in politics. What had made this turn possible? Not, it may be argued, the work of the philologists or the poets who, in the 1840s in particular, had turned to the vernacular. Not the work of Victor Gelu (1856), who wrote poetry in Provençal to document a bygone age, or even that of Simon-Jude Honnorat, the Alpine doctor turned philologist who composed the first general dictionary of the Langue d'oc, one that comprised the main dialects of what was to be perceived as one language in Romance studies (Merle 1986a; Martel 2010a). Instead, the politicisation of the language of the South of France owes much, according to the historian Philippe Martel (1982b), to the work of a southern historian, Jean Bernard Marie Lafon (known as Mary Lafon).

Mary Lafon was born near Montauban near Toulouse in 1810, into a Protestant family. While in Paris at the end of the 1820s, he published a historical novel based on the feats of the Troubadour Bertrand de Born, as well as a number of articles on modern and ancient Occitan (Martel 1982b: 6). In 1840 he published a *Mémoire sur les langues méridionales* and from 1841 a monumental, four-volume, *Histoire politique, religieuse et littéraire du Midi de la France depuis les temps les plus reculés jusqu'à nos jours*. According to Martel (1982b: 5), this last text was instrumental in forging the political consciousness of the generation of the Revival in the 1850s. In his book, Mary Lafon speaks of an antique nation in the South of France, united by one language and a common history, spread across thirty-seven French départements.

The work of Mary Lafon does not, however, emerge in a historical vaccum. Other historians had written about their visions of the splendours of the medieval South, and of the Northern Conquest, carnage and oppression. But the Midi, in that context, was not a nation to be revived, it was a scene against which the politics of the time could be painted, and the struggle of democracy against reactionary France. But, as Martel writes, whereas his forebears were writing a social history of the people,

Mary Lafon makes it the national narrative of a lost people, of those who speak the Langue d'oc. Unlike other historians solely interested in the Middle Ages, Mary Lafon's work roots the nation in Antiquity and writes of its existence until the end of the eighteenth century, that is, long after the annexation of the southern territories by France. In other words, Mary Lafon's perspective is nationalist in essence, and clashes with the much more powerful French nationalism.

8.2.2. Early orthographic debates

The Felibrige was born in this ideological climate of debates over the language, its territory and limits, its origins, and the very reason such a space as the Midi should exist. Disagreements and debates were implicitly contained in its initial revival project: while the organisation sought to embrace the entire domain of the Langue d'oc as it gradually defined it (see Sumien 2009a for different types of proposed classifications), its usual language, which gradually was being established as a literary standard as Mistral's fame grew, was based on the dialect of the Lower Rhône area of Provence (Martel 2012). Should writers in other regions, as they joined the Felibrige movement, write in the literary standard of Mistral and his followers, should they adapt the orthographic principles of the Felibrige to their own variant, or should they devise new solutions? Those debates, when they emerged, concerned in fact the centre of gravity, that is, the centre of power, of the movement (Martel 2012: 24).

In the mid nineteenth century, as the ideological conditions became ripe for the vernacular of Provence to be politicised, the idea that Provençal is dying makes its way into the learned circles of Marseille. As stated previously, Victor Gelu, the celebrated Marseille poet, could write in the early 1840s that the Provençal idiom was dying. While French was indeed making its way into Marseille's everyday life, it is likely that what was at stake was the definition of proper (legitimate) Provençal in the eyes of Gelu, in particular through judgement passed on the growing number of borrowings from French (Gelu 1856: 18). Let it be said that Gelu did not lament the death of Provençal, as he put it. He viewed it as an inevitable fact of life. The Felibrige's intellectual and political proposal emerged in those conditions and in opposition to them, between a nascent discourse of language death, national ideological conditions that make Provençal a possible poetic – and to a certain extent political – resource, and increased contact with the North and a nationalising market of ideas.

Orthographic debates were at the core of the definition of the Felibrige's stance from the very onset of the movement. Among the future founders of Felibrige themselves there were early debates between Mistral and Roumanille regarding how Provençal should be spelt (Mistral 1981), and how the orthographic choices of the Avignon and Marseille poetic schools could be made closer to one another.[25] As an example it is worth noting what Mistral wrote in a 1852 letter to Joseph Roumanille, his mentor and friend, for it condenses all future arguments regarding the weight of etymology,

---

[25] The sections on orthography have been collated by the Centre International de l'écrit en langue d'oc and can be downloaded at the following address: http://www.cieldoc.com/libre/integral/libr0574 (19 December 2016).

phonetics and which ancestors the movement should give itself. Commenting on the movement's orthographic choices, he wrote:

> *A Roumanille*
> *Le 9 janvier 1852*
> *[...] si vous saviez combien ridicule me paraît notre orthographe. Vous seriez stupéfait ! En effet, je vous le demande, quelle est la langue qui n'a ni singulier, ni pluriel et qui peut* établir *de pareils* équivoques:
> *Ama* : *aimer*
> *Ama*: *aimé*
> *Ama*: *vous aimez*
> *C'est se moquer de toutes les règles: c'est vouloir transformer notre belle langue en affreux patois, incompréhensible pour tout autre que pour l'auteur. Je ne puis concevoir quelle divinité malfaisante nous avait rendus si obtus, si bornés, si obstinés, dans un pareil pathos. Je m'en arracherais les cheveux.*

To Roumanille
9 January 1852
[...] If only you knew how ridiculous our orthography seems to me. You would be stupefied! I ask you indeed, what is this language that is without a singular, a plural and that can give rise to such ambiguities:
Ama: to love
Ama: loved
Ama: you (pl) love[26]
This amounts to mocking every rule: it transforms our beautiful language into a horrible patois, unintelligible to all but the author. I cannot fathom what malevolent divinity had made us so obtuse, so narrow-minded, so obstinate, in such respect. I could tear my hair out.[27]

Nevertheless, Mistral ultimately wrote his entire work with the spelling he had derided in the extract above.

A similar argument was developed within the Felibrige after the publication of Damase Arbaud's collection of folk songs in 1862 and 1864. Arbaud was a local doctor from Manosque in the Lower Alpes département turned folklorist. His first volume was reviewed by the Felibre Anselme Mathieu in the Felibrige's annual almanac (the *Armana Prouvençau*), who wrote:

> *L'autour, de parti pres, n'a vougu emplega ni l'ourtougràfi di Troubadour, ni aquelo di Felibre (qu'es la memo), ni meme aquelo de la primiero reneissenço (dóu tèms de La Bellaudière), e a degaia soun libre.*

---

[26] In the Occitan system, those forms, albeit pronounced identically, are rendered as *amar, amat* and *amatz*.

[27] See http://www.cieldoc.com/libre/integral/libr0574 (19 December 2016) for the full collection of letters.

The author, because of his bias, chose not to use the spelling of the Troubadours, or that of the Felibres (which is the same), or even that of the first revival (from the times of La Bellaudière), and wasted his book. (quoted in Arbaud 1864: i)

Damase Arbaud's work was carefully based on the lexicographic work of his fellow Alpine countryman, Simon Jude Honnorat (1846). For example, he maintained the –r in verb infinitives, he noted –m and –tz the first and second person plural of verbs, and noted –t the past participles of verbs. I provide as an example an excerpt from a text collected by Arbaud (1864: 25), and for the sake of comparison the same text in the Felibrige's orthography:

Original text	Felibrige orthography	English
Lou baroun sant Alexi	Lou baroun sant Alèssi	The baron of Sant Alèssi
Se voou pas maridar;	Se vóu pas marida	Does not want to marry
Per oubei' à soun pero	Pèr oubeï à soun pero [paire][28]	To obey his father
La facho demandar,	L'a facho demanda	He asked for her to come
Per oubei' à sa mero	Pèr oubeï à sa mero [maire]	To obey his mother
La vougud' espousar	L'a vóugudo espousa	He wished to marry her

Arbaud first justified his choices by attributing them to his intention to transcribe a heritage from the past, for which the 'modern orthography' (Arbaud 1864: ii), as he called it, would have seemed unfit (he deemed it 'too elastic'). In other words he rejected, for his own usage, the type of modernity indexed by the Felibres' system. However, the bulk of his argument was concerned with the denunciation of the idea put forward by Mathieu that the systems of the Felibres and of the Troubadours are one and the same. On the contrary, Arbaud asserted, his own was much closer to the way the Troubadours had written. In other words, the orthographic quarrel within the movement was a struggle over the right to represent the language, its past and future, and to establish its accepted indexical properties.

8.2.3. *Representing the South*

In order to understand what was at stake more broadly however, it is again essential to bear in mind who the members of the Felibrige were. Its founding members, as stated previously, stemmed mostly from the landed gentry. Its later members were also recruited among the educated and urban wealthy. There was in fact much at stake for both the landed elite and for the intellectual elite of the Felibrige.

The landed elite, on the one hand, used the revival movement for the part it allowed them to take part in the (French) political game on the one hand, and on the other hand to command authority and legitimacy to represent the southern part of the

---

[28] The Felibrige would use the more Provençal forms paire and maire (father, mother) instead of the French loanwords pero, mero.

country. While the Felibrige was (and is) often associated with reactionary politics, the Felibres – who came from all horizons of the political spectrum – were in theory required to leave their political opinions outwith the organisation (Martel 1986, 2010b: 120). But in its local branches, the *escolo*, the Felibrige was also an arena in which left and right party members, and most importantly Republicans and Monarchists, could watch and monitor the other camp in an attempt to maintain control over 'local belonging', a critical category and symbolic resource which one could trade upon in local elections and for which linguistic competence was viewed as essential. As Martel points out, for southern members of parliament or ministers, belonging to a southern literary association as well as celebrating local Letters was also an easy way of buying into localism without being suspected of separatism.

Writers on the other hand were primarily concerned with who would best represent Provence and the Midi more generally, hence their particular interest in the struggle: who would be able to legitimately speak in its name, to illustrate it and to impose a legitimate definition of what it was? The main way this was organised was through literary competitions: 'the true issue at stake in those competitions defining the most beautiful type of Provençal was in fact to determine where the centre of gravity of the Provençal renaissance would be' (Martel 2012: 32). The same issue would later be enacted between Provence and Languedoc, but while Martel sees local nationalism as interfering with linguistic reflection, it might be safer to posit that linguistic reflection is likely primarily a pretext for the staging of the struggle to define intellectual leadership in Southern France.

Dependent on Paris for recognition, the Felibrige could not stand for a contestation of the social or moral order defined in the French capital. Instead, it symbolised the struggle not for balance of power between the North and the South of France, but for the legitimacy to claim the benefits allotted by the elites of the capital to the southern part of the country. At a time of increased contact with the North, the definition of what constituted the true Midi became paramount in political terms; in that respect the Felibrige provided a terrain for a competition between Provence and Languedoc to be played out. But perhaps more importantly, the organisation allowed for southern intellectual elites to position themselves as part of the modernity embodied by France (and especially its capital city), while still claiming the benefits of the association with a local context.

The next section expands this argument and situates it within twenty-first century debates: how do language debates enable social actors to situate themselves both within arguments over globalisation and local issues, and to influence them?

8.3. Contemporary struggles: Provençal as a language in its own right or as an Occitan dialect

I now turn to the analysis of a violent debate that developed along the lines exposed in the previous section at the turn of the twenty-first century in Provence. As in the nineteenth century, it involved a combination of local politics and orthographic issues. It concerned the status of Provençal: was it really to be treated as a dialect of a wider entity, be it called Occitan or Langue d'oc, as had hitherto been customary? Or should it in fact be treated as a language in its own right? I analyse what is at stake in a debate that spanned a decade and is still a major force in Provençal language politics in 2015. Understanding the current debates requires, nevertheless, some elements of comprehension dating back to the late 1970s and early 1980s. I provide those below.

It is worth noting that the more general struggle over categorisations with the French state or with opponents to so-called 'regional languages' discussed in the previous chapters continues throughout the period under scrutiny. This was the case for example in recent tensions over the use of Occitan in the Toulouse metro (in the early 2010s) or over the presence of an Occitan road sign in the Montpellier area, an event analysed by Connor (2011).

8.3.1. *Ideological roots of contemporary linguistic arguments*

By the end of the twentieth century, Provençal was generally considered by language advocates of both the Felibrige and the Occitan movement to be a dialect of a wider entity called either Langue d'oc or Occitan, following in this respect the orthodoxy set by the early language movement. Much has been said until now about the Felibrige, the next paragraph will be devoted to a short introduction to the Occitan movement, an offshoot of the Felibrige after the 1920s, and more particularly after 1945.

The Occitan branch of the language movement was largely structured in the early twentieth century in Languedoc (Abrate 2001), and after the Second World War it coalesced into a publicly recognised organisation, the Institut d'Estudis Occitans (IEO), or Institute for Occitan Studies. This association, founded by intellectuals and members of the *Résistance* such as Tristan Tzara, Max Rouquette or Charles Camproux, was from the onset dominated by people who were close to the Communist Party (Abrate 2001: 390). It also positioned itself strongly against any form of Occitan nationalism (Abrate 2001). Originally an organisation dedicated to the study of language and society in the South of France, the IEO gradually became a language advocacy organisation open to non-researchers, an aspect that was accentuated after the 1980s (Jeanjean 1990).

With around two thousand members in 2010, it is, along with the Felibrige, one of the largest language organisations in Southern France. During my fieldwork, I collaborated with local and national branches of the IEO, in Marseille, the Drôme, the Ardèche, Montpellier and Toulouse. The members were very often teachers, university lecturers or civil servants. Over the period of my work with and within the movement, the links between the IEO and a centre-left political party, the Partit Occitan, intensified. The trajectory of David Grosclaude, IEO president between 2001 and 2010, was instrumental in this respect to establish and strengthen the connection. During his mandate, Grosclaude, also the founder of the Occitan weekly *La Setmana* based in Béarn, in Southwest France, worked as a journalist. After the end of his mandate he was elected to the regional council of Aquitaine thanks to a political alliance between the Partit Occitan, the Green Party and the Socialist Party. There he was instrumental in creating a public interregional language office dedicated to the promotion of Occitan.

Orthography has remained the main terrain for arguments between both sides of a polarised movement throughout the century until the present period, and a number of skirmishes took place in the early 1980s in the domain of education in particular. What set apart both factions was the use of two different and well entrenched spelling systems, the orthography of the Felibres on the one hand, and the Occitan (or 'Classical') orthography, developed from the early work of Honnorat on the other. The Occitan spelling system, developed for the most part in Languedoc, gained importance throughout the twentieth century as the centre of gravity of the language movement moved from Provence to Languedoc (Abrate 2001). By the 1980s however, it had been fully adapted to Provençal, in particular by Lafont (1972). By then, normalisation (as Catalan and Occitan sociolinguistics referred to the processes of standardisation and dissemination; Vallverdú 1990)[29] was well under way, at least as far as orthographic codification was concerned (see however Sumien 2006: 110 for an outline of the various competing norms and subnorms of Occitan).

I provide a summary of the main differences between both norms as well as textual examples below.

Occitan orthography		Felibrean orthography		
Symbol	Example	Symbol	Example	Sound
<ò>	ròsa	<o>	roso	[ɔ]
<o>, <ó>	Tolosa	<ou>	Toulouso	[u]
<-a>	parla	<-o>, <-a>	Parlo, parla	[ɔ], [o], [ə], [a][30]
<lh>	mielhs (better)	<i>, <h>	miés	[j]
<nh>	castanha	<gn>	castagno	[ɲ]
<-r>	cantar (to sing)	-	aima	silent
<-t>	cantat (sung)	-	aima	silent
<-tz>	cantatz (you love, pl)	-	aima	silent
<-s>	camisas (shirts, pl.)	-	camiso	silent

[29] According to Catalan sociolinguists, normalisation (*normalització*) was the combination of political and linguistic action to make Catalan the normal language of communication in society. It involved standardisation (*normativització*), but also the reorganisation of linguistic functions in society (Aracil, 1965; Vallverdú, 1977).

[30] There is a significant amount of geographic variation regarding the pronunciation of the final vowel in words such as *cadiera/cadiero*, a chair, or *canta*, he/she sings. The Occitan system notes all pronunciations with <a>, while the Felibrean system allows for some variation in certain cases (see also Martin & Moulin 2007).

Lafont (1972: 67) supplies an example of a text in both orthographies, which I reproduce here to give the reader an idea of the differences in practice:

Occitan orthography	Felibrean orthography
Una fes que lei dinnadas e lei sopadas dei tropèus son arrestadas e bèn marcadas, lei bailes arriban dins leis Aups onte cadun vai reconóisser lo campèstre de son arrentament. Entrements, ailalin, lei tropèus sarrats coma lei peus de la tèsta, s'avançan plan-plan, buta-tu, buta-ieu, lei fièrs menons en tèsta ! O ! lei polits escabòts ! lei bèleis escarradas d'aver !	Uno fes que li dinado e li soupado di troupèu soun arrestado, e bèn marcado, li baile arribon dins lis Aup ounte cadun vai recounouisse lou campèstre de soun arrentamen. Entremen, eilalin, li troupèu sarra coume li péu de la tèsto, s'avançon plan-plan, buto-tu, buto-iéu, li fièr menoun en tèsto ! Oh ! li poulits escabot ! li bèllis escarrado d'avé !

Batiste Bonet, *Vida d'enfant*

The seeds of discord, handed down throughout the entire twentieth century, were still present in the 1980s and 1990s despite some apparent signs of concord (in particular the establishment of a joint committee to supervise the few Provençal television programmes on the partly decentralised public service channel FR3, later France 3). The existence of competing norms was to prove tremendously fertile ground for the investment of language as a terrain for dispute, for as all protagonists recognised already in the 1970s, the choice of orthography had little to do with language. Consider for example the following texts. In his 1972 book, Lafont wrote (in Occitan):

Coma de bòn entèndre, lei rasons ideologicas son mescladas a aquela situacion (una ortografia es totjorn una ideologia). Lei occitanistas de Provènça son lei que creson a una comunitat occitana modèrna [...], a un combat de recuperacion istorica concrèt. Lei « mistralencs » son lei que creson a l'astrada fòra l'istòria d'une cultura purament literària.

Naturally, ideological reasons are mixed with this situation (an orthography is always an ideology). The Provençal Occitanists are those who believe in a modern Occitan community [...] in a struggle for concrete historical recuperation. The 'Mistralians' are those who believe in the ahistorical destiny of a purely literary culture. (Lafont 1972: 20)

Similarly, in the other camp, Louis Bayle committed an essay (in French) on Provençal orthography (Bayle 1968). Louis Bayle was a teacher and a writer, and a Provençal scholar, editor of the cultural journal *L'Astrado*. In this book, having described the orthography devised by Mistral, he suggested a possible way to bring the Felibrean and the Occitan systems together.[31] According to his solution:

- plurals, infinitives and past participles would be restored in the written language;
- <o> would replace <ou>, as in the Occitan system; and
- the feminine would also be written with a final <a>.

---

[31] Other attemps, on the Occitan side in particular, have been made – without lasting success. See Barthélémy-Vigouroux and Martin (2000) for an example.

The word for anthropology, Bayle (1968: 43) explains, would thus be written *antropologia* instead of *antroupoulougìo*, thus rendering the language more elegant. Among the reasons that led him never to implement this reform, Bayle cites habit, and the 'right of masterpiece': since Mistral produced his work with that orthography, it must be of value. His main argument, nevertheless, was ideological:

> *Enfin, dominant le débat – et c'est en fait cela l'essentiel, la réforme orthographique n'étant qu'un des moyens utilisés pour l'édification d'une « **Occitanie** » supra-provinciale –, il y a, dans le choix que les Provençaux ont à faire entre la langue de Mistral et celle que leur proposent les grammairiens occitaniens, à décider de leur survie en tant que peuple distinct, avec sa langue particulière et sa littérature originale, ou de leur fusion et confusion dans le grand ensemble unifié du Midi de la France, assez barbarement et non sans pédantisme dénommé « Occitanie ».*

Finally, at the core of the debate – and this is in fact the main point, the orthographic reform being only one of the means used towards the construction of a supra-provincial '**Occitania**' – between the language of Mistral and the one that Occitanist grammarians are offering them is the need for Provençals to decide whether they will survive as a distinct people, with its own language and literature, or in a fusion and confusion as part of a larger unified ensemble in the South of France, named rather barbarously and not without pedantism 'Occitania'. (Bayle 1968: 45; emphasis in the original)

Bayle's argument signals ongoing changes in the conception of minority languages. In 1971, Lafont could still write that the general aim of the Occitan reconquest resided in the liberation of a socially condemned voice rather than in and for the language itself (Lafont 1971: 99). Bayle's position was already different, concerned as he was by the dehumanisation of Man leading to a standardised human being (Bayle 1968: 45). The Occitan endeavour was to him the embodiment and the enactment of such a programme, one that would eventually produce cultural uniformity worldwide. The progress of contemporary discourses of cultural diversity and endangerment linked with issues of identity was, in other words, already under way.[32] The next section addresses those changes in the 1980s.

8.3.2. *Diversity and the endangerment discourse of the 1980s and 1990s: setting the old song to a new tune*

The idea that fighting for the Occitan cause was not primarily a linguistic cause but one that addressed the silencing of entire portions of the population appears to have receded by the 1980s.

---

[32] The following obervation goes beyond the scope if this volume, yet it would be useful to trace the various connections between the present discourses of diversity as they emerged in the 1960s and 1970s and previous ideas on the subject, as exposed by Hutton (1999) for example.

First, because Occitan itself continued its slow retreat from the scene, and those for whom it is a primary medium of communication became scarcer. A survey conducted in 1991 by Hammel & Gardy (1994) noted that Occitan has come to be viewed first and foremost as heritage, rather than as an everyday communication tool. Further, the authors found that less than 2% of respondents under 34 used it daily (Hammel & Gardy 1994: 54). Following the politicisation of the language in the 1970s (a trend common to all regional languages in France, see McDonald 1989), its indexical properties were at that point being reduced to acts of southern or local identity and local solidarities. To paraphrase Shandler's (2004, 2006) description of Yiddish as a postvernacular language, at that moment the fact that something was being said in Occitan became more important and significant than what was actually being said: the language became, in a sense, pure connotation, or pure indexicality. But as older traditional speakers of patois disappeared, the language's status as Occitan could be firmly established, and as new positions of authority became available the language too would be available to articulate new types of claims in the early twenty-first century, linked with discourses of globalisation in particular.

Second, perhaps, as was suggested to me by a prominent language advocate active since the 1970s, when François Mitterrand's Socialist Party won the 1981 election it was assumed that some form of victory had been achieved. The new president would honour his electoral campaign promise to grant regional languages some degree of institutionalisation, and it would have been deemed unwise among large swathes of the Occitan movement to generate political unrest while 'our friends are in office'.

The 1980s marked a clear change in politics of minority languages worldwide, not least because on the one hand identity politics were becoming more salient (Michaels 2006), and because, as described in the first part of this book, from the 1990s onward discourses of language endangerment were gaining ground worldwide (Dorian 1989b; Duchêne & Heller 2007). More generally however, the type of political activism of the 1970s gave way to a different type of language politics rooted in universalist discourse that reshaped views on heritage on every continent (Heller & Duchêne, 2007; Bortolotto, 2011).

The project that emerged in the 1980s among linguists and sociolinguists but also among language advocates promoted diversity as a more general and universal concept, paving the way to a different way to conceptualise and manage difference. The trope of diversity (Muehlmann 2007), nevertheless, also opened up spaces to debate what could legitimately count as diverse, and what could not. Within the Occitan movement, this meant that the cultural and linguistic heritage dimensions of the movement took precedence over the more overtly political aspects that had dominated the Occitan movement in the 1970s. In the 1980s, the Occitan movement also ceased to be as unitary as it had previously been, regrouped around the two poles that the Felibrige and the Institut d'Estudis Occitan (IEO) had constituted. According to Martel (1989), there was no longer one Occitanist movement, but several. The same applies to the Felibrige side of the movement, with several other movements stemming from it, for example, Parlaren (originally dedicated to securing television airtime for Provençal on the public service channels) or the Unioun Prouvençalo, both in Provence – the latter being instrumental in the emergence of a debate over the unity of the Langue d'oc vs. the existence of several *langues d'oc.*

But as Martel wrote, in the 1980s:

> [s]ocial demands became defensive: no vine shall be torn, no train line shall be shut down. In the cultural domain, one aspired to find points of reference in an all-too-mobile world. The myth of the good old days and of Paradise lost flourished. We know what happened to certain branches of the ecological movement: less a contestation of polluting capitalism than a way to look for the last oasis of calm and nature. Minority demands followed along the same path: the order of the day was no longer to fight for an oppressed minority. Times were ripe for individual quests towards a childhood culture, one's own or, pending that, one's grandfather's [...]. One did not require protest from the language, or for it to embody the refusal of the death of the land; one demanded that it sang the land, any land. (Martel 1987: 138)

On the market of authenticity, Occitan was well positioned. But this new configuration turned the language into a sought-after resource, one for which competition would increase – in particular in Provence where it met perceptions that the Provençal leadership was in sharp decline. It also met growing fears that the Occitan movement was anchored in left-wing politics that clashed with more traditionally conservative Provençal region of Avignon, the heart of Felibrean country. Those claims and fears, which as we saw above were initially mostly voiced by Louis Bayle (e.g. 1975, 1979, 1982), found a relay in the sociolinguistic work of Philippe Blanchet (1985, 1992, 2002). His writings (although from the left wing of the political spectrum) were instrumental in the creation of the so-called Provençal separatist argument developed by the later associations which this chapter is concerned with.

I now turn to the language debate that derived from those writings at the turn of the twenty-first century. After analysing the conditions in which it developed, the remaining part of this chapter will focus on issues of orthography, language naming and limits, before providing elements of interpretation accounting for the vehemence of those debates and struggles over the definition of what counts as the authentic Provençal language.

8.3.3. *A rose by any other name would not smell as sweet: the* Collectif Prouvènço, *a new player in Provençal language politics*

The orthographic debate acquired renewed importance in the year 2000, after a new organisation, the *Collectif Prouvènço* ('the Provence Collective'), appeared in the field of Provençal language advocacy. It appeared at a time when the Occitan movement was growing stronger again in the aftermath of national debates in 1999 over the signature and ratification of the European Charter for Regional and Minority Languages. While it initially drew mainly on the traditional rhetoric of the Felibrige, the Collectif gradually became autonomous in terms of discourse and aims. Its central aim was (and to this day remains) the establishment of Provençal as a separate language, and the imposition of the written norm designed by the early Felibrige as its only acceptable orthography. In other words, it embarked on a radically new project in terms of groupness and geography. From the onset this movement drew heavily on the work of the sociolinguist Philippe Blanchet, whose numerous publications (e.g. 1985, 1992, 1999) tirelessly advocate the idea that Provençal should be considered a language in its own right, and not a dialect of Occitan. More recently other academics have voiced similar ideas in other parts of Southern France (see in particular Lafitte & Pépin 2009). Those ideas break away from at least two centuries of philological (Sumien 2012) and political discourse, and for that reason should not be underestimated. This section therefore addresses the reasons why not only certain academics would seek to change the rules of the game, but also why, at a particular moment, their ideas are taken on and used in the public sphere by advocacy movements.

It is worth remarking that the outer limits of the domain of the *langueS d'Oc*, as Lafitte & Pépin (2009) call them, emphasising the plural, are strictly the same as the limits of the Langue d'oc or Occitan. The new divisions are internal. Not only are the dialects of the Occitan and Felibrige movements recast as discrete languages; the domain of Provençal is also reshaped so as to encompass all territories east of the Rhône River. In doing so, they transcend the CA/CHA heterogloss (Figure 7, below) that traverses the linguistic domain, as shown on the map below, and acts as a dialectal border between Provençal and Vivaro-Alpine in the Occitanist discourse (see also Bert & Costa 2014). The Collectif Provence thus claims as Provençal all of the Provence-Alpes-Côte d'Azur administrative region as well as the Drôme département, situated in the Rhône-Alpes region.

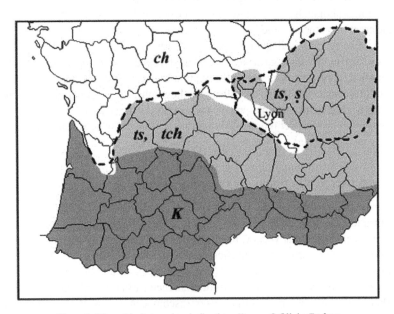

Figure 7: The ca/cha heterogloss in Southern France. © Olivier Bodson

The new organisation campaigned fiercely from the onset against what its founders saw as the 'Occitanisation' of Provence, echoing Bayle's (1968) essay. In the June 2010 of the editorial of the Collectif's quarterly *Me dison Prouvènço* (*'They call me Provence'*), Jean-Pierre Richard, the president of the association, mobilised a number of references to the history of France, including frames recalling the *Résistance* against German Occupation during the Second World War, to issue the following call. It illustrates well the type of rhetoric developed by the organisation:

Nous n'oublierons pas dans cette liste les pressions politiques de certains pseudo-défenseurs de l'environnement, qui camouflent leur engagement en faveur de la « Grande Occitanie » sous l'étiquette « Verte » pour mieux avancer leurs pions. Et que dire de « l'entrisme » cher à Léon Trotsky dans les milieux éducatifs ou dans la presse ?... Ce qui est Provençal y est par essence présenté comme « ringard », « passéiste », « désuet »...voire même « extrémiste ». Mais dès que l'on se pavoise de la croix occitane et que l'on emploie le « gai sabir » des tristement fameux Louis Alibert, François Fontan ou Robert Lafont, là, on est « branché », « in », « ouvert », « généreux », « à la mode »...

A tous ces gens, qu'ils soient décideurs, artistes, responsables politiques ou autres, le temps est venu de dire : cela suffit ! Regardez bien, Mesdames et Messieurs, ce qui se passe en Belgique, un pays quasiment coupé en deux pour des raisons linguistiques et nationalistes ! Les partis occitanistes ne rêvent que de cela, et plus encore... Vous leur ouvrez les bras et vos médias au nom de votre « branchitude » ... Mais soyez conscients de ce qu'ils veulent ... Dès qu'ils le pourraient, ils voudraient créer de toutes pièces une sorte de « Flandre » méridionale séparatiste qui demanderait par la suite des comptes à la France... Cela est d'autant moins acceptable ici que si la Flandre est bel et bien une entité véritable, cela n'a jamais été le cas de cette improbable « Occitanie » recentrée sur le Languedoc.

Cela fait dix ans que nous vous avertissions en affirmant que si l'on n'y prenait pas garde, la croix occitane flotterait bientôt sur les bâtiments publics provençaux. Certains nous répondaient : « vous dramatisez !... ».

A la lecture de ce numéro de notre magazine, vous verrez bien que non !... Comme le Général De Gaulle lança ce même mois son fameux Appel il y a soixante-dix ans, nous lançons un appel solennel pour une mobilisation générale contre l'occitanisation de la Provence. Afin que notre région, dans le cadre de la République française, conserve ses traditions, sa véritable identité. Et en un mot, son âme.

We shall not forget, among all the political pressure, that of certain pseudo-pro-environment activists, who disguise their engagement in favour of a 'Greater Occitania' under the 'Green' label to better further their positions. And what about the entrism – which Trotsky was so fond of – in the domains of education or the media? ... What is Provençal is viewed as essentially 'drab', 'old-fashioned', 'passé' ... even 'extremist'. But as soon as the Occitan cross is displayed or when one uses the 'gai sabir' [a pun on the Occitan term gai saber, or happy science, a term used in the Middle Ages by Occitan poets, and the French word sabir, 'gibberish'] of the infamous Louis Alibert, François Fontan or Robert Lafont[33], then one is 'trendy', 'in', 'open-minded', 'generous', 'fashionable'

To all those people, be they policy-makers, artists, politicians or other, it is now time to tell them: that's enough! Ladies and Gentlemen, look at what is taking place in Belgium, a country almost split in two for linguistic and nationalist reasons! The Occitanist parties dream of nothing else, and more even... You welcome them with open arms because they are fashionable... But be conscious of what they want... As soon as they could, they would create a type of separatist Southern 'Flanders' that would then make France accountable... This is all the more unacceptable that while Flanders is indeed a real entity, that was never the case of the improbable 'Occitania' centred on Languedoc

We have been warning you for the past ten years that if we didn't pay enough attention, the Occitan cross would soon fly over Provençal public buildings. Certain people would tell us 'you're dramatising!'

This issue of our magazine will demonstrate that we were not! ... In the same way that the Général de Gaulle urged us to resist, this very month seventy years ago, I solemnly want to call for general mobilisation against the Occitanisation of Provence. So that our region may keep its traditions and true identity within the French Republic. In other words, so that it may keep its soul.

Claiming to represent both its 8,000 members as well as the entire Provençal people, the organisation is a federation of local associations and municipalities who choose to adhere to the Collectif. In other words, it has few direct members. The organisations that are part of the federation consist of local Felibrean associations, as well as of local associations concerned with the promotion of folk traditions such as the Provençal costume (see Dossetto 2001). The Collectif's missions were thus stated on its website in 2010:

---

[33] Louis Alibert codified Occitan according to the Occitan norm in the 1930s, and was later associated with the Vichy government during the Second World War. François Fontan founded a left-wing political group called 'Ethnism' in the 1970s, which advocated the creation of states based on nations, in turn based on distinct languages. Robert Lafont, a founding figure of the contemporary Occitan movement, bears no connection whatsoever with the ideological options of either Alibert or Fontan.

Ço que voulèn/ Ce que nous voulons:

La reconnaissance de la langue provençale dans ses variétés dialectales, codifiée par Frédéric Mistral comme langue régionale à part entière. De la même façon, nous demandons avec la Fédération des associations du Comté de Nice, la reconnaissance du Nissart.

L'enseignement du provençal dans les écoles, collèges, lycées, et universités de Provence. Nous revendiquons dans le cadre d'une décentralisation accrue, que le choix de la langue régionale enseignée, appartiennent à la région concernée et particulièrement aux habitants de cette région.

Pour cela, nécessité d'augmenter le nombre, et de se doter d'un CAPES résolument provençal (avec d'éventuelles options concernant les autres langues d'Oc). Ce CAPES pourrait s'intituler 'CAPES de langue provençale » avec options langues d'Oc'.

Le Collectif revendique fortement l'enseignement de 3 langues:

- *une langue régionale, fondamentalement le provençal mistralien, celui qui rassemble 90% de locuteurs.*

- *une langue nationale, fondamentalement le Français.*

- *une langue internationale, que devrait être l'Anglais.*

Le changement du nom de 'PACA' par 'Provence' qui est bien entendu le nom historique de cette région. Pour prendre en compte la diversité et la pluralité de cette région, le Collectif propose l'appellation de 'Pays de Provence', la notion de Pays étant ainsi fortement développée.

La nécessité impérative de la reconnaissance respective des langues provençale (dans ses variétés dialectales et codifiées par Frédéric Mistral) et niçoise par l'assemblée régionale.

What we want:

The recognition of the Provençal language through its dialectal variants, codified by Frédéric Mistral as a regional language in its own right. In the same way, we demand, along with the Federation of Associations of the Nice County, the recognition of the Nissart language.

The teaching of Provençal in primary and secondary schools, and in Provençal universities. We demand that as part of increased decentralisation the choice of what regional language can be taught be delegated to the regions, and more specifically to the inhabitants of each region.

To that effect, we demand more [teaching] positions [in Provençal], and the creation of a resolutely Provençal CAPES [teaching certificate].

This CAPES could be called 'Provençal language CAPES' with an 'Oc languages' option.[34]

The Collectif strongly calls for the teaching of three languages:

- a regional language, fundamentally Mistralian Provençal, which currently concerns 90% of the speakers

- a national language, fundamentally French

- an international language, which should be English

The renaming of PACA [the acronym of the administrative region Provence-Alpes-Côte d'Azur] as Provence, naturally the historical name of the region. In order to take into account the diversity and plurality of this region, the Collectif advocated the use of the name 'Pays de Provence' [Provence country, or countries], the notion of pays thus being strongly emphasised.

The imperious necessity for the regional assembly to recognise Provençal (in its dialectal varieties and as codified by Frédéric Mistral) and Nissart.[35]

While the focus of the Collectif's claims in this extract is not purely linguistic, it does emphasise processes of naming: of the language as Provençal, and of the region as Provence. The conflict changes the role of the Institution (here the regional council), from adversary to legitimating authority. 'What we want', in the words of the Collectif, is for the regional assembly to take action to impose language, spelling system and territorial definition. Conversely, the Occitan movement is described as an enemy of the current institutional order, and throughout the Collectif's literature, the links of the Occitan movement with Catalonia is emphasised along with the alleged concomitant pro-independence sentiments.

The conflict thus bears on issues of delimitation of a linguistic and political territory. The association's slogan, *uno regioun, uno identita, uno lengo* ('one region, one identity, one language') is in this respect clear. What is at stake is the identification of a given space, and through that space of a group whose name derives from that of the territory, and finally of a homonymous language. It reproduces the logic of the French or the Occitan processes of groupness: France, French, French; Occitania, Occitan, Occitan; Provence, Provençal, Provençal. This logic derives from a particular

---

[34] The current teaching certificate, or CAPES, is a national exam the modalities of which are determined by the French Ministy for Education. It currently encompasses all the dialectal varieties subsumed under the appellation 'occitan-langues d'oc', and allows candidates to express themselves, in written and oral forms in any of the recognised dialects of the language. The use of any one dialect must however be consistent, and mixing would be viewed as a sign of poor linguistic knowledge and competence.

[35] This version appeared on the organisation's website in 2010. The current version at the time of writing is slightly different.

reading of history, one that considers Provence to have had a historical existence (unlike, according to the Collectif, Occitania, which the association considers to be entirely artificial). Yet just as in the Occitan case, the act of naming seeks to bring into existence the very categories it utters (Bourdieu 1980a) – The term 'Provence' refers to a large number of polities throughout history, none of which apply exactly to the borders of the present administrative region. The Collectif's action is therefore an (attempted) act of authority to contest its competitors the right to speak on language, and through it on placeness and groupeness. Its unique reference to Mistral also signals a competition in historical terms, the reference to the Troubadours being routinely erased in the organisation's discourse. The Collectif's discourse associates the term 'Occitan' with the ideas of 'complicated orthography' (also found in Blanchet 1992), 'archaic', a system that 'defaces [défiguration] the language',[36] and which is 'foreign to Provence'.

The Collectif therefore placed itself from the onset outwith the dynamics of the language movement in Southern France – the Felibrige as well as the Occitan branches – and constituted an attempt not only to redefine it but to replace it, using the strategies used by revitalisation movements identified in the previous chapters. In this respect, neither Occitania nor Provence is more legitimate than the other. Rather, and as stated by Canut (2000), naming strategies are always implicitly or explicitly strategies of domination. What we must concern ourself with is the aim of this naming conflict through the study of the discourses through which it is materialised.

The organisation's discourse evolved over time. Initially, it claimed that Mistral had only ever referred to the Langue d'oc as the sole language of Provence, and more specifically of the Provençal of the Rhône region.[37] Over time however, and possibly inspired by the sociolinguistic work of Philippe Blanchet or the example of Corsican (viewed as an Italian dialect until the 1970s when it became recognised as a language in its own right), the Collectif came to consider the possibility that new languages could be born of changing sociolinguistic conditions.

The debates sparked by the organisation outgrew largely the sphere of its members, and until recently the Collectif could claim the support of the Provence region's president, Michel Vauzelle, whose electoral base is in Arles – a town often thought to be, in popular discourse, the Provençal heartland. The arguments put forward by the Collectif were often echoed in the local press, and a debate in 2003 at the regional assembly opposed two diverging positions regarding the language. On 17 October 2003, the Provençal Regional Council voted in favour of a proposition supported by

[36] From the Collectif's website: http://www.collectifprovence.com/spip.php?article179 (12 September 2009).
[37] See a letter published by the then monthly letter of the Bouches-du-Rhône region of the IEO, L'Estaca, of which I was at the time the editor. The letter is reproduced in the following account of the language debate by Josiane Ubaud on her website: http://www.josiane-ubaud.com/Occitan%20et%20graphie%20archaique.pdf (8 August 2013, page 5). The Collectif wrote: 'quand Mistral parlait de langue d'oc unique, sa langue de référence n'était pour lui que le seul provençal rhodanien en graphie mistralienne' ('When Mistral spoke of one 'Langue d'oc' his language of reference was the sole Rhône Provençal using the Mistralian [Felibrean] orthography').

its president, Michel Vauzelle. It sought to recognise symbolically that Provençal and Niçois (or Nissart, the variety spoken in Nice) were the regional languages of the Provence-Alpes-Côte d'Azur region. This immediately caused an upsurge of indignation among Occitan activists in Provence, on the grounds that both were dialects of Occitan. On 5 December 2003, the Council voted in a new resolution submitted by the Communist party and claiming that Occitan or Langue d'oc was the true language of the region, in its various dialectal forms (including Provençal and Nissart but also Alpine dialects). The resolution also asserted that all varieties were of equal value. Both resolutions remained purely on the symbolic level, however, and entailed no consequences in terms of policies.

In order to understand this debate, and before proposing an interpretation as to why it ever came to be and why it generated disproportionate debates given the lack of political importance of linguistic issues in Provence, it is important to bear in mind the sociological base of the Collectif – or at least the one it claims to represent. Whereas both the Felibrige and the Occitan movements are mainly middle-class movements, the Collectif views itself as an emanation of the people. It claims not only to represent the people but also to be the people, and ascribes to the Occitan movement a middle-class, urban (and thus illegitimate) identity.

What was at stake in this debate and conflict is not only the general direction of the language movement in Provence but clearly the establishment of new regimes of truth, new discursive regimes to talk about the linguistic reality of the whole of Southern France. This new regime of truth concerns three main elements: first, what Provençal ought to be, and what centres of power are legitimate in deciding its future and the future of its speakers as speakers of a legitimate linguistic variety. This involves, among other elements, defining conflict in terms of working class versus middle class and country versus towns. Second, what the place of Provence should be in an increasingly globalised environment, both culturally and economically. And third, what it means to be a legitimate Provençal in the early twenty-first century. The Collectif redefines this latter question in terms of autochthony. The general programme of the organisation is captured in this next extract from its website, which brings together the main tropes it commonly summons – globalisation, ideology, identity:

> *Au nom de la liberté, jamais nous ne laisserons les tenants d'une langue d'oc unique et d'un OCCITAN globalisateur capter nos identités et nos langues au profit d'un occitanisme idéologique. Au noum de la liberta, jamai!*[38]

> In the name of freedom, never shall we let the proponents of a unique Langue d'oc and of a globalising OCCITAN capture our identities and our languages for the benefit of an ideological Occitanism. In the name of freedom, never!

---

[38] From the Collectif's website: http://www.collectifprovence.com/spip.php?article109 (1 September 2008).

8.3.4. *Occitan globalisation and the shaming of the Occitan middle class*

The discourse of the Collectif Provence evolved over the years, in particular with respect to its characterisation of Provençal as a language in its own right as we saw. Overall its main argument remains stable to this day, and its ideas spread over time to other regions such as the Cévennes, Béarn and Auvergne, or met similar existing local movements. The Collectif is now part of an Alliance for the Langues d'oc, a loose organisation which aims to redefine the internal organisation of the linguistic domain of Southern France. Its main actions consist in mobilising members of the French Parliament to get the ministries of culture and education to recognise Provençal as a separate language, and in organising a number of cultural events. Its initial plan to launch private Provençal immersion schools never saw the light of day, and its project of an observatory of the Provençal language has not made much progress over the past few years.

Interpreting the conflict generated around issues of language in Provence is a complex matter. It must certainly be read in light of the paucity of resources allocated to language advocacy in Provence. In an environment where money is scarce, and where many well-established organisations already exist, an aggressive approach can be an efficient way to market oneself, and to gain access to financial resources. One way of entering the market that public subsidies constitute and of quickly gaining shares is to portray the situation as inherently dramatic and to depict (and construct) a situation of ever-growing crisis, hence the discourse on the dangers of an imminent Occitanisation of Provence. Given how, only a few years after its creation, the organisation was able – according to members of the IEO I spoke to, and judging by the type of manifestations it organised – to attract a large part of the available funding (mostly for large cultural events), it seems undeniable that this strategy was successful.

But in terms of gaining any symbolic benefits, in the form of a governmental recognition of the discreteness of Provençal, the organisation's strategy has until now proved unfruitful. Its action has, it must be noted, led to a split within the Felibrige around the idea of Provençal as a separate language, but the Felibrige board has until now remained faithful to the idea of the Langue d'oc as one single language. How, then, can this ongoing war be explained, given how few people effectively care about regional language issues in Provence, whatever its name? In order for a satisfactory interpretation to be reached, this debate needs to be replaced within wider, worldwide debates on autochthony and globalisation.

The following text was published on the Collectif's website, and was written by one of its main leaders, Rémi Venture. The author presents it as a response to Occitan militants and, more particularly, to their attempt to use the figure of Frédéric Mistral as part of their own discourse for legitimation purposes. The text, posted on the organisation's website in October 2009, was specifically written for fellow members of the association, and yet its very publication on the internet makes it clear that beyond the association it was meant to be read by Occitan activists and politicians. Five arguments were presented that should be opposed to the Occitanist discourse.

Here I reproduce the first three of them, illustrating the construction of indexical connections between language and strictly bounded regional identity:

> *A - Se fau ramenta que pèr Mistral i'a d'acò dous siecle – bord que sian dins lou XXIen e qu'éu visquè dins lou XIXen !...– LA lengo d'o «pèr dre de cap d'obro», èro soulamen lou prouvençau. E lou Maianen aurié ama que tout lou Miejour s'aprouvençaliguèsse!*

> *B- Adounc, se lis óucitanisto volon tant èstre mistralen que ço que d'afourtisson, faudrié que se diguèsson soulamen que Prouvençau, em'uno identita prouvençalo : emplé dóu prouvençau mistralen en grafìo mistralenco, evoucacioun de l'istòri prouvençalo – rèi d'Arle, comte catalan em'anjóuvin, emai de persounage coume Mirabèu o Pascalis...–, drapèu prouvençal, etc.*

> *C- Es en reacioun à-n-aquelo pensado – e bouto, li coumprene proun !... –, que li Lengadoucian – o Óucitan, bord que li dous mot soun sinounime...-, creèron uno autro ideoulougìo, aqueste cop que soun cèntre èro lou Lengadò, emé lou biais lengadoucian – parla lengadoucian em'uno grafìo mais asatado à soun gàubi, drapèu lengadoucian, istòri lengadouciano – albigeïsme, comte de Toulouso, crousado albigeso.*

A. One should bear in mind that for Mistral, two centuries ago – we live in the 21st century, he lived in the 19th century! – the Langue d'oc, as a 'right of masterpiece', meant only Provençal.

B. Therefore, if the Occitanists wish to become as Mistralian as they claim, they should call themselves Provençal only, with a Provençal identity: use of Mistralian Provençal and Mistralian spelling, evocation of Provençal history – king of Arles, Catalan and Angevin counts, and also characters such as Mirabeau or Pascalis ... Provençal flag, etc.

C. It is in reaction to that train of thought – and I don't blame them! ... – that Languedocians – or Occitans, because both terms are synonymous – created another ideology, the centre of which, this time, was Languedoc, with a Languedocian style – the Languedoc way of speaking with a spelling system better suited to their ways, Languedocian flag, Languedocian history – Catharism, Count of Toulouse, Albigensian Crusade.[39]

The Collectif presents itself as a contemporary movement and rejects potential claims to look back to the founding myth of the Felibrige/Occitan movement as backward. It further defines which historical references are legitimate and which are not, and projects onto the medieval period the divisions that it promotes: medieval Languedoc and Provence are framed as discrete and bounded territories, with

---

[39] From the Collectif's website: www.collectifprovence.com/spip.php?article215 (23 October 2009).

different (competing) allegiances that paved the way to contemporary regional identities, associated with flags that signal continuity since the Middle Ages. The main social fear it points to nevertheless lies in the idea of mixing and the loss of perceived homogeneity – of the impure. To one territory corresponds one, and only one, history, language and orthography. Denying this is putting one's own identity at risk. The entire group is thus connected to the literary revival of the nineteenth century, pushing to its paroxysm the revivalist ideology of the redeeming text that pervades the entire language movement in Southern France, as identified by Lafont (1997: 114).

In expressing its fears, the Collectif expresses through language and issues of autochthony highly contemporary (and international) fears about the alleged loss of homogeneity of the very structure of society (Appadurai 2006). Those in turn are very much connected with issues of globalisation and of identifying or defining 'us' and 'them' in late modernity.

Globalisation is summoned in many of the organisation's texts through its association with the Occitans. In 2013 for instance, it was the object of a public petition for preventing Provençal from being dissolved into 'Occitan globalisation'. Earlier, in 2009, the expression was used as a central part of a call to take part in a demonstration (called *Sian e saren*, 'we are and we will be') that took place at the same time as another demonstration – convened by the Felibrige, the IEO and a number of other organisations such as the FELCO (*Fédération des enseignants de langue et de culture d'oc*), an Occitan teachers' association. The text read:

> *La reconnaissance des langues d'oc est plus que jamais à l'ordre du jour. La globalisation occitane ne peut conduire qu'à l'échec de la mise en œuvre d'une politique régionaliste authentique.* [the entire extract appears in bold in the original text]
>
> The recognition of the Langues d'oc is more than ever on the agenda. The Occitan globalisation can only lead to the failed implementation of authentic regionalist policies.[40]

It is the opposition to this 'Occitan globalisation' that makes possible the definition of a good regionalist policy, that is to say an authentic one – none of those terms apparently requiring any explanation. It is hard not to see in the use of the term 'globalisation' an echo of the debates concerning 'globalisation' in general. In particular, the opposition between 'authenticity' and 'globalisation', or at least the need to redefine authenticity in conditions of globalisation (Heller 2005; Heller et al. 2014) is well-known in anthropological literature. In particular, authenticity may serve as refuge against the forces of globalisation perceived as disembodied and threatening, as a source of unrest and decomposition, and as the cause of the overthrow of traditional values (Ali-Khodja & Boudreau 2009). Globalisation is by now a familiar trope, one that summons negative associations such as business relocations in parts of the world

---

[40] Collectif Provence website: http://www.collectifprovence.com/spip.php?article175 (25 August 2013).

offering cheaper conditions of labour, job losses, or the loss of traditions, values and ways of life.

The defence of traditions is a central part of the Collectif's activities. In particular, the costume, traditional gastronomy and the right to wear the traditional Camargue hat rather than a helmet (as required by French law) while riding horses are focal points of the organisation's activities. Through the association of the terms 'globalisation' and 'Occitan', I suggest that the Collectif may hope to rally some of those who oppose the anonymous forces of economic and cultural globalisation by identifying and designating a common enemy. The Occitan becomes, in other words, the identifiable face of globalisation.

Within this framework, the Collectif is able to gather (or at least, to summon) around its ideas the victims of globalisation, the Provençal working class, and especially its rural component and to oppose the purported beneficiaries of globalisation, the middle classes. The Occitan movement is associated with those middle classes in a number of instances – Occitanists are for example called 'Bo-b'oc' in at least two texts. 'Bo-b'oc' is a compound word made up of the French term *bobo* (or hipster) and *oc* for Occitan. The Bob'oc is part of an urban intellectual elite, whose language is usually deemed inauthentic by the Collectif as well as by its main academic sources of inspiration (Blanchet 1999, 2002). In a text published on its website, and no longer available online, the Collectif wrote:

> *Nous en avons assez de ces « Bo-b'oc » qui vous disent que la Provence n'est qu'une partie de la grande Occitanie dont la langue se dit « langue d'oc » au singulier, ou « provençal occitan ».*

> We are fed up with those 'Bo-b'oc' who tell you that Provence is but a part of a greater Occitania whose language is 'Langue d'oc' in the singular, or 'Provençal Occitan'.[41]

The interests represented by the Occitan movement are thus, in this discourse, those of the wealthy middle classes understood as being favourable to the ideals of globalisation. The identifiable face they provide makes a discourse of resistance easier to convey.

---

[41] Collectif Provence website: http://www.collectifprovence.com/spip.php?article107 (25 August 2013). The term was also in a different (but similar) text in its internal journal *Me dison Prouvènço*, issue 21, and reproduced on the following website: http://fr.academic.ru/dic.nsf/frwiki/1885903 (19 December 2016). The text reads:

> *Nous en avons assez de ces 'Bo-b'Oc' qui vous disent que la Provence n'est qu'une partie de la grande Occitanie dont la langue se dit 'langue d'oc' au singulier, ou 'provençal occitan' ... pour ne pas dire 'occitan' tout court. Une langue qui ne pourrait s'écrire que d'une manière autoproclamée 'classique' c'est-à-dire d'une façon archaïque, tout en prononçant autrement. Le tout en se référant à une identité qui n'est pas la nôtre, mais recentrée sur la seule 'Occitanie' au sens étymologique du terme.*

> We are fed up with those 'bo-b'Oc' who tell you that Provence is but a part of a greater Occitania whose language is 'Langue d'Oc' in the singular, or 'Provençal Occitan' ... not to say 'Occitan' full stop. A language that could only be written in a self-proclaimed classical style, i.e. in an archaic way, but pronounced differently. All this in reference to an identity that isn't ours, but centred on 'Occitania' only, in its etymological sense [that is to say, for the authors of the text, Languedoc].

With regard to the highly disembodied but anxiety-inducing processes of globalisation, personifying it through the figure of the Occitanist may allow for protagonists to re-appropriate the discursive space and to renegotiate a minority position within that space, by aligning with the French state against those who are constructed as its enemies. Language becomes an ideologically acceptable fetish to produce a discourse on the unnameable, on processes for which nobody is apparently accountable. Naming the language (Provençal rather than Langue d'oc or Occitan) may in this configuration be a way to claim agency with regard to otherwise elusive processes. Beyond the language itself, the act of naming an object which one may shape allows for the appropriation of a story, one through which a more favourable future might be told. In this respect, the progressive demise of traditional speakers of the vernacular in Provence leaves a legitimacy gap, one that becomes available for diverse – and competing – appropriations.

8.4. CONCLUSION

In this chapter, I sought to show that debates over linguistic issues within language advocacy movements had little to do with ideological clarification. Instead, such debates concern the right and capacity to name the world and to impose one's own narrative upon it. They concern the ability to name groups, and determine who should be part of them, and who should not. But more significantly, such internal debate fractally replicate the type of categories that revitalisation movements generate in the first place to assert their existence in the eyes of the dominant group against which they pit their action. Categories of majority and minority are thus replicated within the minority group, and the same strategies are then used to achieve different goals and agendas, to command the necessary authority to impose different views over the categories that are deemed important at the time they are contested. What should therefore be borne in mind when analysing such movements is that they are not intrinsically about right or wrong, but about the capacity to create and recreate groups and meaningful categories. In that sense, no amount of ideological clarification or purification will ever settle internal debates or provide necessary impetus for the success of revitalisation as an endeavour. Instead such movements and debates need to be studied for what they are: struggles for the legitimate definition of social categories, whose legitimacy is a function of the myths they can summon on of the authority they can come to exert over them.

LEGITIMACY

The final two chapters of this book are concerned with the necessity for the charter myth of language revitalisation movements to summon certain figures to legitimise its claims while simultaneously coming to terms with the discrepancies it might encounter in terms of the expectations those categories of people might hold regarding the language. The question addressed here is therefore that of the construction of the legitimate member of the group under construction in revitalisation, and how that legitimacy derives from certain types of language use. I also address how issues of legitimacy are contested by those very social actors the revitalisation movements needs to further its claims.

Within the Occitan language movement, the explicit take on groupness is that all inhabitants of the linguistic domain (or of Occitania) are Occitan (or in some versions potentially so depending on whether they identify as such or not). This principle is generally replicated within the other sectors of the language movement that identify with the *langues d'oc* in the plural option. In that case, all people living in Provence are (potentially) Provençal, and the same goes with Gascony and other regions. In other words, the Occitan language revitalisation project (just as most, if not all similar projects in Europe) is viewed as inclusive, and seeks to promote an open approach to identity. In fact, Occitan language advocates often voice the idea that the local language is a way for immigrants from North Africa or Eastern Europe to integrate into the local community. This idea is present among diverse sectors of the movement: the music band Dupain claims that Polish immigrants could find integration into local working class communities during the 1980s in areas such as Fos-sur-Mer, then famous for its shipyards (further examples of such claims are given by Merle 1977). A similar idea is developed by such organisations as the *Association des enseignants de langue d'oc* (AELOC), an organisation of teachers and parents promoting the teaching of Occitan in the public sector of education. In this particular case, the claim is that learning the regional language is one way for immigrants or descendants of immigrants to learn about the region and its culture. Similar views were expressed by some of my own pupils' parents in Marseille when I taught Occitan there between 2003 and 2005. Most of them had migrated from the other side of the Mediterranean and thought it important for their children to acquire some Occitan.

Language revitalisation is, this book contends, about imposing new categories and new definitions of former categories – most conspicuously in the Occitan case, it is about bringing into existence a group called 'the Occitans' who speak 'Occitan' in 'Occitania' (Bourdieu 1991b: 223). This entails, to varying degrees, replacing the categories of 'Southern French', 'patois' and 'Le Midi'. The place-based narrative of the Occitan movement, as well as the need for that narrative to appeal to the widest possible audience demand broad inclusiveness. It implies defining or redefining groupness not in terms of origin but at least in part according to chosen affiliation in order to incorporate a broader base, including people of Southern descent born outwith the traditional Occitan-speaking area but who have chosen to learn and use Occitan, and to move to the area. This approach echoes general concerns within language-based movements in Europe. Tadhg Ó hIfearnáin (2015: 82) suggests for example that the association of language to territory (rather than only people) is well anchored among minority language movements in Europe – the implication being that the said language belongs to all contemporary inhabitants of a given territory, irrespective of their origins. The Occitan movement's approach also fits into a prevalent ideology in France that associates belonging with choice rather than birth to promote a view that anyone can be or become Occitan (or Provençal, or Gascon) as long as they choose to be so. A related view postulates that all people born in Occitania are Occitan, whether they know it or not: the rejection of this identity is then equated with alienation. In a response to a comment to one of his weekly blog post on the online Occitan media *Jornalet*, the linguist and self-identified Occitan nationalist Domergue Sumien wrote: *'Lo pòble occitan subís una alienacion extrèma'* ('The Occitan people is undergoing extreme alienation').[42] 'Occitan' here referred to the entire population of the South of France, together with the Occitan parts of Italy and Spain.

In the next chapters I argue that the all-encompassing equation posited in the Occitan movement, as in many language-based movements in Europe, is not as straightforward as it appears. Despite its ideology of inclusiveness, the Occitan language movement, together with most language movements founded predominantly on Herderian principles, struggles to consider all linguistic practices as being of equal value, and to consider everyone as equally legitimate. In fact, the question of what constitutes good or legitimate language is paramount to discussions among language advocates and is, I argue, central to the very operation of language revitalisation for it determines the conditions under which social actors may or may not be included. In other words, in societies where inclusion is a founding principle, the nature of language allows us to determine who is in and who is out, and to hierarchise individuals within the language movement and society at large. In other words, language revitalisation is perhaps not about *what* language is being revived. It is, rather, about *whose* language is, and how.

One domain in which heated discussions often occur in revitalisation movements is the language of younger speakers. Let us consider a telling example: in a recent book, Eric Fraj (2013), a musician and a teacher of Occitan in secondary education, contrasted his view on traditional and youth (acquired through formal education) speech. On the one hand, he rejected the very notion of a linguistic standard, arguing instead that the language is constituted of nothing but its various vernacular instantiations:

> *En réalité l'occitan n'est nulle part ailleurs que dans cette pluralité linguistique pratiquée à l'oral comme à l'écrit sur son territoire linguistique.*

> In reality Occitan does not exist outwith this linguistic plurality as practiced orally and through the written medium on its linguistic territory. (Fraj 2013: 129)

---

[42] *Jornalet*, 13 May 2013: http://opinion.jornalet.com/lenga/blog/518/lenga-e-accion-armadasubre-lflnp.

On the other hand however, he condemned the speech of new speakers and deems it often influenced by French, thus reproducing a hierarchy between acceptable authentic forms of language and unacceptable ones:

> *Combien de nouveaux locuteurs du languedocien entendons-nous (souvent passés par une Calandreta et les cours du secondaire) qui le prononcent à la française, de l'ouverture des voyelles au déplacement d'accent tonique [...] ? En l'occurrence ces néo-locuteurs prononcent comme c'est écrit, ce qui signale alors une pédagogie inadaptée car trop basée sur l'écrit et/ou un oral professoral lui-même déjà inauthentique.*

> How many new speakers of Languedocian do we hear (even though they often went through the Calandreta [immersion] system and attended high school classes [in Occitan]) pronouncing the language in a French way, from the opening of vowels to the shifting of stress patterns [...]. In effect those new speakers pronounce as written, which thus signals inadequate methodologies of teaching, too focused on the written word and/or an already inauthentic teacher speech. (Fraj 2013: 129)

Legitimate language is defined by Bourdieu as:

> uttered by a legitimate speaker, i.e. by the appropriate person, as opposed to the impostor [...] it is uttered in a legitimate situation, i.e. on the appropriate market [...] and addressed to legitimate receivers; it is formulated in the legitimate phonological and syntactic forms [...] except when transgressing these norms is part of the legitimate definition of the legitimate producer. (Bourdieu 1977: 650)

But in Fraj's perspective, what characterises legitimate language is its (inherent) authenticity, its link with inherited speech (as opposed to the artificial speech based derived from books), its capacity to index place, and its 'properly contextualised performance' (Silverstein 2014). In other words, legitimate Occitan, for a long-time language advocate such as Fraj, is the opposite of the 'voice from nowhere' that standard languages are thought to embody (Gal & Woolard 2001).

Yet if Bourdieu's framework is to be followed, legitimate language is only ever legitimate on a given market on which the value ascribed to speech is only defined with respect to a particular field, that is, a structured space of power relations (Bourdieu 1993: 72). The task of language-based social movements consists largely in appropriating the current market conditions to transform them and regiment them so that new types of power relations may exist within what ultimately emerges as a new field. Recategorisation is, in this respect, a central operation. Such changes (e.g. the switch from 'patois' to 'language') restructure the very way individuals interact and the type of linguistic authority that social actors resort to.

The nature of the legitimate language and groupness membership criteria, I argue, are comprised in the charter myth of any revitalisation movement – but in ambiguous ways. In the Occitan case, legitimate language is, according to the language movement's narrative, simultaneously the written language whose roots lie in the prestigious literature of the Middle Ages, as well as the everyday language of traditional speakers. In both cases, legitimacy is founded on tradition, but on two very different versions of tradition. To a certain extent, the tensions which arise from those two visions of tradition play out the antagonism between Lockean and Herderian types of ideologies (Bauman & Briggs 2003): in the former perspective good language is anonymous and is valued for its clarity and transparency; in the latter, it is steeped in and indexically linked with people and place.

Since theoretical membership in the group ('the Occitans') as defined by the revitalisation movement is, on the surface of things, merely a matter of claiming affiliation, the real question becomes not only who is a legitimate member of the group, whose language is legitimate, but also: who gets to decide on that matter? Who can, as a consequence, speak on behalf of the group, and who can speak authoritatively on issues of language – thereby defining both legitimate language and legitimate speakerhood. Such issues are constantly stirred up within language movements and often generate the types of heated debates that I analysed in the previous section.

The next two chapters analyse how two ambiguous categories of social actors, both central to revitalisation movements, yet constantly under suspicion, shape their understanding of the language movement, and how they resist its agenda. Analysing those categories in turn helps understand how legitimacy is constructed and established among such movements. The two categories, defined for practical purposes in terms of speakerhood (see each chapter for a critical discussion) are the traditional speakers and the children who acquire Occitan through schooling. The first are essential for they provide numerical strength (in the Occitan case they are the overwhelming majority of the three million people said to speak the language – see Sibille 2002) the connection with an unbroken tradition as well as with authentic language-as-*emplaced* (indexing place). Yet their failure to pass on the language as well as their attachment to very localised forms of language, and their possible rejection of the language movement's project of an all-encompassing language makes them potentially suspicious. The young are both the future of the language; yet they are also suspicious in many ways. In particular, their speech tends to display many signs of contact with the dominant language, in particular in prosodic terms as exemplified by Fraj's comment above.

9

LEGITIMATE LANGUAGE AND TRADITIONAL SPEAKERS

9.1. INTRODUCTION: FINDING THE 'TRADITIONAL SPEAKER'

When I first became acquainted with the Occitan language movement in Provence in 2003, I was initially surprised by the discrepancy between two types of arguments I would hear about language rights: Occitan needed to be given status because of the large proportion of speakers in the population. Yet those remained largely mythical as I was regularly told that there were no native speakers left, at least in the Marseille area where I was based. Native speakers never seemed to attend any of the cultural events organised by the local branch of the Institut d'Estudis Occitans (IEO) whose activities I attended. Two consequences resulted from this: first, claims were made on behalf of Occitan as 'the language of the country'; second, activism was focused on language rather than people, and on training new speakers rather than on catering for the remaining, and ageing, speakers.

I later discovered exceptions, for example the work conducted in Cucuron, near Aix-en-Provence, which led to the publication of Alain Barthélémy-Vigouroux and Guy Martin's (2000) book and CD, designed to learn Occitan as spoken in Provence (their own terms). Many other such exceptions exist. But traditional speakers are always a challenge to a language revitalisation movement: they are paramount in such a movement's definition, and yet they belong to the old order of things. They are useful as figures, less so as individuals. The language movement purports to speak on their behalf, and yet often those people have no interest in the movement, or even in reviving the language. Some may even forcefully oppose it, as did a woman who was 91 when, in 2005, I visited an old people's home in northern Provence with a group of 13 year-old pupils who were learning Occitan. She argued angrily that her parents and herself had struggled hard to rid themselves of the patois and to invest in French, and could not understand why it was being brought back.

Revitalisation movements extoll elders whose usual language of childhood sociali-sation had been patois (in their own words) or Provençal/Occitan (in the words of the language advocates). They are the 'traditional speakers', the true bearers of language and tradition. Yet they are also responsible for not passing on the language to their children and grandchildren: in that sense they are both culprits (non-transmitters) and victims (they did not pass on the traditional language because they were alien-ated). Those people are often summoned in discourse, and ignored in actual fact. Their speech is often viewed as a model, and yet in many ways it is embarrassing: it is marked by contact with the dominant language, most often in the form of abundant lexical borrowings. In other words, such people are both a necessity and an impediment for language movements as they act as a constant reminder of the condition such movements strive to overcome.

The term 'traditional speaker' is heavily loaded and while it is used by language advocates themselves it also belongs to a wider discussion on speaker typologies in documentary linguistics (Bert & Grinevald 2010; Grinevald & Bert 2011). Use of this terminology tends to restrict social actors to a set of linguistic competences which, as Muehlmann (2012b: 164–5) points out, is highly problematic for it reduces individuals to the sole status of 'speaker', leaving aside other competences that they or their relatives might value more. In her example the 'last speaker of Cucapá' was also an excellent fisher and singer. As Muehlmann writes, the intention of the radio show host who announced the passing of this 'last speaker of Cucapá' was to raise support for extending medical services into this community. But the implication was that an indigenous fisherwoman who has died in a poor Mexican settlement needs an entire indigenous classification in her head alone for her death to matter. Identifying what is lost in an individual's death by pointing out she is a "last speaker" prioritises the "speaker" rather than the mother, the wife or the fisherwoman' (Muehlmann 2012b: 165). The term 'traditional speakers' also tends to dehistoricise the people it refers to, and automatically categorises other speakers as non-traditional. In this chapter I focus on the claims to legitimacy that those people can claim on the basis of their speakerhood.

In order to explain the apparently paradoxical treatment of those individuals in the Occitan language revitalisation narrative, this section analyses some of the ideological underpinnings of how those 'traditional speakers' view the language movement. It shows how the narrative wrought within the advocacy movement remains opaque to those very people it aims to serve, and ultimately how language advocates and traditional speakers function within two radically distinct indexical orders, that is, layers of indexical associations and 'constellations of ideologically related meanings' (Eckert 2008: 454) which come to refer to different cultural and social experiences (Silverstein, 2003). The introduction in this chapter of terminology from semiotic anthropology (see Mertz 2007) is particularly useful to understand how the terms 'Occitan', 'Provence' and even 'language' come to index very dissimilar social worlds for both categories of actors. Traditional speakers are ultimately left to occupy on the one hand a totemic role as ancestors, and on the other to feature as figures to legitimise claims made by the language movement.

In the following sections I focus on how language features in the indexical order of the traditional speakers I met in Provence, and on how their approach to categorising speech differs from the discourse of proponents of either a single language in Southern France or of several languages. The discrepancy between the orders of indexicality in which traditional speakers and language advocates take part in helps explain, I argue, why the former are often reduced to symbols (or rather, indexes) in the discourse of the latter – and why, despite the apparent overvaluation of traditional speech forms their speakers are not fully members of the revitalisation movement.

9.2. 'LANGUAGE' ACCORDING TO TRADITIONAL SPEAKERS IN PROVENCE

The very existence of a language-based social movement in Southern France rests upon the premises that there is such a thing as a discrete, bounded, identifiable linguistic entity which can collectively be termed 'Occitan' or 'Langue d'oc' (or 'Provençal', or 'Gascon' and so on in the competing groups – the dynamics are fundamentally alike). Yet for the individuals who had learnt the language in their homes in the 1920s or 1930s such an object was usually non-existent.

Lafont (1984) identified a number of layers of language in Southern France which all exist in an interrelated way and which index different orders and different social worlds. First, an 'inherited Occitan' (*'Occitan hérité'*), the one dialectologists are interested in: '[t]his usage constitutes the now residual majority of Occitan usage, used to count natural Occitan speakers' (Lafont 1984, reproduced in Lafont 1997: 97). This is the language of the people I refer to in this chapter. Second, a 'reconstituted Occitan', the consequence of 'the successive waves of normalisation' applied to the inherited language. But, Lafont adds, in the absence of a truly standardised language, what obtains is 'a mobile arrangement from subject to subject, and from moment to moment for each subject, between elements borrowed from the norm, that is, to a written language, and to natural dialectology, in more or less direct relation with the subject's own biography and geographic base' (Lafont 1997: 98). This is the general speech of most language advocates in Southern France, who view the inherited variety both as an unreachable ideal and as the sign of a bygone age. Next to those Occitan usages Lafont identifies a range of local or imported varieties of French.

Michel Bert's (2001) linguistic and sociolinguistic work in the Pilat region near Saint Etienne in Central France also showed that speakers saw no particular linguistic difference where linguists identify two distinct languages, 'Occitan' and 'Francoprovençal' (see also, on that subject, Bert & Costa 2014). While studying a local association of language enthusiasts where (mostly elderly) speakers from the north-western area of the Pilat region and others from further south met on a regular basis, Bert found that participants consistently overlooked the difference in stress placement pattern that linguists draw upon to distinguish the two languages, among other criteria. Members from the various locations did not recognise that (measurable) difference as meaningful, and consequently did not turn it into a feature that allows for the construction of a discourse of difference.

The recategorising work of the revitalisation movement therefore involves taking into account and transforming both the dominant discourse of the State, and that of the traditional speakers in order to naturalise its own – hence the insistence on the part of the Provençal-as-a-separate-language proponents to portrait the Occitan movement as artificial (Blanchet 2002), in order to naturalise its own construction as 'Provençal'.

Let us take one example from the Drôme area in Northern Provence (Figure 8). The entire Occitan domain is traversed by innumerable heteroglosses, few of which are rendered meaningful within a 'language framework' by the revitalisation movement, backed by linguistics.

Figure 8. Heteroglosses in the Drôme area of Northern Provence (Map © Olivier Bodson)

Conversely, informants regularly reported the Rhône Valley, which corresponds to no particular heterogloss, as a meaningful linguistic and cultural border. The river was, however, an important political border in the Middle Ages between Provence and Languedoc, between the Holy Roman Empire and France. The next section will illustrate further how 'language' indexes very different realities for traditional speakers.

9.3. TERMINOLOGICAL CONFUSION IN ORANGE

During my fieldwork in the Orange region (2007–2009), traditional speakers took the shape and the voice of three women aged 67 to 88. This section analyses how they categorised language, and how they viewed revitalisation efforts. I wish to illustrate that the mismatch between them and language advocates stems from radically diverging ideologies of place in particular, leading to a notion of groupness at odds with the agenda of the revitalisation movement (see also Milhé 2008). For this reason, this section argues that the legitimacy that traditional speakers are thought to possess among language advocate can only remain symbolic: they belong to different worlds. While they might also be thought of as constituting the logical target of the language movement, my experience in several sectors of revitalisation has informed me that they more often than not are not. They are nevertheless essential figures for the revitalisation movement, living incarnation of ancestors and proof that the language once had, and still has, a sociological and substantial numerical basis.

Mrs R. was 88 when I met her in 2008 in her suburban home in Orange. She had never been part of any language organisation. Her son-in-law, who was active with the local Occitan immersion school and who had learnt Occitan in evening classes, introduced us. Mrs R. had grown up in the Nice area until she was ten. She grew up speaking the Nice patois, as she called it, or, to use the generally accepted terminology among linguists, the Nice dialect of Occitan Provençal. She then moved to the Orange area to work on a farm, where she remained all her life. There she learnt the (linguistically relatively close) local vernacular to avert mockery, she told me. Until our meeting, she had not spoken Occitan to anyone since 1991, when her husband died. She had never wanted to use that language with her son-in-law. Our conversation lasted for two hours, and covered topics related to her personal biography.

The case of Jouseto and Mireio is a little more complex. They were 75 and 67 when I encountered them in 2008 after a Provençal class organised by a local language organisation (affiliated to the Felibrige), *Lou Cieri* (the local Provençal name of the Roman theatre in Orange). The organisation was at the time concerned with folklore and language, and as far as Provençal was concerned organised two weekly classes – one for beginners and one for advanced participants (involving between five and ten participants each). The classes I attended consisted in reading and translating classical texts by nineteenth century Felibres, Mistral in particular. Jouseto and Mireio grew up hearing 'patois', as they called it, but considered their competence to be fragmentary. In fact, their competence was probably not the cause for their attendance: rather, attending the class was a way for them to socialise around something which they saw as theirs and as a reminder of their childhood, and which they could no longer share with anyone else. Our two-hour conversation took place mostly in that language however.

This chapter is also informed by my work as a teacher of Occitan at secondary level in public education in five nearby schools, as well as by a survey of the nearby Southern Drôme area I conducted as part of the *Francoprovençal and Occitan in Rhône-Alpes* (FORA) project between 2007 and 2009 (Bert et al. 2009).[43] This particular project involved numerous conversations and interviews with older speakers in the North Vaucluse and Southern Drôme areas.

9.3.1. *Categorising speech and language: 'patois' and 'mistralien'*

Mrs R. lived through the linguistic change from what she always called 'patois' to French, a process she said was completed by the 1970s. As far as I could assert, and despite her son-in-law being very much invested in the life of the local Occitan immersion school she seemed indifferent to the language promotion discourse. Jouseto and Mireio had been exposed to the discourse of the Félibrige, a discourse they had interpreted in their own way. During our conversation they used the term 'patois' three times, 'Provençal', 'Occitan' and 'Langue d'oc' once, and 'Mistralien' (i.e. derived from the name of Frédéric Mistral) three times. Among members of the Félibrige 'Mistralien' is usually reserved to describe a spelling system or Mistral's literary style and language, but they used it to refer to their own speech, as in the exchange below. I transcribe the interview in the Mistralian orthography they would have used, and I refer to myself as 'James'.

1	**James**	*e l'ideio de Calandreto aloro pensas que pòu ajuda a*
		and so this idea of Calandreta do you think it can help to
2		*countinua la lengo?*
		maintain the language?
3	**Jouseto**	*ben vo mais / ei pas lou mistralen*
		ah yes but / it's not Mistralian
4	**James**	*non non*
		no no
5	**Jouseto**	*mais enfin euh si pòu*
		but really er you can
6	**James**	*mai / lou mistralen es ço que se parlo vo es unicamen la*
		but is Mistralian what people speak or is it only the
7		*grafio vo lou biais d'escriure?*
		orthography or the way to write?
8	**Jouseto**	*oh non / escriure / ei pas lou biais d'escriure / crese que*
		oh no / writing / it's not the way to write / I think that
9	**James**	*la lengo que parlas / vous / coumo la sounas?*
		this language you speak / yourself / what do you call it?

[43] The FORA project was commissioned by the Rhône-Alpes regional government in order to inform the elaboration of a public policy for Occitan and Francoprovençal in the region. It consisted in a combination of quantitative and qualitative surveys in two selected villages in each of the region's *départements*.

10	**Jouseto**	*mistralen mai / par exemple vau dire Aurenjo [ur'ɛŋdʒə] /*
		Mistralian but / for example I'll say Aurenjo [ur'ɛŋdʒə] /
11		*Aurenjo [ur'ɛŋdʒə] nousautri l'apelèn disèn [ur'ɛŋdʒə]*
		Aurenjo [ur'ɛŋdʒə] we call it we say [urɛŋdʒə]
12		*coume Mistral mai elei dison [urɛŋ] [urɛŋ] Aurenjo*
		like Mistral but they say [urɛŋ] [urɛŋ] Aurenjo
13		*[ur'ɛŋdʒa]*
		[ur'ɛŋdʒɑ]
13	**James**	*d'accord*
		alright
14	**Jouseto**	*prounouncion pas tout à fait la / m'enfin bon / mai*
		they don't pronounce exactly the / but
15		*comprenès quand parlon*
		you understand when they talk
16	**James**	*ah vo: vo*
		ah ye:s yes

In Jouseto's mouth, 'Mistralien', usually an adjective, turned glossonym in the context of the rivalry between 'Provençal' and 'Occitan'. 'Provençal' is also used to indicate an opposition to 'Occitan':

1	**James**	*vo / vo / que n'en pensas de la calandreto / vousautri?*
		Yes / yes / so what do you think of the Calandreta?
2	**Mounico**	*ben c'est pas tout à fait pareil*
		Well it's not exactly the same thing
3	**Jouseto**	*nousautrei*
		we
4	**Mounico**	*eux c'est l'occitan nous c'est le provençal*
		they [speak] Occitan and we [speak] Provençal
5	**Jouseto**	*vaqui*
		that's it

In the next extract the term 'patois' is used to refer to the language of childhood and home, and alternates with 'Provençal':

1	**Jouseto**	*dounco esplicave que nosti parent voulién pas que*
		so I was explaining that our parents didn't want us to
2		*parle:ssian patois*
		speak patois
3	**Mounico**	*c'est vrai / ma ma maire un còp èro vengu un ome dins sa*
		that's true / once a man came to my my mother's
4		*granjo / e / e li a di a sa maire ei vengu un ome / e sa*
		farm and she told her mother a man [ome] came / and her
5		*maire li a di que l'ome se cresié ((inaud.)) li a di fau*
		pas dire
		mother told her the man thought ((inaud.)) she said don't

6   *ven un ome fau dire ven un moussu / e amé moun fraire*
                say [ome] say [moussu][44] with my brother
7   *se parlavo toujour patois abitave amé moun fraire que ei*
                it was always patois I used to live with my brother who
8   *mort i a dous an aurié / quatre vint / mai alors li sabié*
                died two years ago he would be / eighty / but then he
9   *touti li prouverbi en prouvençau j'en ai au moins n'ai au*
                knew all the proverbs in Provençal I have
10   *mens tres pajo quand ça me revient*
                at least three pages when I can remember [them

In this extract 'patois' is used in opposition with the 'Mistralien' of the class, and the term 'Provençal' might have benefited from positive associations with the type of knowledge associated with proverbs. What emerges overall is a system of two parallel systems of nomination: 'patois' on the one hand and 'Mistralien' vs. 'Occitan' on the other, both referring to different spheres of usage and knowledge. 'Patois' is for the home, the past, and childhood. The opposition between 'Mistralien' and Occitan refers to current issues linked with language advocacy movements. Later they refer to the speech of one of the Calandreta school's main advocates, and say they understand her perfectly and state that they speak the same language. What seems at play in the case of Jouseto and Mireio is the re-entextualisation (i.e. decontextualised and recontextualised in different texts or narratives; Blommaert 2005: 47) of notions of speech-as-language ('Provençal', 'Occitan') derived from the language advocacy narrative within pre-existing ideologies of vernacular speech as 'patois'. Hence the uncertainties of 'Mistralien' and 'Provençal', a confusion which, according to the leader of the group *Lou Cieri* did not originate in his own discourse. In other words, the main figure of the language myth, Mistral, eventually stands for the language itself, and the written word takes precedence over the spoken one, represented by the term patois.

The apparent opposition between a Mistralien-speaking 'us' and an Occitan-speaking 'them' remains theoretical and exists mostly at the level of committed language advocates: Jouseto confirms twice that she has no trouble understanding the 'Occitans'. At one point during the interview Mireio informs Jouseto that she had recently seen a well-known figure in Occitan circles (whom she also was acquainted with) on the Provençal/Occitan programme on regional television. She makes no specific comment about that person's accent or any other aspect of her speech. And when both women refer to patois, their references are not to either version of the language myth, but to their own life experiences. There is no myth in their time frame, and the only golden age is their youth.

---

[44] The opposition between *'ome'* and *'moussu'* is one of second order indexicality: the former is a native term, whereas the latter is a borrowing from formal French (< *monsieur*, a man or gentleman). The French loanword thus refers to a higher status than the term *ome*, 'man'.

9.3.2. *Language and place*

In this section, I seek to show that while emic categorisations of speech are often invoked in the language debate to justify or legitimate various positions, traditional speakers themselves do not appeal to ideologies of language that link language and territory in the way that language advocates do. This further emphasises the absence of convergence between the interests of advocates and traditional speakers, and helps understand perhaps both the latter's lack of engagement and their reduction to numbers in the discourse of the language movement.

To Mrs R., the discourse of one or two languages, rife in the debate among participants on both main sides of the language movement, is not relevant to her argument about accent and place. On several occasions, she mentioned certain differences between her original Nice accent and the accent of the Orange region, as well as certain lexical differences between my own speech and hers – without being able to place mine. She recalled how differences between her speech and that of locals would make the latter laugh, leading to her eventually adapting her accent to suit the local pronunciation. But while she did mention the existence of different patois, she would not necessarily associate them with what sociolinguists such as Blanchet (e.g. 2007) have otherwise been tempted to call different 'languages'. At one point she turned to her son-in-law and said, referring to his father who lived in Montpellier, a town located further South in Languedoc, and speaking a variety which would normally be classified as a different dialect or language by linguists: *'Avec votre père à Montpellier, ça arrivait qu'on parle patois tous les deux'* ('With your father in Montpellier, I would sometimes speak patois').

Jouseto also referred to nearby ways of speaking in similar ways when I asked her if she understood people in the Gard and Ardèche, the départements on the other side of the Rhône:

1	James	*e de l'autre cousta en Ardècho e dins lou Gard?*
		and on the other side in Ardèche and the Gard?
2	Jouseto	*o o o dins lou Gard proche se parlo coume nousautre /*
		oh oh oh in the Gard nearby they talk like us /
3	James	*e après mai luenh es encaro la memo lengo? ounte*
		and then further is it still the same language? where does it
4		*s'arresto a pau pres?*
		stop more or less?
4	Jouseto	*ecoutez escoutas li gens li gens de l'Ardècho li comprenen / oh meme*
		listen listen people people in Ardèche we understand them
5		*meme / pas lou catalan*
		even / not Catalan
6	James	*l'occitan? a Toulouso?*
		Occitan? in Toulouse?

7	**Jouseto**	*Toulouso? ben un pau mens ben*
		Toulouse? well a little less well
8	**James**	*e lou catalan de Barcelouno o de Perpignan?*
		and what about the Catalan of Barcelona or Perpignan?
9	**Jouseto**	*ah non / non // se deu / on doit en comprendre*
		quelques uns
		ah no / no // we must / we must understand a bit also
10		*tanben*
		also
11	**James**	*dounco finalament es la lengo d'oc tout acò*
		so in the end all this is part of the Langue d'oc
12	**Jouseto**	*vaqui / vo / es la lengo d'oc*
		that's it / yes / it's the Langue d'oc

Throughout my conversations with traditional speakers in Orange or the nearby Drôme area, it soon became obvious that none of the categorisations I was suggesting made much sense. It also became clear that language and place were linked in a way that fitted none of the language advocacy movement's agendas. Language, to the people I spoke to, was only linked to place insofar as they personally knew those places or people from there. In other words, they could identify whether people spoke like them or not only if and when they had encountered other people from those areas. Pending this, they would make no definite judgment. So in the case of Mrs R., Montpellier could be brought into the realm of the known and of the same, but areas between Orange and Montpellier less so. In Jouseto's case, the nearby Gard was well known and prompted no hesitation. For other places, she hesitated, and summoned hesitant knowledge acquired through the local language association. Her adhesion to the term 'Langue d'oc' can of course also be ascribed to her participation in the same organisation. But 'patois' is a fluid notion, susceptible to encompass new experiences as they are lived, a community of linguistic practice rather than a fixed linguistic community.

9.4 CONCLUSION

The notion of patois is informed by ideologies of place as lived reality, not as imagined, abstract homogenous, mappable territory. The universe it refers to can be known only through first-hand experience. 'Patois' and 'language' are therefore not merely different terms used to name the same reality; they are connected to different individual and collective projects, and to divergent ontologies. The close-knit networks developed through experience that 'patois' indexes are increasingly linked with recollections of the past as it ceases to be transmitted, as with a community consisting of immediate antecedents, as well as with allegiance (if only through alienation; Lafont 1997) to the French national project and subordination to French as *the* language *par excellence* (Lafont 1977). Occitan or Provençal on the other hand index partly abstract imagined communities, sophisticated narratives of ancestors and group, and a strong relation between language, place, culture and people. In this sense the terms 'Provençal' as well as 'Occitan' belong to the same ideological world, that of modernity and nation states – the same plane occupied by the French national myth, which they directly engage with. Neither term can, in this regard, replace the term 'patois', as they refer to very different sets of lived experiences. The indexical discrepancy between patois and Occitan thus makes it easier for proponents of the language revitalisation movement to view traditional speakers as figures and numbers rather than as social actors with an actual voice in a project they cannot comprehend. By so doing, language advocates can hold the speech, practices and views on language of traditional speakers both at an idealised and secure distance.

10

CHILDREN AS AMBIGUOUS PARTICIPANTS IN LANGUAGE REVITALISATION[45]

10.1. INTRODUCTION: THE DUBIOUS CHILD

In August 2008 I presented some early results from my work to an audience of language advocates during a language summer school in the Provençal Alps. Such events allow speakers of the language to gather in an environment where Occitan becomes the dominant language as well as to work on their language skills and to learn about Occitan history, literature, fauna and flora (through hikes) in the minority language. On that occasion I played some recordings I had made of children speaking Occitan in a Provençal immersion school, thinking that long-standing language advocates might be pleased to hear the language of pupils who attended the school system they had campaigned for from the 1970s onward. In fact, most participants were horrified by the children's language, and one participant told me, while leaving the room, that if this was to be the Occitan of the future, then perhaps it wasn't worth fighting for. Evidently the children's prosody, which displayed clear marks of contact with that of French, had come as a surprise to advocates who had committed their lives to a particular version of Occitan.

So while the ambiguous position of traditional speakers in language revitalisation movements can be addressed by turning them into ancestral figures or into anonymous numbers, the position of children is more difficult to handle. On the one hand, they embody the future of the language, and thus of the group that is supposed to speak it. On the other hand they are often accused of not speaking the minority language properly: they mix languages, they do not perform the right accent, and so forth. Adults tend to view them with suspicion, a pattern reproduced within many language revitalisation movements (for similar developments in Brittany see Le Nevez 2006; Hornsby & Quentel 2013; Hornsby 2015).

Children are present in language revitalisation movements in two ways: first as children, that is, as the embodiment of the group's future, as pure potentiality and as image. Second, as pupils whose task it is to learn and use the language. This dual role can lead to tensions: on the one hand, as legitimate members of the group and heirs to its values, the minority language is construed as rightfully theirs (hence the type of discourse common across minority language contexts that posits that all children who live in the traditional language area context must be able to learn their language at school). On the other hand, they still have to be taught it, that is, they (most often) do

---

[45] Parts of this chapter are loosely based on Costa (2015b).

not speak it already. In other words, they are both legitimate and illegitimate, and they are often the object of conflicting ideologies and projections of groupness and language.

As children, they are used in discourse as the embodiment of the ideal of language transmission in the home, an ideal that grew in the Occitan movement at the beginning of the twenty-first century since little collective effort had previously been invested in the promotion of family language transmission. As pupils, they are simultaneously the justification for a number of language schemes through which thousands of pupils are schooled throughout the South of France.

The importance of children in revitalisation movements is tied with the necessity to invest in education in order to control part or all of the schooling system. Within the nation-state framework, education is theoretically a key site for defining legitimate language, as well as legitimate knowledge (Heller & Martin-Jones 2001; Heller 2006). In effect, it was one of the main focuses of language movements in France and in the rest of Europe for decades (Heller 2006; Hornberger 2008), an approach that remains largely dominant. But that investment goes beyond the teaching of language to children. It provides an outlet for the employment of Occitan studies graduates. The existence of an Occitan education sector has provided for many years the main rationale for the existence of teacher training in Occitan, and for the maintenance of Occitan as a university academic subject at Montpellier, Toulouse or Aix-en-Provence.

For two decades it was the main area in which graduates in Occitan could find employment. The situation only changed recently (at the turn of the 2010s) with the rise of opportunities for employment in the private sector.

But whether the mere presence of the language in education, or even the existence of bilingual classes (involving just over seven thousand pupils in 2012–2013)[46] 'has an important role to play in the definition of the value of symbolic capital, in its legitimation and in mediating access to it' (Heller 2003: 7) remains to be seen. Indeed, the value of Occitan as linguistic capital remains limited on all markets, and its (already small) share in the field of education (i.e. the number of posts necessitating the language) is at best stable, and constantly under threat from the education system.

As the objects of discourse on language, children are thus both the site of considerable (emotional, discursive and financial) investment in their disembodied form, and a regular source of disappointment when incarnated in actual flesh. Based on ethnographic fieldwork in an Occitan immersion school in the Orange area, the next sections will consider first, children as symbols of language revival, then children as pupils in the education system. The material analysed in this chapter derives from fieldwork conducted in an immersion school in the Orange region of Provence as well as from conversations with pupils and teachers in other schools in Orange (in particular at the local high school where Occitan is taught) and in Marseille. The chapter is also based on my own experience as a secondary education Occitan teacher.

The language movement's charter myth provides a way to narrate, justify and organise the regimentation of the type of society (or societies, since as seen previously

---

[46] These figures are provided by the (Federation for regional languages in public education): http://www.flarep.com/cartes (25 August 2013).

there is no one single project within revitalisation movement) social actors seeks to bring into being. In particular, education is the locus where the following questions can be addressed:

- Who is part of the group – who will be accepted as a pupil?
- Can pupils of non-local descent be accepted? Can the language be shared with pupils who have no group ancestry?
- What language will be taught, or more specifically whose language? What norms and spelling conventions should be implemented?
- How should interferences with the dominant language be treated?
- How will the language be framed: in terms of intergenerational links, of connection with a territory, sacred or otherwise, or as a badge of identity?
- How will language usage outwith the school be dealt with? Should traditional speakers be brought into the school, should pupils visit said speakers, or should this not be considered important and left to private (family) initiative?

And above all, how are those questions framed, by whom, and to what end? In this chapter I focus on issues of language legitimacy, and on how children are construed as both essential and problematic within the movement, as well as on how they affirm their own status as legitimate speakers.

10.2. CHILDREN AS CHILDREN: TOKENS OF GROWTH AND OF A FUTURE FOR THE COMMUNITY

Children are the objects of intense investment within language revitalisation movements in the sense that they represent the future of the language, and therefore the future of the group imagined around language. Whereas traditional speakers are useful as numbers, children are part of a wider imaginary which connects the social movement with a future. Children are thus best thought of as images, or perhaps icons in the Peircean sense: they resemble the future of the language. Numbers, it should be noted, are also important, for example, the number of pupils attending bilingual education.

For Joshua Fishman (1991), reversing language shift entails family language transmission. Although children were always at the front of the language movement's preoccupations through a concern for education, language transmission in the home became central to the Occitan movement at the turn of the 2000s when a new generation of language advocates came to the fore. Children, and families, acquired the position of societal regenerators.

In Southern France this was rendered particularly salient in a number of posters and leaflets published while I was conducting fieldwork. I mention here a few examples from Occitanists as well as from proponents of Provençal as an autonomous language. In 2008, the Institut d'Estudis Occitans (IEO) published an issue of its journal, (Issue 130) on 'natural and family language transmission'. The front cover depicted a father carrying his young daughter in his arms. The background was green, and the child was wearing a white shirt. In 2010, the IEO published a small free information booklet on Occitan entitled *L'occitan, qu'es aquò?* (What is Occitan?). Several thousand copies were printed for distribution in touristic locations across the South of France over the summer. The front page again depicted a young boy, possibly aged 10. The background was again green, and the child was wearing a white shirt. In his hands he carried a bunch of paper flowers, one of which bore an Occitan cross. Finally, when the Collectif Prouvènço scheduled a demonstration in Beaucaire (Provence) to compete against another demonstration, organised by the IEO and the Felibrige (and other Occitanist organisations) in Carcassonne (Languedoc), the association chose to depict a young girl, set against a Provençal flag (red and gold) background and wearing a white shirt. A text written across the poster stated (in French):

> *Je m'appelle Mayane, j'ai deux ans et je manifesterai pour la Provence. Et vous?*

> My name is Mayane, I'm two years old and I'll be demonstrating for Provence. What about you?

All three posters associate images of youth and growth to symbolise the action they stand for. While this is by no means surprising, it also illustrates how children can serve as images or figures in the same that 'last speakers' do to stand for language endangerment. How exactly children fit in language revitalisation, how their participation is determined, and how they are legitimised as speakers remains a more thorny issue.

10.3. Children as pupils

Education has historically been the main domain that language movements have invested. Three reasons can explain this. First, its public status makes it an easier target than the private domain of the home. Second, the oft-articulated rationale among language advocates is that since compulsory schooling uprooted traditional languages, it should consequently be the ideal way to reintroduce it. Third, schools are key institutions for the establishment, reproduction and dissemination of national ideologies and for the definition of legitimate language (Bourdieu 1991b; Heller & Martin-Jones 2001; Heller 2006). In the words of Monica Heller and Marilyn Martin Jones, education is:

> an institution of social and cultural production and reproduction, that is, a discursive space in which groups with different interests struggle over access to symbolic and material resources and over ways of organizing that access that privilege some and marginalize others on the basis of criteria of evaluation that have collective applications and effects. (Heller & Martin-Jones 2001: 5–6)

A central institution to all contemporary European language movements, it comes as no surprise that education in the Occitan domain has been particularly scrutinised in academic circles – in studies on present-day issues (Burban & Lagarde 2007; Lieutard

& Verny 2007) or from a historical perspective (Martel 2007). Likewise, the Calandreta immersion schools have attracted a fair amount of attention (Dompmartin-Normand 2002; Boyer 2005a; Sumien 2009b). Before discussing how the status of legitimate speakers of the children-as-pupils is construed, I briefly sketch the debates in which Occitan as an educational issue has found itself entangled.

Institutional recognition began in 1951 with the which allowed for a small number of languages to be taught optionally on a voluntary basis (see Gardin 1975; Martel 2007: 131–141). Gradually the language movement secured more recognition until the establishment of specific teaching positions in a number of minority languages and (mostly at primary level) state-funded bilingual education in the 1980s. Teaching in or of 'Occitan-Langue d'oc' (as it is officially called by the French Education ministry) is available in public and private schools from preschool to secondary schools, concerning several thousand pupils. The private sector consists in the Catholic network of schools as well as in the Calandreta system a parent-run system which runs mainly primary schools throughout Southern France.

The Calandretas, the system in which the pupils I followed for my doctoral thesis were involved, were first established in 1979 in Pau, in Southwestern France. The schools are secular (*laïques*) and tuition is free for parents. In 2014 they taught a total of 3,471 pupils in sixty primary schools and three high schools[47] mainly in the western part of the linguistic domain as defined by the language movement and linguists – as shown in Figure 9.

Figure 9. Map of Calandreta schools (2013). Dots represent individual primary schools, squares areas with more than one primary school, and triangle secondary schools (From the Calandreta federation website: http://www.calandreta.org/IMG/jpg/mapa_sept_2013-2.jpg (29 September 2014)).

[47] According to the Calandreta federation website: http://www.calandreta.org/Nouvelle-traduction-20-Objectif.html (29 September 2014).

Calandreta schools use Occitan as the main medium of instruction, and only introduce French once the pupils can read and write (in Occitan), that is, in the second year
of primary education at the age of seven. In the school where I conducted fieldwork in
2007 and 2008, French could only be used in a separate, designated classroom. The
schools employ teaching methods derived from the early pedagogical work of Célestin
Freinet (1896–1966) which aims to put the children at the centre of their own learning experience and to emphasise communication in all aspects of learning (Legrand
1993: 406). In this particular school, those principles took the form, for example, of
a class currency, which could be earned by taking part in community activities (such
as filling out a weather chart) and which could be spent at a class market held once
a week on a Friday. On that occasion, the children would bring in items they had
made or owned but no longer wanted, and they could exchange it for that currency at
a price they set themselves. Another class institution was the *Qué de nòu?* ('What's
new?'), a short session held once or twice a week during which general class affairs
are collectively discussed. Class rules were collectively devised by the pupils and
the teachers, and ratified by individual vote at the beginning of each school year.[48]

Where they exist, Calandreta schools are an important focus of the language movement's life and economics. While the state pays teachers (after a period of probation),
the input of parents (i.e. the organisation of public events to provide funding) is
essential to maintain buildings and to fund school material and outings. The schools
are also the main outlet for Occitan language textbooks, often the translation into
Occitan of French manuals (the schools follow the official French programmes), and
they provide a venue for Occitan theatre companies.

Equally importantly, the Calandretas provide a locus of the instantiation or
implementation of the movement's charter myth, in terms of providing historical,
geographic and group representations (e.g. Lafont 2003, a history manual for children
and teenagers).

10.4. Bilingual education pupils as 'new speakers'

The term 'new speaker' has recently gained popularity in sociolinguistic studies,
in particular among scholars studying processes whereby people adopt Catalan,
Galician or Irish as their primary language of use or affiliation (O'Rourke & Pujolar
2013; O'Rourke & Ramallo 2015; O'Rourke & Walsh 2015). Within that field of
studies new speakers are defined as individuals 'with little or no home or community exposure to a minority language but who instead acquire it through immersion
or bilingual educational programmes, revitalisation projects or as adult language
learners' (O'Rourke et al. 2015: 1). The Calandreta pupils fall, for the most part,
under this category. As Jaffe (2015: 25) points out, as a category 'new speaker' can be

[48] For an overview of distinctive activities, see the following webpage which explains to parents the
way one particular Calandreta school functions: http://calandreta-candola.org/siti/?page_id=166
(21 December 2016).

'an explicit/relatively established or an emergent/implicit emic category'. She also states that 'if the 'new speaker' contrasts in a positive way with the 'semi-speaker', he or she also contrasts with the 'native speaker'' (Jaffe 2015: 23). What I suggest lies at the core of this dichotomy is the question of legitimate language, very much present in the Occitan summer school event I recounted at the beginning of this chapter. The very category of 'new speaker' is neither a given nor a purely descriptive label, it is an issue over the definition of which social actors struggle, in order to impose positive or negative connotations, and ultimately to gain control over the definition of legitimate language.

In revitalisation movements, immersion or bilingual education should, in theory, bridge the generational gap between so-called traditional and new speakers. In the Calandreta where I conducted fieldwork, most pupils only had a faint idea of what traditional speakers sounded like. Some had first hand experience with distant relatives who spoke Occitan, or more likely, 'patois'. When in the school, I followed a group of six pupils aged nine to eleven, who attended the Calandreta's CM2 (last year of primary education) but were grouped with children aged seven and eight. The complete group numbered just over twenty pupils. Together (on the playground) they spoke mostly French, but no French was allowed in the classroom (any unauthorised use of French would be discussed collectively, and the wrongdoer might be fined in the class currency). All informal conversations with myself as well as interviews were conducted in Occitan, at the children's own request.

The 'new speaker' label is, of course, not one children used naturally. Why would they? Occitan was their everyday classroom language and the pupils had spoken it since they had started school, typically at the age of two.[49] This label is nevertheless used in various academic and activist conversations to refer to children in particular. In the remaining part of this section I analyse how this label is both a contested issue as well as an instrument to impose particular views on what legitimate language is. I will then turn to a discussion I had with a group of three pupils over issues of new and traditional language.

10.4.1. *New speakers and legitimate language on the Provençal linguistic market*

In the South of France, the term 'new speakers' has recently acquired some currency. Some language advocates do tend to increasingly refer to themselves newspeakers, or rather *néo-locuteurs* (neo-speakers) either apologetically or with pride to emphasise their language-learning efforts. The term, however, is also used in a derogatory way in some sectors of the language movement as well as in academia. Consider for example this contribution to a discussion thread on the Projetbabel.org forum, a French forum designed for language lovers at large. The thread itself is entitled: *Eth gascoûn: ua auta lenga que l'ouccitân?* (Gascon: a language other than Occitan?]:

[49] This section reproduces, albeit in modified form, an article published in 2015 in a special issue of the *International Journal of the Sociology of Language* on new speakers, edited by Bernadette O'Rourke, Joan Pujolar and Fernando Ramallo (Costa 2015b).

La novlang que parlent les néo-locuteurs est un dialecte pour le coup occitan de vague inspiration gasconne, qui si on l'analyse proprement, n'est que du français traduit mot à mot. Et encore, je parle d'une génération qui a eu la chance d'avoir des enseignants parfois fins locuteurs. La génération nouvelle des Calandretas parle une langue complètement loufoque, une sorte de titi parisien super-nasal avec des -o à la fin (qu'ils prononcent -e en fait).[50]

The newspeak used by new speakers is clearly a form of Occitan with a vague Gascon inspiration, which, if properly analysed, is but word for word French. And I'm speaking of a generation that was lucky enough to be taught by teachers who were fine speakers. The new Calandreta generation speaks a completely barmy language, a sort of super-nasal Parisian slang with -o at the end [of words] (which in fact they pronounce -e).

The author establishes a seemingly obvious connection between the type of Gascon used by neo-speakers and Orwellian newspeak, suggesting both the artificial nature of the language as well as its use for manipulative purposes. This type of (very habitual) comment underlines, however, the current struggle that pervades the Occitan language movement as to what counts as legitimate language, in particular at a time when traditional speakers are fast disappearing – positions of authority are, so to speak, there for the taking.

10.4.2. New speakers for academics: a descriptive category?

The term *néo-locuteur* is also used in academic (mostly sociolinguistic) conversations, where it can also acquire both apparently neutral and derogatory meanings. As an apparently neutral category, consider the following excerpt from Martel (2001b), a book chapter on language policy in Southern France:

Mais contradictoirement, les langues de France fonctionnent – et on l'a vu depuis plusieurs décennies déjà – comme langues choisies par des néo-locuteurs qui sont le plus souvent de purs produits de l'école française.

But contradictorily, the languages of France now function – and have been for several decades now – as languages chosen by neo-speakers who are most often pure products of the French school system. (Martel 2001b: 383)

While Martel intends the category to be a descriptive one, he does not specify what it describes, other than that it relates to individuals who have consciously made the choice to learn Occitan. He says nothing of the status of such individuals in the South of France, of their position on the Occitan linguistic market, or of the linguistic varieties they speak.

---

[50] Available on the Projetbabel.org website: http://projetbabel.org/forum/viewtopic.php?p=165312 (15 August 2016).

Another academic who uses the term while referring to Provence is the sociolinguist Philippe Blanchet, a staunch advocate of Provençal as a distinct language. He correlates new speakers with what he terms neo-Provençal as well as with signs of distinct lack of legitimacy. He construes neo-Provençal as an index of youth, urban and middle-class lifestyles, all of which are, according to him, far removed from what authentic Provençal ought to be. Consider for instance the following two excerpts from his writings, the first from a sociolinguistic study, the second from a teach-yourself Provençal manual:

(1) *Le « néo-provençal » est un provençal fortement francisé, surtout dans ses structures syntaxiques et phraséologiques, réguliers chez les jeunes militants urbains.*

'Neo-Provençal' is a highly frenchified Provençal, especially in its syntax and phraseology, regular among young urban activists. (Blanchet 2002: 33)

(2) *On notera surtout une différence entre le provençal des conversations spontanées des locuteurs « naturels » et celui des activistes, enseignants, écrivains, présentateurs à la télévision etc. qui l'ont parfois appris volontairement et plus ou moins artificiellement. Les locuteurs « naturels » utilisent davantage de mots empruntés au français mais ont une syntaxe et une stylistique typiquement provençales. Les locuteurs volontaires ont un vocabulaire « épuré » (parfois au point d'utiliser des formes curieuses) mais une syntaxe et une stylistique influencées par le français normatif (parfois calquées mot à mot). Les seconds se recrutent heureusement parfois parmi les premiers !*

One will note in particular a difference between the Provençal of 'natural' speakers in spontaneous conversations and that of activists, teachers, writers, television presenters, etc. who have sometimes learnt it on a voluntary and more or less artificial basis. 'Natural' speakers use more words borrowed from French but their syntax and stylistics are typically Provençal. Willful speakers have a 'purified' vocabulary (sometimes to the point that they use curious forms) but their syntax and stylistics are influenced by normative French (sometimes claqued on a word for word basis). Fortunately, the latter [i.e. Teachers, presenters, etc.] are sometimes recruited among the former! (Blanchet 1999: 22)

This discourse draws on several layers of meaning in Provence, in particular on the aforementioned divide between proponents of Provençal as a dialect of Occitan and those who view Provençal as an independent language (see chapter 7). While the former are usually viewed as younger and more often as leading urban lifestyles, the latter are believed to come from more rural backgrounds, and to have more contact with native speakers. 'Wilful speakers' are here supposed to be recruited among the former. Two types of potentially legitimate language are at play: one derived from the social symbolic benefits associated with urban culture in modernity, and the other from traditional patterns of language use and from the prestige of the native speaker.

What emerges is the construction of an apparently clear-cut dichotomy between new and traditional speakers, indexed through the type of speech that users display (see also O'Rourke & Ramallo 2011: 150–151).

Table 2. Summary of the main dichotomies between traditional and new speakers

Ordinary speakers	New speakers
Rural	Urban
Old	Young
Working class	Middle class
Continuity, tradition, authenticity	Rupture, artificiality

The language of new speakers of minority languages is variously termed néo-breton (Le Berre & Le Dû 1999), néo-provençal (Blanchet 2002) etc. It often refers to standardised or literary varieties (Hincks 2000), that is, varieties deemed invented or artificial. Mari Jones (1995: 437), speaking of Breton, quotes language advocates as referring to the language of new speakers as 'a form of Celtic Esperanto'. This in turn echoes the term 'newspeak' that was used by the Gascon activist above. This 'new language' is often understood as artificial, literary, normative, reconstituted or idiosyncratic (Lafont 1984), urban, young, and displaying the wrong aspects of contact with the dominant language. Syntactic and prosodic features influenced by the dominant language and thus largely condemned. On the contrary, the lexical borrowings of traditional speakers embedded in more traditional syntax are construed as authentic and as indexing the true native speaker.

'New speakers' is a discursive category based not only on the appreciation of recent acquisition of a language but also on the very type of language that those associated with it use. In that respect, calling certain people 'new speakers' serves the interests of some, those who have the authority to define legitimate Provençal. On the other hand this category can be summoned to force others to either align with what legitimate language ought to be, or to establish parallel, separate linguistic markets.

What this points to is also the existence of idealised varieties of minority languages, what the French sociologist of language Pierre Achard (1982) called the myth of the lost language, in turn hinting at the existence of legitimacy in language use as lying elsewhere, in an indeterminate locus, in the hands or minds of indeterminate others. The advantage of this particular locus being of course that its definition is variable, and can be adapted by different actors to suit various needs in various occasions. Of key importance here is the potentially fuzzy and uncertain type of differentiation it generates, which can for instance be used by teachers to justify the existence of evening classes, by native speakers to exclude younger people from conversations etc. The notion of 'new speakers' is therefore loaded with a wealth of political, social and moral issues. It is connected with the type of language that should be taught to children in schools, and the types of social and indexical links social actors seek to foster, e.g. repairing a broken connection with older generations (Le Berre & Le Dû 1999) or battling against an ongoing diglossic complexus (Lafont 1997).

10.4.3. *Legitimacy among bilingual school pupils in Provence*

I now turn to my fieldwork among the pupils of the Orange Calandreta to explore precisely how issues of legitimacy are problematised for the children involved in the Calandreta immersion programme. I focus more specifically on a one-hour interview with three girls Léa (then aged ten), Carla (eleven) and Safia (twelve). Not only did the pupils interact with me, they also interacted with each other, displaying the very mechanisms that serve to establish authority and legitimacy locally, as well as making clear how Occitan was relevant to their everyday lives and socialisation processes as children, as pre-adolescents, as girls, and as participants in activities such as football or music associations.

In order to understand how the pupils constructed their positions of legitimate speakers (or not) of Occitan, I draw on Jaffe's (2009) notions of epistemic and affective stances to analyse the various positions that the girls display in interaction. Epistemic stances refer to 'claims to know' and serve 'to establish the relative authority of participants, and to situate the sources of that authority in a wider sociocultural field' (Jaffe 2009: 7). Affective stances 'represent emotional states of the speaker' and have two main functions: they relate to evaluation, presentation and positioning of the self; they can also 'index shared, culturally specific structures of feeling and norms [...] and can thus be mobilised in the drawing of social boundaries that is central to the work of social differentiation and categorisation' (Jaffe 2009: 7).

Throughout the interview, the pupils alternated between epistemic and affective stances. Léa, Carla and Safia used both types as ways to establish (and further) their own position with respect to one another, to display legitimacy in the eyes of the interviewer (e.g. through the insertion of short narratives explaining that the girls often lapse into Occitan on occasions when it is not expected, for instance at home with their parents). In the context of the interview, linguistic resources are managed in a very normative way: infelicitous utterances (e.g. marked by contact with French, grammatical errors) are immediately corrected by Léa and Carla, who establish themselves as authorities with regard to Safia. Correct language is however not the only element that establishes authority. In the following extract, Carla interrupts the flow of the conversation to ask Léa why she speaks such good Occitan, since she arrived in the school several years after herself and Safia:[51]

---

[51] I transcribe the interview using the Occitan orthographic system, that is, the one used in the Calandreta system.

1	Carla	*una question mai just per ca es per Léa / es ti*
		a question but just for ca its for Léa / did you
2		*avans / avans que sias venguda aqui an aquesta escòla eh*
		before / before you came here in this school well
3		*ben coneisses lo provençau ? coneissiáu / coneissiás*
		did you know Provençal? knew / know
4	Léa	*coneissaviás lo provençau*
		[proposes to correct Carla] knew provençal
5	James	[I provide the correct form] *coneissiás*
		know
6	Carla	*òc coneissiás lo provençau ?*
		yes did you know Provençal?
7	Léa	*euh //// bòna question [laughs] alòra es parier que mei*
		well //// good question [laughs] so it's like my
8		*copinas a la dança ai vist de paneus e tot / mai euh*
		friends at the dance I had seen signs and all / but
9	Carla	*coneissiás pas*
		you didn't know it
10	Léa	*mai aviau jamai entendut [parlAR*
		I'd never heard it [spoken
11	Carla	*[pas un* mòt euh
		[not a word
12	Léa	*ja aviáu jamai entendut parlar d'una escòla / Calandreta*
		to begin with I'd never heard of a school / Calandreta
13		*e siáu fòrça d'alhors contenta de la de lo saupre / ara*
		and I'm really happy to know it / now
14		*e d'i èstre*
		and to be here
15	Carla	*en tot cas a fòrça lèu aprés lo provençau*
		anyway you learnt provençal really quickly
16	Léa	*pense COma / ditz Danieu es perdequé es coma èstre fòrt*[52]
		I think like / Daniel[52] says it's because it's like being
17		*en provençau ajuda en francés / èstre fòrt en francés*
		good at Provençal helps for French / to be good at
18		*ajuda au provençau / va dins lei dos sens / pense*
		French helps for Provençal / it goes both ways / I think

In the extract above, Carla derives her own legitimacy from the fact that she has been in the Calandreta system all her life. Her hesitations at first on the past tense form of the verb *conéisser* (to know; lines 2–3) do not alter her own status with respect to the other two girls. In contrast to Carla, who derives her own position on the linguistic market from interplay between epistemic and affective stances (she regularly

---

[52] Daniel is the teacher.

proclaims her loyalty to Occitan as a beautiful language, and as a language related to Italian, a language spoken in her family – see also Costa 2014), Léa draws her overall legitimacy from epistemic stances. In the extract above, Léa infers her ability to learn Occitan quickly from her (good) knowledge of French, not from language loyalty – an argument she borrows from the ultimate source of authority in the class: the teacher.

Carla and Léa share the floor, competing internally for a dominant position within the classroom linguistic market on different grounds; Safia on the other hand repeatedly displays marks of linguistic insecurity. The issues that are questioned internally reflect those that are questioned outside the classroom: the capacity to produce felicitous utterances on the linguistic market as well as seniority in terms of group membership. 'Newspeakerhood', or rather the types of behaviours that seniority implies in terms of legitimate language, is recursively projected and contested within the group. The example above shows how primacy (or lack thereof) in a group is but one element among others in the evaluation of utterances (and of individuals) on a linguistic market. Legitimacy, or acceptability, occurs at the crossing between many elements that involve a combination of epistemic as well as affective stances, of grammatically correct language use as well as of the ability to speak with authority on language through the use of appropriate metalinguistic language and comments.

10.4.4. *Encountering the native speaker: reframing language into old vs. new Provençal*

Classroom rules have a life of their own however, and the girls' language is evaluated in different ways outside the classroom in a variety of situations that are related to their status as pupils in an Occitan school, as speakers of Occitan, as girls and as children.

All three pupils are fully aware of the price of Provençal on linguistic markets when school is over. Carla thus repeatedly resorts to the notion of 'shame' to describe why she does not use (or talk about) Provençal outwith the school, in particular when playing football in her club – where other participants are predominantly boys. It is, in her own words, difficult enough to be a young girl without adding the mockery that revealing the Provençal component of her linguistic repertoire would entail. Negative social evaluation is therefore connected as much to Provençal itself as to a particular variety of the language – to the language itself rather to what is said or how it is said. However, one may also suggest that the lack of value of Provençal outwith the school is precisely what confers its value within the school. The virtual absence of social evaluation other than that of the teacher allows Provençal to function as a commodity that is easily controlled by a small group of children within the school. In that respect, confrontation with a more unified linguistic market may question this very legitimacy internally, as in the next extract from the same interview as above.

I presented the pupils with an extract from an interview I had conducted with an eighty-seven year old woman, Mrs R. (see also chapter 9). I originally intended to observe how the children would evaluate her speech. Provençal was her first and only language until the age of ten (roughly the age of the girls at the time of the interview), when she learnt French at school. In the extract I played, Mrs R. recounts a dream she had in Provençal some months before. At first, because of the pupils' evaluation of Mrs R.'s articulation as old, Carla asked what was wrong with the woman and the children made fun of her. The situation was thus framed as us (young people) vs. her (old woman), with the usual loading of stereotypes attributed to age – stuttering and memory loss in particular. I then intervened and explained that the woman learnt French at a much later age, and that Provençal was in fact her first language:

1	Carla	*DETZ ANS / avans parli provençau* [at] TEN YEARS OLD / before I spoke provençal[53]
2	James	*parlava QUE provençau* she spoke only provençal
3	Carla	*la cha::nce* how lucky:
4	All	*la cha:nce* how lucky
5	Carla	*elle est* née quand? when was she born?
6	James	*elle a vuechanta vuech ans doncas elle est née en 1921 euh* She is eighty eight so she was born in 1921 er what am I
7		*qu'est-ce que je vous dit 1921 22 quelque chose comme ça* saying 1921 22 something like that
8	Carla	*ouh la la* O:h
9	Léa	*en 1921* In 1921
10	Carla	*1921 ! mai alòra perqué siáu pas nascuda en 1921?* 1921! But so why wasn't I born in 1921?

This information, which I initially gave in defence of the women I had interviewed, proved more powerful than intended. It revealed an aspect of Provençal history which the girls were unaware of – that Provençal was once the first language of people in their area. The new element of information prompted a change in footing expressed through switching to French, that reframed the interaction as one where linguistic authority, that is, the capacity to mobilise and affirm legitimate language, shifts from the girls to the interviewed woman. I interpret this shift as informed by an ideology that confers natural legitimacy onto the native speaker and monolingualism, in keeping with the prevalent ideology of both the Occitan movement and French society at large. In the extract, Carla finally resumes using Occitan when she seeks to align with the aged woman by wishing she also had been born in 1921.

[53] What Carla expresses here is stupefaction at the fact that Mrs. R spoke no French before the age of ten.

However, this second shift in legitimacy is only partially solved through alignment. In a third movement, after hearing a longer excerpt from the interview with Mrs R., the girls analyse the type of language they have heard with respect to their own, and frame differences as naturally occurring variation:

1	**James**	*vaquí / doncas aquò es una dòna d'------ / doncas / vos*
		right / so this is a woman from ------ / so / does your
2		*sembla different lo provençau que parlatz vosautrei de son*
		Provençal seem different
3		*provençau an ela?*
		to hers?
4	**Carla**	*[ouh la la vò vò vò*
		[oh yes yes yes
	[...]	
5	**Léa**	*[vò mai es de vielh / de vieux vieux vieux provençau aquò*
		[yes but this is old / old old old Provençal
6	**Carla**	*[vò ieu ai pas tròp comprès çò qu'a dich*
		[yes I didn't quite understand what she said
7	**James**	*de qu'a fòrça cambiat* *[entre vòstre accent e*
		what has changed a lot [between your accent and
8	**Carla**	*[ben sabe pas euh / ja*
		[well I don'y know er
9		*son accent / son accent e puei euh /// quelque chose qu'ai*
		her accent / her accent and er /// something I didn't
10		*pas trò:p comprès en fach es lei es lei mòts ai pas tròp tròp*
		quite understand in fact is the is the words I didn't quite
11		*tròp comprès / l'accent parlava lèu ja / un pichòt pauc lèu e*
		quite understand / the accent she spoke fast / a little too
12		*puei euh / es vielha doncas a pas lo meme provençau que*
		fast and er / she's old so she doesn't have the same
13		*nosautrei / mai a due èstre fòrça contenta / d'èstre pendent*
		provençal as us / but she must have been very happy / to
14		*tres tres oras*
		be speaking for three hours
15	**James**	*quand dises qu'es vielha doncas a pas lo meme*
		when you say she's old so she doesn't have the same
16		*provençau que nosautrei perqué dises aquò?*
		Provençal as ours why do you say that?
17	**Carla**	*ben perqué es un nov alòra es un novèu provençau çò que*
		well because it's a ne so it's a new provençal what
18		*parlam / ela fin i a plusiors provençaus e ela fasiá un*
		we speak / she I mean there are several Provençals and she
19		*provençau different de nosautrei pensi*
		has a different Provençal I think

20	**James**	*vòs dire que avans lo provençau èra different o qué ?*
		you mean Provençal was different before is that it?
21	**Carla**	*ben avans lo provençau pensi qu'èra qu'èra presque parier mai un*
		well before Provençal I think was almost the same but a
22		*autre provençau en fach / aquò es un novèu provençau*
		but a different one in fact / this is a new Provençal
23		*e euh en mila / quauquaren là eh ben èra un autre provençau /*
		and er in nineteen er something it was another Provençal

The tension identified between different forms of Provençal is likely one of authority and legitimacy. The elderly speakers' language is potentially more valuable on a Provençal linguistic market not only because it is intrinsically better than theirs, or because it could index more authentically Provençal values, but because she is a native speaker, and can boast a state of monolingualism until the age of ten. This potentially threatening situation is therefore reframed into one of 'difference but equality' between varieties. This enables both varieties to be equally authoritative, in the sense that the issue is not one of 'proper Provençal vs. neo-Provençal', but one of 'old vs. new', of natural change.

This last extract therefore shows that while the notion of 'new language' language is available, it may be appropriated and negotiated in different ways that all encompass a dimension of authority and legitimacy on a given market, be in a unified linguistic market where old and new co-exist, or a more restricted linguistic market such as the classroom. Linguistic forms are used in particular ways that make use of categories of 'old' and 'new' in creative ways that allow the girls to position themselves in the world. It enables Carla to claim legitimacy through seniority, and Léa to state that she may be a bright student because she managed to learn Provençal in a shorter period of time. It permits a naturalised opposition between old and new that resolves the potential ideological tension between the monolingual native speaker and the second language learner by reducing both categories to naturally occurring variation. Finally, old and new can acquire different meanings on different markets according to what type of status participants wish to acquire; while in the school seniority may be an advantage, in other minority language contexts showing the goodwill of a new speaker may also bring symbolic benefits. In other words, one is always a new speaker for a particular purpose – be it to gain something, or to be prevented from achieving some form of status.

10.5. CONCLUSION

Children are, as initially stated, ambiguous figures within language revitalisation movements. They are both hope for a future, but the type of future they embody might not be the one hoped for within the movement. Children often do not grasp the charter myth of the language movement (Costa 2014); they frequently do not speak well enough in the eyes of weary language advocates who have spent their lives fighting for a certain ideal. Children are all at once symbols, icons, numbers, pupils, and they are expected to take part in a number of performances in which they are required to act according to norms they might not grasp – for example in orthographic contests (see also Jaffe 1996).

Increasingly, children as well as younger participants in language revitalisation movements are approached as 'new speakers'. This is occurring in a number of conversations, among language advocates as well as among academics. While potentially positive, the term also comes with a whiff of suspicion, and is inevitably associated with the idea of new language – itself carrying associations at worst with Orwellian Newspeak, or at best with nineteenth century invented languages (recall Jones's 1995 *Celtic Esperanto*). In other words, what finds itself at stake with 'new speakers' is the ability to control the definition of what counts as genuinely Provençal or Occitan. The complexity of the interests at stake is also made more salient by the dearth of available resources, the passing of the traditional speakers, and the open conflict between proponents of Provençal-as-Occitan vs. Provençal-as-a-discrete-language. The gradual postvernacularisation of Occitan generates a number of available positions of authority which make the definition of legitimate language an ever-more contested issue, and the capacity to intervene in the debate an object of personal and academic pride as well as a motif of distinction (see Bourdieu 1977).

What the examples from language advocates, academics and pupils also highlight is the importance of the ideology of the native speaker and, above all, the monolingual speaker as the arch-legitimate speaker. What particularly impressed the Calandreta pupils was the fact that Mrs R. had learnt French at the age of ten. This commanded respect, and led to the necessity for the children to redefine their own practice. It is therefore noteworthy that as traditional speakers die out, minority languages do not necessarily become the spaces of freedom where artistic experiments can be conducted without judgement, as some claim in Provence and elsewhere. New linguistic regimes generate new conditions of legitimacy, and new questions about how social actors negotiate positions, identities and roles in a world where post-vernacular languages have largely become badges, used for a wide array of purposes. What counts is more often that they are used at all and not what is said in them. In this respect, 'new speakers' are not simply 'learners' of a given language: they use language in particular semiotic ways that relate to what it means to do 'Provençal', 'Occitan', or, for that matter, 'Irish' or 'Nahuatl' in the world today. They also raise further questions, in particular: why is this important, and to whom?

Paradoxically perhaps, while language revitalisation is in principle about empowerment and returning legitimacy to speakers, the language movement in Southern France finds itself in a position in which it struggles to construct the very people it seeks to empower as legitimate in an everyday sense – other than as icons.

11

CONCLUSION:
WRESTLING WITH CLASSIFICATIONS IN A
WORLD OF SIGNS

Language revitalisation, this book has argued, is primarily a process of struggle over classifying the world by specific social actors in specific social and historical conditions problematised as a form of contact. Contact, constructed as conflict through the establishment of a charter myth, is an essential and inherent dimension of any revitalisation project. Language revitalisation is a social project, articulated in the name of language by people who act on behalf of a group that they construct as a minority in opposition to another group featuring as 'the majority'. The revitalisation process aims to renegotiate the very terms of contact between itself and the majority group, but this it may only achieve by acting upon categories that the dominant group views as important. In that sense, revitalisation is not an inward looking process, as it is sometimes portrayed in the media or by its opponents; it is clearly outward looking in the sense that it addresses an 'Other', viewed as dominant or majoritarian. Language becomes a terrain for debate, contestation and negotiation if it is considered an important category among the dominant group. In other words, if revitalisation movements are organised around language, it is because language is important to those who have the power to set agendas according to which legitimate categories are shaped in late modernity.

Given the long-standing genealogy of the importance of language in modernity, it is perhaps no surprise that it is being used as an increasingly popular terrain to articulate debates over issues of land or legitimate knowledge (as exemplified also by Gustafson 2009 in Bolivia). In the Occitan case, language has been used as a terrain in very different circumstances to serve very different causes over the past century and a half. But the Occitan case is particularly useful to help problematise the various shifts that may occur historically and to show how language may be appropriated in different ways to serve different political and social projects. From nineteenth century political struggles between republicans and monarchists to debates over globalisation, language has proved an essential component of political life in Southern France. In other parts of the Occitan speaking territory, language is being turned into an issue for local elections, in Languedoc and Aquitaine in particular. It bears particular significance in Aquitaine, where Basque already benefits from public support from regional authorities.

At the core of the classification struggle initiated by language revitalisation is the question of legitimacy: legitimate language, legitimate speakers, and legitimate participants in the group the movement defines. Language revitalisation is fundamentally about the idea that some people, for whatever reason, do not or cannot speak in the right way. Language revitalisation movements rely on a number of categories of social actors mobilised to sustain and further the cause: committed language advocates, traditional speakers and children, in particular. But language revitalisation is not just about 'language': it is about somebody's language, and about the type of indexical order that different forms of language can summon. Language revitalisation movements are deeply engaged in a form of verbal hygiene, one that seeks to bring into being not any form of 'the language', but a particular one. In the Occitan case, one whose dignity can be put on a par with that of French – that is to say, a language which linguists can describe as autonomous (in terms of internal structure, vocabulary, orthography), one that is not a hybrid, one that has a respectable pedigree. Conflicts over what constitutes legitimate knowledge about language and about who counts as a legitimate speaker are therefore inevitable. They raise the question of who, ultimately, has authority over the language: authority to decide what forms legitimately count as part of the language, and which ones do not.

Processes of classification are therefore external as well as internal, a movement that institutes the revitalisation processes as a field in the Bourdieusian sense. They situate members of the minority group with respect to a majority group and, within the minority group, establish hierarchies and objective relations of power between individuals. The struggles entailed by processes of classification are by nature unstable and they find new terrains within the language movement throughout the process. One unexpected example was provided to me as I was finishing this book in the form of a comment to a blog post published on an Occitan online news site. Its author, a well-known young language advocate, implied that speaking Occitan at home and passing on the language to one's children should be a basic criterion to be considered a true 'Occitanist' (Occitan language advocate). This criterion would in effect exclude many historic figures of the movement, as it only became an important theme at the turn of the twenty-first century. On 25 August, he wrote:

> *Un occitanista, militant de la lenga occitana parla e transmet sa lenga.*
> *Siegem clars sobre las definicions elementàrias !*

> An Occitanist, an Occitan language advocate, speaks his/her language and passes it on. Let's be clear when it comes to elementary definitions.[54]

What exactly he meant by speaking (all the time? as much as possible? to everyone?) is not clearly spelt out. Yet what is apparent is how language revitalisation functions like a field, in which a constant wrestle with categories defines and redefines what counts as legitimate knowledge and action. In a world of words and signs, language revitalisation is about whose words we use, to do what and for whom.

I started this book by stating that I did not know whether the types of processes currently subsumed under the label 'language revitalisation' were 'worth doing' or

---

[54] Comment to the linguist Domergue Sumien's blogpost in the Occitan online daily (25 August 2015), entitled 'Leis Occitans devèm pas defendre lo francés' ('We Occitans shouldn't defend French'): http://opinion.jornalet.com/lenga/blog/1509/leis-occitans-devem-pas-defendre-lo-frances-i#comentaris (28 August 2015).

not, quoting Nancy Hornberger (2008). Certainly they are worth investigating, for individually as well as collectively those movements tell us something about ideologies of difference in late modern societies. They show how, to be heard, groups must be organised according to terms that will make them audible and visible, and language constitutes an ideal terrain in this respect. While direct issues of land rights, self-determination or labour rights might'prove too contentious, language constitutes a respectable terrain, one which is immediately classified within international organisations and governments as pertaining to the cultural sphere rather than the political.

Current regimes of classification of groups constructed as 'endangered language groups' or 'minority language groups' shed light on how difference is currently understood. Diversity is part of a political project that professes to respect all differences equally, and uses the respect for difference to erase class-based conflicts on the one hand, and on the other hand hierarchises various levels of legitimate difference. Within the diversity paradigm, languages are more valued than dialects, to give but one example. This raises the possibility of new struggles over classification to gain access to this regime of diversity and to sustain a position as part of the 'legitimately diverse'. In this respect, and despite the fact that 'in liberal polities [language struggles] have become less intense and intractable' (Brubaker 2015: 99) as opposed to religious struggles, the possibility for language to be a terrain of persistent struggles is likely to endure.

REFERENCES

ABLEY, M. 2003. *Spoken here*. Montreal: Random House of Canada.

ABRAMS, DANIEL M. & STEVEN H. STROGATZ. 2003. 'Modelling the dynamics of language death', *Nature* 424(900).

ABRATE, L. 2001. *Occitanie 1900–1968: des idées et des hommes*. Puylaurens: Institut d'Etudes Occitanes.

ACHARD, P. 1982. 'Prefaci', in Lluís Aracil, *Lo bilingüisme coma mite*. Magalàs: Institut d'Estudis Occitans. 9–27.

ALÉN GARABADO, M. C. 1999. *Quand le "patois" était politiquement utile...: l'usage propagandiste de l'imprimé occitan à Toulouse durant la période révolutionnaire*. Paris: L'Harmattan.

ALI-KHODJA, M., & BOUDREAU, A. 2009. 'Du concept de minorité à la pensée de l'exiguïté: Pour une autre compréhension des phénomènes linguistiques', *Langage et Société*, 3(129). 69–80.

AMERY, R. 2001. 'Language planning and language revival', *Current Issues in Language Planning*, 2(2&3). 141–221.

ANDERSON, B. 1983. *Imagined communities: reflections on the origin and spread of nationalism*. London: Verso.

APPADURAI, A. 2006. *Fear of small numbers: an essay on the geography of anger*. Durham, NC: Duke University Press.

ARACIL, L. V. 1965. *Conflit linguistique et normalisation dans l'Europe nouvelle*. Nancy: Centre Européen Universitaire.

ARACIL, L. V. 1997. Historia inédita de la llengua catalana. *Caplletra*, 21. 185–190

ARBAUD, D. 1864. *Chants populaires de la Provence*. Spéracédès (Provence): TAC Motifs & Association Canta lou Pais / Cantar lo Païs.

ARE, O. B. 2015. 'Bridging the gap between theory and practice in language revitalization efforts in Africa. *Ghana Journal of Linguistics*, 4(1). 15–31.

ASCOLI, G. I. 1878. Schizzi franco-provenzali. *Archivio Glottologico Italiano*, 3. 61–120.

AUROUX, S. 1995. *La révolution technologique de la grammatisation*. Paris: Mardaga.

AUSTIN, P. K. 2008. *One thousand languages, living, endangered and lost*. Berkeley, CA: University of California Press.

AUSTIN, P. K., & SALLABANK, J. (eds.). 2011. *The Cambridge handbook of endangered languages*. Cambridge: Cambridge University Press.

AUSTIN, P. K., & SALLABANK, J. (eds.). 2014. *Endangered languages: Beliefs and ideologies in language documentation and revitalisation*. Oxford: Oxford University Press / British Academy.

BALIBAR, R. 1985. *L'institution du français: Essai sur le colinguisme des Carolingiens à la République*. Paris: Presses Universitaires de France.

BARTHÉLÉMY-VIGOUROUX, A., & MARTIN, G. 2000. *Manuel pratique de provençal contemporain*. Aix en Provence: Edisud.

BAUMAN, J. A. 1980. *A guide to issues in Indian language retention*. Washington, DC: Center for Applied Linguistics.

BAUMAN, R., & BRIGGS, C. L. 2003. *Voices of modernity: Language ideologies and the politics of inequality*. Cambridge: Cambridge University Press.

BAYLE, L. 1968. *Dissertation sur l'orthographe provençale (comparée à la graphie dite occitane)*. Toulon: L'Astrado.

BAYLE, L. 1975. *Procès de l'occitanisme*. Toulon: L'Astrado.

BAYLE, L. 1979. *Huit entretiens sur l'occitanisme et les Occitans*. Toulon: L'Astrado.

BAYLE, L. 1982. *La Provence en danger (Second dossier occitan)*. Toulon: L'Astrado.

BEC, P. 1973. *La langue occitane. Que sais-je?* Paris: PUF.

BERGOUNIOUX, G. 1984. 'La science du langage en France de 1870 à 1885: Du marché civil au marché étatique', *Langue Française*, 63(1). 7–41.

BERGOUNIOUX, G. 1989. 'Le francien (1815–1914): la linguistique au service de la patrie', *Mots. Les langages du Politique* 19(1). 23–40.

BERGOUNIOUX, G. 1992. 'Les enquêtes de terrain en France', *Langue française* 93(1). 3–22.

BERT, M. 2001. Rencontre de langues et francisation: l'exemple du Pilat. Thèse de doctorat. Lyon: Université Lyon 2.

BERT, M., & COSTA, J. 2014. 'What counts as a linguistic border, for whom, and with what implications? Exploring Occitan and Francoprovençal in Rhône-Alpes, France', in C. Llamas & D. Watt (eds.), *Language, borders and identity*. Edinburgh: Edinburgh University Press. 186–205.

BERT, M., COSTA, J., & MARTIN, J.-B. 2009. *Etude FORA: francoprovençal et occitan en Rhône-Alpes*. Lyon: Institut Pierre Gardette, INRP, ICAR, DDL.

BERT, M., & GRINEVALD, C. 2010. 'Proposition de typologie des locuteurs de LED', *Faits de Langues* 35/36. 117–132.

BLACKWOOD, R. J. 2008. *The state, the activists and the islanders: Language policy on Corsica*. Amsterdam: Springer.

BLANCHET, P. 1985. *La langue provençale: unité et variété. Lou Prouvençau a l'escolo (Cahier no 4)*. Marseille: Centre international de recherches et d'études provençales.

BLANCHET, P. 1992. *Le provençal: Essai de description sociolinguistique et différentielle*. Louvain-la-Neuve: Peeters.

BLANCHET, P. 1999. *Parlons provençal*. Paris: L'Harmattan.

BLANCHET, P. 2002. *Langues, cultures et identités régionales en Provence: la métaphore de l'aïoli*. Paris: L'Harmattan.

BLANCHET, P. 2007. Une ou plusieurs langue(s) d'oc? *Langues et Cité*. 10. 6.

BLOMMAERT, J. 1999a. *Language ideological debates*. Berlin: Mouton de Gruyter.

BLOMMAERT, J. 1999b. 'The debate is open', in J. Blommaert (ed.), *Language ideological debates*. Berlin: Mouton de Gruyter. 1–38.

BLOMMAERT, J. 2005. *Discourse*. Cambridge: Cambridge University Press.

BORTOLOTTO, C. 2011. 'Le trouble du patrimoine culturel immatériel' in C. Bortolotto (ed.), *Le patrimoine immatériel: enjeux d'une nouvelle catégorie.* Paris: Éditions de la Maison des sciences de l'homme. 21–43.

BOULARD, G. 1999. 'L'ordonnance de Villers-Cotterêts: le temps de la clarté et la stratégie du temps (1539–1992)', *Revue Historique* 301(609). 45–100.

BOURDIEU, P. 1976. 'Le champ scientifique', *Actes de la recherche en sciences sociales* 2(2–3). 88–104.

BOURDIEU, P. 1977. 'The economics of linguistic exchanges', *Social Sciences Information* 16(6). 645–668.

BOURDIEU, P. 1980a. 'L'identité et la représentation: éléments pour une réflexion critique sur l'idée de région', *Actes de la recherche en sciences sociales,* 35(1). 63–72.

BOURDIEU, P. 1980b. 'Le Nord et le Midi: Contribution à une analyse de l'effet Montesquieu', *Actes de la recherche en sciences sociales,* 35(1). 21–25.

BOURDIEU, P. 1991a. 'Identity and representation', in P. Bourdieu, *Language and symbolic power.* Cambridge: Polity Press. 220–228.

BOURDIEU, P. 1991b. *Language and symbolic power.* Cambridge: Polity Press.

BOURDIEU, P. 1993. *Sociology in Question.* London: Sage.

BOURDIEU, P., & EAGLETON, T. 1991. Doxa and common life: An interview. *New Left Review,* I(191). 111–121.

BOURDIEU, P. & WACQUANT, L. 1992. *An invitation to reflexive sociology.* Chicago, IL: Chicago University Press.

BOYER, H. 1991. *Langues en conflit: Etudes sociolinguistiques.* Paris: L'Harmattan.

BOYER, H. 2005a. *De l'école occitane à l'enseignement public: Vécu et représentations sociolinguistiques. Une enquête auprès d'un groupe d'excalandrons.* Paris: L'Harmattan.

BOYER, H. 2005b. '"Patois": Continuité et prégnance d'une désignation stigmatisante sur la longue durée', *Lengas* 57. 73–92.

BOYER, H., & GARDY, P. 2001. *Dix siècles d'usages et d'images de l'occitan – des troubadours à l'internet.* Paris: L'Harmattan.

BRADLEY, M. 2014. 'Is it possible to revitalize a dying language? An examination of attempts to halt the decline of Irish. *Open Journal of Modern Linguistics* 4(4). 537–543.

BRANCA-ROSOFF, S. 1998. 'De la culture de la vigne à la cueillette des fleurs des champs. Les noms de la langue dans la dialectologie française du XIX° siècle', *Langue française* 85(1). 48–67.

BRENNAN, S. 2013. 'From political independence to the current economic crisis: A look at the institutional promotion of Irish', *Langage et Société* 3(145). 35–53.

BRUBAKER, R. 1998. 'Myths and misconceptions in the study of nationalism', in J. A. Hall (ed.), *The State of the Nation: Ernest Gellner and the Theory of Nationalism.* Cambridge: Cambridge University Press. 272–306.

BRUBAKER, R. 2002. 'Ethnicity without groups', *Archives européennes de sociologie* 43(2). 163–189.

BRUBAKER, R. 2004a. *Ethnicity without groups*. Cambridge, MA: Harvard University Press.

BRUBAKER, R. 2004b. 'Rethinking classical theory: The sociological vision of Pierre Bourdieu' in D. L. Swartz & V. L. Zolberg (eds.), *After Bourdieu: Influence, critique, elaboration*. Amsterdam: Kluwer. 25–64.

BRUBAKER, R. 2015. *Grounds for difference*. Cambridge, MA: Harvard University Press.

BRUN-TRIGAUD, G. 1990. *Le croissant: Le concept et le mot. Contribution à l'histoire de la dialectologie française au XIXe siècle*. Lyon: Centre d'Etudes Linguistiques.

BURBAN, C., & LAGARDE, C. 2007. *L'école, instrument de sauvegarde des langues menacées?* Perpignan: Presses Universitaires de Perpignan.

CAMERON, D. 1995. *Verbal hygiene*. London: Routledge.

CAMERON, D. 2007. 'Language endangerment and verbal hygiene: History, morality and politics', in A. Duchêne & M. Heller (eds.), *Discourses of endangerment*. London: Continuum. 268–285

CAMPBELL, L., & MUNTZEL, M. C. 1989. 'The structural consequences of language death', in N. C. Dorian (ed.), *Investigating obsolescence: Studies in language contraction and death*. Cambridge: Cambridge University Press. 181–196

CANUT, C. 2000. 'Le nom des langues ou les métaphores de la frontière', *Ethnologies comparées* 1. 1–18.

CASANOVA, J.-Y. 2004. *Frédéric Mistral: l'enfant, la mort et les rêves*. Perpignan: Trabucaire.

CAVAILLÉ, J.-P. 2008. Villers-Cotterêts et la langue qui n'avait pas de nom. *Mescladis E Còps de Gula*. http://taban.canalblog.com/archives/2008/12/17/11786374.html (15 August 2015).

CERQUIGLINI, B. 2007. *Une langue orpheline*. Paris: Editions de Minuit.

CERTEAU, M. DE, JULIA, D., & REVEL, J. 1975. 'Une ethnographie de la langue: L'enquête de Grégoire sur les patois', *Annales. Histoire, sciences sociales* 30(1). 3–41.

CEUPPENS, B., & GESCHIERE, P. 2005. 'Autochthony: Local or global? New modes in the struggle over citizenship and belonging in Africa and Europe', *Annual Review of Anthropology* 34. 385–407.

CHABAUD, S. 2013. 'Le chant en occitan, une expérience récente et originale de prise en main d'une culture et d'une langue', Lengas 74. http://lengas.revues.org/375 (29 December 2016).

CHAMBERS, J. K., & TRUDGILL, P. 1980. *Dialectology. Cambridge textbooks in linguistics*. Cambridge: Cambridge University Press.

CHAMPAGNE, P. 2013. 'Note sur quelques lectures du concept de champ', *Actes de la recherche en sciences sociales* 5(200). 38–43.

CITRON, S. 2008. *Le mythe national: L'histoire de France revisitée*. Ivry-sur-Seine: Editions de l'Atelier.

CLIFFORD, J. 1986. 'Introduction: Partial truths', in J. Clifford & G. E. Marcus (eds.), *Writing culture: The poetics and plitics of ethnography*. Berkeley, CA: University of California Press. 1–26.

CLIFFORD, J. 1987. 'The politics of representation. Of other peoples: Beyond the "Salvage Paradigm"', in H. Foster (ed.), *Discussions in contemporary culture – number one*. Seattle, WA: Bay Press. 121–130.

CLIFFORD, J. 2013. *Returns: Becoming indigenous in the twenty-first century*. Cambridge, MA: Harvard University Press.

COLLEY, L. 1986. 'Whose nation? Class and national consciousness in Britain 1750–1830', *Past and Present* 113(1). 97–117.

COMAROFF, J. L., & COMAROFF, J. 2009. *Ethnicity, Inc*. Chicago, IL: Chicago University Press.

CONNOR, J. 2011. National standardization or strength in diversity? Language ideological debates in the South of France. BA Dissertation. University of Chicago.

COSTA, J. 2009. Language history as charter myth? Scots and the (re)invention of Scotland. *Scottish Language* 28(1). 1–25.

COSTA, J. 2010. 'Language, ideologies, and the "Scottish voice"', *International Journal of Scottish Literature* 7.

COSTA, J. 2012. 'Mythologie(s) occitane(s) et figures de l'autorité: Le rôle du linguiste dans l'imaginaire de l'aménagement linguistique'. *Cahiers de l'observatoire des pratiques linguistiques* 3, 107–117.

COSTA, J. 2013. 'Language endangerment and revitalisation as elements of regimes of truth: Shifting terminology to shift perspective', *Journal of Multilingual and Multicultural Development* 34(4), 317–331.

COSTA, J. 2014. 'Must we save the language? Children's discourse on language and community in Provençal and Scottish language revitalisation movements', in P. K. Austin & J. Sallabank (eds.), *Endangered languages: Beliefs and ideologies in language documentation and revitalisation* Vol. 199. Oxford: Oxford University Press / British Academy. 195–214.

COSTA, J. 2015a. 'Can schools dispense with standard language? Some unintended consequences of introducing Scots in a Scottish primary school', *Journal of Linguistic Anthropology* 25(1), 25–42.

COSTA, J. 2015b. 'New speakers, new language: On being a legitimate speaker of a minority language in Provence', *International Journal of the Sociology of Language* 2015(231). 127–145.

COSTA, J., & GASQUET-CYRUS, M. 2012. 'Introduction: Aspects idéologiques des débats linguistiques en Provence et ailleurs', *Lengas* 72, 9–22.

COUPIER, J., BLANCHET, P. & Association Dictionnaire français-provençal. 1995. *Dictionnaire français-provençal = Diciounàri francés-prouvençau*. Marseille: Association Dictionnaire français-provençal.

COUROUAU, J.-F. 1999. *Bertrand Larade. La margalide gascoue et meslanges 1604, édition critique*. Toulouse: Section française de l'Association internationale d'études occitanes.

COUROUAU, J.-F. 2001a. 'La deffence de Du Bellay et les apologies de la langue occitane, XVIe-XVIIe siècles', *Bulletin de l'association d'étude sur l'humanisme, la réforme et la renaissance* 53(1). 9–32.

COUROUAU, J.-F. 2001b. *Premiers combats pour la langue occitane: Manifestes linguistiques occitans XVIe-XVIIe siècles*. Anglet: Atlantica & Institut Occitan.

COUROUAU, J.-F. 2003. 'Les apologies de la langue française (XVIs siècle) et de la langue occitane (XVIe-XVIIe siècles), naissance d'une double mythographie. Première partie', *Nouvelle revue du XVIe siècle* 21(2). 35–51.

COUROUAU, J.-F. 2004. 'Les apologies de la langue française (XVIs siècle) et de la langue occitane (XVIe-XVIIe siècles), naissance d'une double mythographie. Deuxième partie', *Nouvelle revue du XVIe siècle* 22(2). 23–39.

COUROUAU, J.-F. 2006. 'La plume et les langues', *L'Homme*, 177–178, 251–278.

COUROUAU, J.-F. 2012. *Et non autrement. Marginalisation et résistance des langues de France (XVIe-XVIIe siècle)*. Paris: Droz.

CRAIG, C. 1992a. 'A constitutional response to language endangerment: The case of Nicaragua', *Language* 68(1). 17–24.

CRAIG, C. 1992b. 'Language shift and language death: The Case of Rama in Nicaragua', *International Journal of the Sociology of Language* 93(1). 11–26.

CROWE, R. 2005. 'Iolo Morganwg and the dialects of Welsh', in G. H. Jenkins (ed.), *A rattleskull genius: The many faces of Iolo Morganwg*. Cardiff: Gwasg Prifysgol Cymru. 315–331.

CRYSTAL, D. 2000. *Language death*. Cambridge: Cambridge University Press.

CRYSTAL, D. 2005. Revitalizing the Celtic Languages. XI Annual Conference of the North American Association for Celtic Language Teachers. University of Wales, Bangor.

DARNELL, R. 1998. *And along came Boas: Continuity and revolution in Americanist anthropology*. Amsterdam: John Benjamins.

DARQUENNES, J. 2007. Paths to language revitalization'. *Plurilingua*, 30(1). 61–77.

DAUENHAUER, N. M., & DAUENHAUER, R. 1998. 'Technical, emotional and ideological issues in reversing language shift: Examples from Southeast Alaska'. in L. A. Grenoble & L. J. Whaley (eds.), *Endangered languages: Language loss and community responses*. Cambridge: Cambridge University Press. 57–98.

DAUZAT, A. 1938. *Les patois*. Paris: Librairie Delagrave.

DAVIS, W. 2009. *The wayfinders: Why ancient wisdom matters in the modern world.* Toronto: Anansi Press.

DEL PERCIO, A., FLUBACHER, M., & DUCHÊNE, A. (forthcoming). 'Language and political economy', in O. Garcia, N. Flores, & M. Spotti (eds.), *Oxford handbook of language in society*. Oxford: Oxford University Press.

DELLA PORTA, D., & DIANI, M. 2006. *Social movements: An introduction* (2nd edn). Oxford: Blackwell.

DIDEROT, D., & D'ALEMBERT, J. L. R. (eds.). 1765. *Encyclopédie ou dictionnaire raisonné des sciences, des arts et des métiers* (Vol. 12). Paris.

DIXON, R. M. W. 1997. *The rise and fall of languages*. Cambridge: Cambridge University Press.

DOMPMARTIN-NORMAND, C. 2002. 'Collégiens issus de Calandreta: Quelles représentations de l'occitan?', *Etudes de Linguistique Appliquée*, 101. 35–54.

DORIAN, N. C. 1981. *Language death: The life cycle of a Scottish Gaelic dialect*. Philadelphia, PA: University of Pennsylvania Press.

DORIAN, N. C. 1989a. 'Introduction', in N. C. Dorian (ed.), *Investigating obsolescence: Studies in language contraction and death. Studies in the social and cultural foundations of language*. Cambridge: Cambridge University Press. 1–10.

DORIAN, N. C. 1989b. *Investigating obsolescence: studies in language contraction and death. Studies in the social and cultural foundations of language*. Cambridge: Cambridge University Press.

DORIAN, N. C. 1993. 'A response to Ladefoged's other view of endangered languages', *Language* 69(3). 575–579.

DOSSETTO, D. 2001. 'En "Arlésienne" ou "le voile islamique" à l'envers?', *Terrain* 36(1). doi:Terr.036.0011

DOUJAT, J. (ed.). 1811. *Las obros de Pierre Goudelin*. Toulouso: J.-A. Caunes.

DROTT, E. 2011. 'The Nòva Cançon Occitana and the internal colonialism thesis', *French Politics, Culture & Society* 29(1). 1–23.

DUCHÊNE, A. 2008. *Ideologies across nations: The construction of linguistic minorities at the United Nations*. Berlin: Mouton de Gruyter.

DUCHÊNE, A., & HELLER, M. (eds.). 2007. *Discourses of endangerment: Ideology and interest in the defense of language. Advances in sociolinguistics*. London: Continuum.

DUCHÊNE, A., & HELLER, M. (eds.). 2011. *Language in late capitalism: Pride and profit*. London: Routledge.

ECKERT, P. 2008. 'Variation and the indexical field', *Journal of Sociolinguistics* 12(4). 453–476.

ELLIS, P. B., & MAC A'GHOBHAINN, S. 1971. *The problem of language revival*. Inbhir Nis: Club Leabhar.

EQUIPE "18ème et Révolution" (ed.). 1991. *Dictionnaire des usages socio-politiques (1770–1815). Fascicule 5: Langue, occitan, usages*. Paris: Klincksieck.

ERRINGTON, J. 2003. 'Getting language rights: The rhetorics of language endangerment and loss', *American Anthropologist* 105(4). 723–732.

EVANS, N. 2009. *Dying words: Endangered languages and what they have to tell us*. Malden, MA: Wiley-Blackwell.

FELSKI, R. 2011. 'Context stinks', *New Literary History* 42(4). 573–591.

FISHMAN, J. A. 1964. 'Language maintenance and language shift as a field of inquiry: A definition of the field and suggestions for its further development', *Linguistics* 9(1). 32–70.

FISHMAN, J. A. 1982a. 'The role of the Tshernovits Conference in the rise of Hebrew', in R. L. Cooper (ed.), *Language spread*. Bloomington, IN: Indiana University Press. 220–291.

FISHMAN, J. A. 1982b. 'Whorfianism of the third kind: Ethnolinguistic diversity as a worldwide societal asset (The Whorfian hypothesis: Varieties of validation, confirmation, and disconfirmation II)', *Language in Society* 11(1). 1–14.

FISHMAN, J. A. 1991. *Reversing language shift: theoretical and empirical foundations of assistance to threatened languages.* Clevedon: Multilingual Matters.

FISHMAN, J. A. 1996. 'Language revitalization', in J. A. Fishman, N. H. Hornberger & M. Pütz (eds.), *An international handbook of contemporary research / Manuel international des recherches contemporaines / Ein internationales Handbuch zeitgenössischer Forschung.* Berlin: Walter de Gruyter. 902–906.

FISHMAN, J. A. 2001. *Can threatened languages be saved? Reversing language shift, revisited: A 21st century perspective.* Clevedon: Multilingual Matters.

FISHMAN, J. A., HORNBERGER, N. H., & PÜTZ, M. 2006. *Language loyalty, language planning, and language revitalization: recent writings and reflections from Joshua A. Fishman.* Clevedon: Multilingual Matters.

FLOR, V. 2011. *Noves glòries a Espanya: Anticatalanisme i identitat valenciana.* Catarroja: Editorial Afers.

FOUCAULT, M. 1988. 'Truth and power', in C. Gordon (ed.), *Michel Foucault: Power/knowledge. Selected interviews and other writings 1972–1977.* New York: Pantheon Books. 109–133.

FOUCAULT, M. 2000. *Power.* New York: The New Press.

FOUCAULT, M. 2003. *Society must be defended: Lectures at the Collège de France, 1975–76.* New York: Picador.

FOUILLÉE, A. 1877. *Le tour de la France par deux enfants.* Paris: Belin.

FRAJ, E. 2013. *Quel occitan pour demain? Langage et démocracie.* Pau: Reclams.

FREELAND, J., & PATRICK, D. 2004. 'Language rights and language survival: Sociolinguistic and sociocultural perspectives', in J. Freeland & D. Patrick (eds.), *Language rights and language survival.* Manchester: St Jerome Publishing. 1–33.

GAL, S. 1989a. 'Language and political economy', *Annual Review of Anthropology*, 18. 345–367.

GAL, S. 1989b. 'Lexical innovation and loss: The use and value of restricted Hungarian', in N. C. Dorian (ed.), *Investigating obsolescence: Studies in language contraction and death.* Cambridge: Cambridge University Press. 313–334.

GAL, S. & WOOLARD, K. A. 2001. 'Constructing languages and publics authority and representation', in S. Gal & K. A. Woolard (eds.), *Languages and publics: The making of authority.* Manchester: St Jerome Publishing. 1–12.

GARDIN, B. 1975. 'Loi deixonne et langues régionales: représentation de la nature et de la fonction de leur enseignement', *Langue française* 25(1). 29–36.

GARDY, P. 1990. 'Aux origines du discours francophoniste: le meurtre des patois et leur rachat par le français', *Langue française* 85(1). 22–34.

GARDY, P. 1991. 'Langue d'oc (patois, gascon, provençal, languedocien, langue vulgaire, moundi...)', in Equipe "18ème et Révolution" (ed.). *Dictionnaire des usages socio-politiques (1770–1815). Fascicule 5, 'Langue, occitan, usages'*. Paris: Klincksieck. 117–157.

GARDY, P. 2001. 'Les noms de l'occitan / nommer l'occitan', in H. Boyer & P. Gardy (eds.), *Dix siècles d'usages et d'images de l'occitan: Des troubadours à l'Internet*. Paris: L'Harmattan. 43–64.

GARDY, P., & LAFONT, R. 1981. 'La diglossie comme conflit: L'exemple occitan', *Langages*, 15(61). 75–91.

GELU, V. 1856. *Chansons provençales* (2nd edn). Marseille: Lafitte et Roubaud.

GIPPERT, J., HIMMELMANN, N. P., & MOSEL, U. (eds.). 2006. *Essentials of language documentation*. New York: Mouton de Gruyter.

GOODWIN, C., & DURANTI, A. 1992. 'Rethinking context: An introduction', in A. Duranti & C. Goodwin (eds.), *Rethinking context: Language as an interactive phenomenon*. Cambridge: Cambridge University Press. 1–42.

GRANADILLO, T., & ORCUTT-GACHIRI, H. A. 2011. *Ethnographic contributions to the study of endangered languages*. Tucson, AZ: University of Arizona Press.

GRENOBLE, L. A., & WHALEY, L. J. 1998a. *Endangered languages: Current issues and future prospects*. Cambridge: Cambridge University Press.

GRENOBLE, L. A., & WHALEY, L. J. 1998b. 'Toward a typology of language endangerment', in L. A. Grenoble & L. J. Whaley (eds.), *Endangered languages: Language loss and community responses*. Cambridge: Cambridge University Press. 22–54.

GRENOBLE, L. A., & WHALEY, L. J. 2006. *Saving languages – an introduction to language revitalization*. Cambridge: Cambridge University Press.

GRINEVALD, C. 2003. 'Speakers and documentation of endangered languages', In Peter K. Austin (ed.) *Language documentation and description*, vol 1. London: SOAS. 52–72.

GRINEVALD, C., & BERT, M. 2011. 'Speakers and communities', in P. K. Austin & J. Sallabank (eds.), *The Cambridge handbook of endangered languages*. Cambridge: Cambridge University Press. 45–65.

GRINEVALD, C., & BERT, M. 2014. 'Whose ideology, where and when? Rama (Nicaragua) and Francoprovençal (France) experiences', in P. K. Austin & J. Sallabank (eds.), *Endangered languages: Beliefs and ideologies in language documentation and revitalization*. Oxford: Oxford University Press. 000–000.

GRINEVALD, C., & COSTA, J. 2010. 'Langues en danger: Le phénomène et la réponse des linguistes', *Faits de Langues* 35–36, 23–37.

GRUBER, J. W. 1970. 'Ethnographic salvage and the shaping of anthropology', *American Anthropologist*, 72(6). 1289–1299.

GUSTAFSON, B. 2009. *New languages of the state: Indigenous resurgence and the politics of knowledge in Bolivia*. Durham, NC: Duke University Press.

HABERMAS, J. 1991. *The structural transformation of the public sphere: An inquiry into a category of bourgeois society*. Cambridge, MA: The MIT Press.

HADDON, A. C. 1898. *The study of man*. New York: G.P. Putnam's Sons.

HAGÈGE, C. 2000. *Halte à la mort des langues*. Paris: Odile Jacob.

HAGÈGE, C. 2009. *On the death and lfe of languages*. New Haven, CT: Yale University Press.

HALE, K. 1992. 'Endangered languages: On endangered languages and the safeguarding of diversity', *Language* 68(1). 1–3.

HALE, K., KRAUSS, M., WATAHOMIGIE, L. J., YAMAMOTO, A. Y., CRAIG, C., JEANNE, L. M., & ENGLAND, N. C. 1992. 'Endangered languages', *Language* 68(1). 1–42

HALPERN, B. 1961. '"Myth" and "ideology" in modern usage', *History and Theory* 1(2). 129–149.

HAMES, R. 2007. 'The ecologically noble savage debate', *Annual Review of Anthropology* 36. 177–190.

HAMMEL, E., & GARDY, P. 1994. *L'occitan en Languedoc-Roussillon: 1991*. Perpinyà: El Trabucaïre.

HARKIN, M. E. 2004a. 'Introduction: Revitalization as history and theory', in M. E. Harkin (ed.), *Reassessing revitalization movements: Perspectives from North America and the Pacific Islands*. Lincoln, NE: University of Nebraska Press. xv–xxxvi.

HARKIN, M. E. (ed.). 2004b. *Reassessing revitalization movements: Perspectives from North America and the Pacific Islands*. Lincoln, NE: University of Nebraska Press.

HARRISON, K. D. 2007. *When languages die: The extinction of the world's languages and the erosion of human knowledge*. Oxford: Oxford University Press.

HARRISON, K. D. 2010. *The last speakers*. Washington, DC: National Geographic.

Heller, M. 2003. *Crosswords: Language, education and ethnicity in French Ontario*. Berlin: Mouton de Gruyter.

HELLER, M. 2004. 'Analysis and stance regarding language and social justice', in J. Freeland & D. Patrick (eds.), *Language rights and language survival*. Manchester: St Jerome Publishing. 283–286.

HELLER, M. 2005. 'Language, skill and authenticity in the globalized new economy', *Noves SL. Revista de Sociolingüística* 1–7.

HELLER, M. 2006. *Linguistic minorities and modernity: A sociolinguistic ethnography. Advances in sociolinguistics* (2nd edn). London: Continuum.

HELLER, M. 2008. 'Doing ethnography', in Li Wei & M. G. Moyer (eds.), *The Blackwell guide to research methods in bilingualism and multilingualism*. Oxford: Blackwell. 249–262.

HELLER, M. 2011. *Paths to post-nationalism: A critical ethnography of language and identity*. Oxford: Oxford University Press.

HELLER, M. 2014. 'The commodification of authenticity', in V. Lacoste, J. Leimgruber, & T. Breyer (eds.), *Indexing authenticity: Sociolinguistic perspectives*. Berlin: De Gruyter. 136–155.

HELLER, M., & DUCHÊNE, A. 2007. 'Discourses of endangerment: Sociolinguistics, globalization and social order'. in A. Duchêne & M. Heller (eds.), *Discourses of endangerment: Ideology and interest in the defense of language*. London: Continuum. 1–13.

HELLER, M., JAWORSKI, A., & THURLOW, C. 2014. 'Introduction: Sociolinguistics and tourism', *Journal of Sociolinguistics* 18(4). 425–458.

HELLER, M., & MARTIN-JONES, M. 2001. 'Introduction: Symbolic domination, education and linguistic difference', in M. Heller & M. Martin-Jones (eds.), *Voices of authority: Education and linguistic difference*. Westport: Ablex Publishing. 1–28.

HILL, J. H. 1989. 'The social functions of relativization in obsolescent and non-obsolescent languages', in N. C. Dorian (ed.), *Investigating obsolescence: Studies in language contraction and death*. Cambridge: Cambridge University Press. 148–164.

HILL, J. H. 2002. '"Expert rhetorics" in advocacy for endangered languages: Who Is listening, and what do they hear?', *Journal of Linguistic Anthropology* 12(2). 119–133.

HIMMELMANN, N. P. 2006. 'Language documentation: What is it and what is it good for?', in J. Gippert, N. P. Himmelmann, & U. Mosel (eds.), *Essentials of language documentation*. Berlin & New York: Mouton de Gruyter. 1–30.

HINCKS, R. 2000. *Yr iaith lenyddol fel bwch dihangol yng Nghymru ac yn Llydaw [The literary language as a scapegoat in Wales and Brittany]*. Aberystwyth: Adran y Gymraeg, Prifysgol Cymru Aberystwyth.

HINTON, L. 2001. 'Language revitalization: An overview', in L. Hinton & K. Hale (eds.), *The green book of language revitalization in practice*. San Diego, CA: Academic Press.

HINTON, L., & HALE, K. 2001. *The green book of language revitalization in practice*. San Diego, CA: Academic Press.

HINTON, L., VERA, M., & STEELE, N. 2002. *How to keep your language alive: a commonsense approach to one-on-one language learning*. Berkeley, CA: Heyday Books.

HOBSBAWM, E. J. 1990. *Nations and nationalism since 1780* (2nd edn). Cambridge: Cambridge University Press.

HOBSBAWM, E. J. 1996. *The age of revolution 1789–1848*. New York: Vintage Books.

HONNORAT, S. J. 1846. *Dictionnaire provençal-français, ou dictionnaire de la langue d'oc, ancienne et moderne* (Vol. 1). Digne: Repos.

HORNBERGER, N. H. 2008. 'Introduction', in N. H. Hornberger (ed.), *Can schools save indigenous languages? Policy and practice on four continents*. Basingstoke: Palgrave MacMillan. 1–12.

HORNBERGER, N. H., & CORONEL-MOLINA, S. M. 2004. 'Quechua language shift, maintenance, and revitalization in the Andes: The case for language planning', *International Journal of the Sociology of Language* 167(1). 9–67.

HORNSBY, M. 2005. 'Neo-Breton and questions of authenticity', *Estudios de Sociolingüística* 6(2). 191–218.

HORNSBY, M. 2015. 'The "new" and "traditional" speaker dichotomy: Bridging the gap', *International Journal of the Sociology of Language* 2015(231). 107–125.

HORNSBY, M., & QUENTEL, G. 2013. 'Contested varieties and competing authenticities: Neologisms in revitalized Breton', *International Journal of the Sociology of Language* 2013(223). 71–86.

HUSS, L. 2008a. 'Researching language loss and revitalization', in K. A. King & N. H. Hornberger (eds.), *Encyclopedia of language and education* (Vol. 10). Springer. 69–81.

HUSS, L. 2008b. 'Revitalization through indigenous education: A forlorn hope? in N. H. Hornberger (ed.), *Can schools save indigenous languages? Policy and practice on four continents*. Basingstoke: Palgrave MacMillan. 125–135.

HUSS, L., & LINDGREN, A.-R. 2011. 'Introduction: defining language emancipation', *International Journal of the Sociology of Language* 2011(209). 1–15.

HUTTON, C. M. 1999. *Linguistics and the Third Reich: Mother-tongue fascism, race and the science of language*. London: Routledge.

HYMES, D. 1981. *In vain I tried to tell you*. Philadelphia, PA: University of Pennsylvania Press.

IRVINE, J. T. 1989. 'When talk isn't cheap: language and political economy', *American Ethnologist* 16(2). 248–267.

ISRAEL, P. 2001. 'Acheminement vers la parole unique', *Cahiers d'Etudes Africaines*, 163–164, 815–832.

JAFFE, A. 1996. 'The Second Annual Corsican Spelling Contest: Orthography and ideology', *American Ethnologist* 23(4). 816–835.

JAFFE, A. 1999. *Ideologies in action: Language politics on Corsica. Language, power and social process*. Berlin: Mouton de Gruyter.

JAFFE, A. 2009. 'Introduction: The sociolinguistics of stance', in A. Jaffe (ed.), *Stance: Sociolinguistic perspectives*. Oxford: Oxford University Press. 3–28.

JAFFE, A. 2015. 'Defining the new speaker: Theoretical perspectives and learner trajectories', *International Journal of the Sociology of Language* 2015(231). 21–44.

JEANJEAN, H. 1990. *De l'utopie au pragmatisme? Le mouvement occitan 1976– 1990*. Perpinyà: El Trabucaïre.

JONES, M. C. 1995. 'Atwhat price language maintenance? Standardization in Modern Breton', *French Studies* XLIX(3). 428–436

JOUVEAU, R. 1984. *Histoire du Félibrige* (Vol. 1). Nimes.

KING, K. A. 2001. *Language revitalization: Processes and prospects – Quichua in the Ecuadorian Andes. Bilingual education and bilingualism*. Clevedon: Multilingual Matters.

KRAUSS, M. 1992. 'Endangered languages: The world's languages in crisis', *Language* 68(1). 4–10.

KRAUSS, M. 2007. 'Classification and terminology for degrees of language endangerment', in M. Brenzinger (ed.), *Language diversity endangered*. Berlin: Mouton de Gruyter. 1–8.

KREMNITZ, G. 2007. La langue d'oc, une et plurielle. *Langues et Cité*, (10), 7.

KROSKRITY, P. V. 2000. 'Regimenting languages: Language ideological perspectives', In P. V Kroskrity (ed.), *Regimes of language: Ideologies, polities and identities*. Santa fE, NM & Oxford: SAR Press & James Currey. 1–34.

KROSKRITY, P. V. 2009. 'Language renewal as sites of language ideological struggle. The need for "ideological clarification"', in J. Reyhner & L. Lockard (eds.), *Indigenous language revitalization: Encouragement, guidance & lessons learned*. Flagstaff, AZ: Northern Arizona University. 71–83.

KROSKRITY, P. V, & FIELD, M. C. (eds.) 2009. *Native American language ideologies: Beliefs, practices and struggles*. Tucson, AZ: University of Arizona Press.

LADEFOGED, P. 1992. 'Another view of endangered languages', *Language* 68(4). 809–811.

LAFITTE, J., & PÉPIN, G. 2009. *La "Langue d'Oc" ou leS langueS d'oc?* Monein: Pyremonde / Princi Negue.

LAFONT, R. 1954. *Mistral ou l'illusion* (2nd edn). Valderiès: Vent Terral.

LAFONT, R. 1971. 'Un problème de culpabilité sociologique: la diglossie francooccitane', *Langue française* 9(1). 93–99.

LAFONT, R. 1972. *L'ortografia occitana: lo provençau*. Montpelhièr: Centre d'Estudis Occitans, Universitat de Montpelhièr III.

LAFONT, R. 1977. 'Sobre el procés de patoisització', *Treballs de Sociolingüística Catalana*, 1. 131–135.

LAFONT, R. 1982. 'Le "Midi" des troubadours: Histoire d'un texte', *Romantisme* 35(1). 25–48.

LAFONT, R. 1984. 'Pour retrousser la diglossie', *Lengas* 15. 5–36.

LAFONT, R. 1991. *Temps tres*. Perpinyà: El Trabucaïre.

LAFONT, R. 1997. *Quarante ans de sociolinguistique à la périphérie*. Paris: L'Harmattan.

LAFONT, R. 2003. *Petita istòria Europèa d'Occitània*. Perpinyà: El Trabucaïre.

LAFONT, R. 2004. 'Préface', in G. Agresti (ed.), *Anthologie de la nouvelle écriture occitane*. Montpeirós: Jorn.

LAFONT, R., & ANATOLE, C. 1970. *Nouvelle histoire de la littérature occitane* (Vol. 2). Paris: Presses Universitaires de France.

LATOUR, B. 2005. *Reassembling the social: An introduction to actor-network theory*. Oxford: Oxford University Press.

LAURENDEAU, P. 1994. 'Le concept de patois avant 1790, vel vernacula lingua', in R. Mougeon & É. Béniak (eds.), *Les origines du français québécois*. Montréal: Presses de l'Université Laval. 131–166.

LAURENT, J.-P. 1989. 'L'Ordonnance de Villers-Cotterêts (1539) et la conversion des notaires à l'usage exclusif du français en pays d'oc', *Lengas* 26. 59–94.

LE BERRE, Y. & LE DÛ, J. 1999. 'Le qui pro quo des langues régionales: sauver la langue ou éduquer les enfants?', in C. Clairis, D. Costaouec, & J.-B. Coyos (eds.), *Langues et cultures régionales de France – etat des lieux, enseignement, politiques*. Paris: L'Harmattan. 1–83.

LE NEVEZ, A. 2006. Language diversity and linguistic identity in Brittany: A critical analysis of the changing practice of Breton.

LEGRAND, L. 1993. 'Célestin Freinet (1896–1966)', *Prospects: The Quarterly Review of Comparative Education*, XXIII(1/2). 403–418.

LÉVI-STRAUSS, C. 1956. 'Sorciers et psychanalyse', *Le Courrier de l'Unesco*, July-August. 8–10.

LÉVI-STRAUSS, C. 1973. *Anthropologie structurale deux*. Paris: Plon.

LÉVY-BRUHL, L. 1999. '"Primitive Mentality" and Religion', in J. Waardenburgh (ed.), *Classical approaches to the study of religion*. Berlin: Walter de Gruyter. 335–352.

LEWIS, M. P., & SIMONS, G. F. 2010. 'Assessing endangerment: Expanding Fishman's GIDS', *Revue Roumaine de Linguistique* 55(2). 103–120.

LIEBMANN, M. 2008. 'The innovative materiality of revitalization movements: Lessons from the Pueblo Revolt of 1680', *American Anthropologist* 110(3). 360–372.

LIEUTARD, H., & VERNY, M.-J. 2007. *L'école française et les langues régionales – XIXe-XXe siècles. Etudes occitanes*. Montpellier: Presses Universitaires de la Méditerranée.

LINCOLN, B. 2000. *Theorizing mth: Narrative, ideology, and Scholarship*. Chicago, IL: University of Chicago Press.

LINTON, R. 1943. 'Nativistic movements', *American Anthropologist* 45(2). 230–240

LODGE, R. A. 1993. *French: From dialect to standard*. London: Routledge.

LODGE, R. A. 2005. 'Le clivage oc-oïl au moyen âge: Fiction méthodologique', *Mélanges de l'Ecole Française de Rome. Moyen Age* 117(2). 595–613.

LOETHER, C. 2009. 'Language revitalization and the manipulation of language ideologies. A Shoshoni case study', in P. V Kroskrity & M. C. Field (eds.), *Native American language ideologies* (pp. 238–254). Tucson, AZ: University of Arizona Press. 238–254.

MAFFI, L. 2000. 'Language preservation vs. language maintenance and revitalization: Assessing concepts, approaches, and implications for the language sciences', *International Journal of the Sociology of Language* 142. 175–190.

MALINOWSKI, B. 1954. *Magic, science and religion and other essays*. New York: Doubleday Anchor Books.

MARTEL, P. 1982a. 'Les historiens du début du XIXème siècle et le Moyen Âge occitan: Midi éclairé, Midi martyr ou Midi pittoresque', *Romantisme* 12(35). 49–72.

MARTEL, P. 1982b. 'Les Occitans face à leur histoire: Mary Lafon, le grand ancêtre', *Amiras / Repères occitans* 1. 5–16.

MARTEL, P. 1986. 'Bleu, blanc ou rouge: La politique félibréenne autour de 1870', *Amiras / Repères occitans* 13. 116–132.

MARTEL, P. 1987. 'Vingt-cinq ans de luttes identitaires', in G. Vermes & J. Boutet (eds.), *France, pays multilingue. Tome 1: Les langues de France, un enjeu historique et social.* Paris: L'Harmattan. 125–142.

MARTEL, P. 1989. 'Un peu d'histoire: Bref historique de la revendication occitane, 1978–1988', *Amiras / Repères occitans*, 20. 11–23.

MARTEL, P. 1997. 'Le Félibrige', in P. Nora (ed.), *Les lieux de mémoire.* Vol. 3. Paris: Quarto Gallimard. 3515–3553.

MARTEL, P. 1998. 'Les "patois" pendant la période révolutionnaire: Recherches sur le cas occitan', *Mots. Les langages du politique* 16(1). 191–194.

MARTEL, P. 2001a. 'Autour de Villers-Cotterêts: Histoire d'un débat', *Lengas* 49. 7–25

MARTEL, P. 2001b. 'La France et l'occitan à l'époque contemporaine: Histoire d'une étrange politique linguistique', in H. Boyer & P. Gardy (eds.), *Dix siècles d'usages et d'images de l'occitan.* Paris: L'Harmattan. 367–384.

MARTEL, P. 2004. 'Le Félibrige: Un incertain nationalisme linguistique', *Mots. Les langages du politique* 74. 43–56.

MARTEL, P. 2007. *L'école française et l'occitan – le sourd et le bègue.* Montpellier: Presses Universitaires de la Méditerranée.

MARTEL, P. 2010a. 'Du parler local à la langue: le docteur Honnorat à la découverte de l'unité de la langue d'oc', *Chroniques de Haute Provence*, 365.

MARTEL, P. 2010b. *Les Félibres et leur temps: Renaissance d'oc et opinion (1850-1914).* Bordeaux: Presses universitaires de Bordeaux.

MARTEL, P. 2012. 'Une norme pour la langue d'oc? Les débuts d'une histoire sans fin', *Lengas* 72. 23–50.

MARTEL, P. 2013. 'La Nòva Cançon occitana: révolution en occitan, révolution dans la chanson occitane?', *Lengas* 74(303).

MARTIN-JONES, M. 1989. 'Language, power and linguistic minorities: The need for an alternative approach to bilingualism, language maintenance and shift', in R. Grillo (ed.), *Social anthropology and the politics of language.* London: Routledge. 106–125.

MARTIN, G., & MOULIN, B. 2007. *Grammaire Provençale / Gramatica Provençala.* Aix en provence: CREO Provença.

MAURON, C. 1993. *Frédéric Mistral.* Paris: Fayard.

MAY, S. 2013. *Language and mnority rights: Ethnicity, nationalism and the politics of language.* London: Routledge.

MAZEROLLES, V. 2008. *La chanson occitane, 1965–1997.* Bordeaux: Presses universitaires de Bordeaux.

MCDONALD, M. 1989. *We are not French: Language, culture and identity in Brittany.* London: Routledge.

MCMULLEN, A. 2004. '"Canny about conflict": Nativism, revitalization, and the invention of tradition in native Southeastern New England', in M. E. Harkin (ed.), *Reassessing revitalization movements. perspectives from North*

America and the Pacific Islands. Lincoln, NE: University of Nebraska Press. 177–261.

MEEK, B. A. 2009. *Language ideology and aboriginal language revitalization in the Yukon, Canada*. Tucson, AZ: The University of Arizona Press.

MEEK, B. A. 2010. *We are our language: An ethnography of language revitalization in a Northern Athabaskan Community*. Tucson, AZ: University of Arizona Press.

MERLE, R. 1977. *Culture occitane per avançar*. Paris: Editions Sociales.

MERLE, R. 1986a. 'Le chemin d'Honnorat: Histoire d'A, ou la langue telle qu'elle doit être. *Amiras / Repères occitans* 13. 85–98.

MERLE, R. 1986b. 'Préfélibrige: "Lou fué eïs estoupes?"', *Amiras / Repères occitans* 13. 6–36.

MERLE, R. 1990. *L'écriture du provençal de 1775 à 1840*. Béziers: Centre international de documentation occitane.

MERLE, R. 2002. *Le couteau sur la langue*. Marseille: Jigal.

MERLE, R. 2010. *Visions de "l'idiome natal" à travers l'enquête Impériale sur les patois (1807–1812): langue d'oc, catalan, francoprovençal – France, Italie, Suisse*. Perpinyà: El Trabucaïre.

MERLIN-KAJMAN, H. 2011. 'L'étrange histoire de l'ordonnance de Villers-Cotterêets: Force du passé, force des signes', *Histoire, epistémologie, langage* XXXIII(2). 79–101.

MERTZ, E. 2007. 'Semiotic anthropology', *Annual Review of Anthropology* 36. 337–353.

MICHAELS, W. B. 1992. 'Race into culture: A critical genealogy of cultural identity', *Critical Inquiry* 18(4). 655–685.

MICHAELS, W. B. 2006. *The trouble with diversity: How we learned to love identity and ignore inequality*. New York: Holt McDougal.

MICHELET, J. 1840. *Œuvres de M. Michelet* (Vol. 3: Histoir). Bruxelles: Meline, Cans et Compagnie.

MILHÉ, C. 2008. *'Pragmatique de l'utopie occitane: le point de vue béarnais'*, Thèse de doctorat. Bordeaux: Université Victor Segalen - Bordeaux 2.

MISTRAL, F. 1859. *Mirèio: Pouèmo prouvènçau*. Avignon: Roumanille.

MISTRAL, F. 1867. *An English version of Mr Frédéric Mistral's Mirèio from the Original Provençal under the author's sanction*. (C. H. Grant, Trans.). Avignon: Roumanille.

MISTRAL, F. 1879. *Lou tresor dóu Felibrige, ou Dictionnaire provençal-français embrassant les divers dialectes de la langue d'oc moderne*. Aix-en-Provence: J. Remondet-Aubin.

MISTRAL, F. 1907. *Memoirs of Mistral*. (C. E. Maud, Trans.). London: Edward Arnold.

MISTRAL, F. 1981. *Correspondance Mistral-Roumanille 1847–1860*. Raphèle-les-Arles: Culture Provençale et Méridionale.

MOORE, R. E., PIETIKÄINEN, S., & BLOMMAERT, J. 2010. 'Counting the losses: Numbers as the language of language endangerment', *Sociolinguistic Studies* 4(1). 1–26.

MUEHLMANN, S. 2007. 'Defending diversity: Staking out a common global interest?', in A. Duchêne & M. Heller (eds.), *Discourses of endangerment: Ideology and interest in the defense of languages.* London: Continuum. 14–34.

MUEHLMANN, S. 2008. '"Spread your ass cheeks": And other things that should not be said in indigenous languages', *American Ethnologist* 35(1). 34–48.

MUEHLMANN, S. 2009. 'How do real Indians fish? Neoliberal multiculturalism and contested indigeneities in the Colorado Delta', *American Anthropologist* 111(4). 468–479.

MUEHLMANN, S. 2012a. 'Rhizomes and other uncountables: The malaise of enumeration in Mexico's Colorado River Delta', *American Ethnologist* 39(2). 339–353.

MUEHLMANN, S. 2012b. Von Humboldt's parrot and the countdown of last speakers in the Colorado Delta. *Language & Communication* 32(2). 160–168.

MUFWENE, S. S. 2004. 'Language birth and death', *Annual Review of Anthropology* 33. 201–222.

MUFWENE, S. S. 2008. *Language evolution: Contact, competition and change.* London: Continuum.

NAUDET, M. 1827. 'De l'état des personnes en France sous les rois de la première race', in I. R. de France (ed.), *Histoire et mémoires de l'Institut royal de France, Académie des inscriptions et belles-lettres.* (Vol. VIII). Paris: Imprimerie royale. 401–597.

NETTLE, D., & ROMAINE, S. 2000. *Vanishing voices: The extinction of the world's languages.* Oxford: Oxford University Press.

Ó HIFEARNÁIN, T. 2015. 'La pratique de l'irlandais et la minorité irlandophone', *La Bretagne linguistique* 19. 81–97.

Ó LAOIRE, M. 2008. 'Indigenous language revitalisation and globalization', *Te Kaharoa* 1(1). 203–216.

O'ROURKE, B., & PUJOLAR, J. 2013. 'From native speakers to "new speakers" – problematizing nativeness in language revitalization contexts', *Histoire, epistémologie, langage* 35(2). 47–67.

O'ROURKE, B., & PUJOLAR, J. 2015. 'New speakers and processes of new speakerness across time and space', *Applied Linguistics Review* 6(2). 145–150.

O'ROURKE, B., PUJOLAR, J., & RAMALLO, F. 2015. 'New speakers of minority languages: The challenging opportunity', *International Journal of the Sociology of Language* 231. 1–20.

O'ROURKE, B., & RAMALLO, F. 2015. 'Neofalantes as an active minority: Understanding language practices and motivations for change amongst new speakers of Galician', *International Journal of the Sociology of Language* 231. 147–165.

O'ROURKE, B., & RAMALLO, F. F. 2011. 'The native-non-native dichotomy in minority language contexts: Comparisons between Irish and Galician', *Language Problems & Language Planning* 35(2). 139–159.

O'ROURKE, B., & WALSH, J. 2015. 'New speakers of Irish: Shifting boundaries across time and space', *International Journal of the Sociology of Language* 231. 63–83.

ORMAN, J. 2013. 'Linguistic diversity and language loss: A view from integrational linguistics', *Language Sciences* 40(6). 1–11.

ORTNER, S. 1984. 'Theory in anthropology since the sixties', *Comparative Studies in Society and History* 26(1). 126–166.

PARAYRE, C. 2015. 'Occitan studies: Literature, modern period', *The Year's Work in Modern Language Studies* 75. 165–170.

PERLEY, B. C. 2012. 'Zombie linguistics: Experts, endangered languages and the curse of undead voices', *Anthropological Forum* 22(2). 133–149.

PHILIBERT, C. 2005. 'Le complexe du santon: Le provençal et son image', Thèse de doctorat. Université Lumière-Lyon 2.

PIVOT, B. 2014. 'Revitalisation de langues postvernaculaires: le francoprovençal en Rhône-Alpes et le rama au Nicaragua', Thèse de doctorat. Université Lumière-Lyon 2.

RAITHBY, J. (ed.). 1811. *The statutes at large, of England and of Great Britain: From Magna Carta to the Union of the Kingdoms of Great Britain and Ireland* (Vol. III). London: George Eyre and Andrew Strahan.

RAYNOUARD, F. J. M. 1816. *Choix des poésies originales des troubadours* (Vol. 1). Paris: Imprimerie de Firmin Didot.

RENAN, E. 1882. *Qu'est-ce qu'une nation? Conférence faite en Sorbonne, le 11 mars 1882.* Paris: Calmann Lévy.

REYHNER, J. 1999. 'Some basics of indigenous language revitalization', in J. Reyhner, G. Cantoni, R. N. St Clair, & E. P. Yazzie (eds.), *Revitalizing indigenous languages.* Flagstaff, AZ: Northern Arizona University.

REYHNER, J., CANTONI, G., ST CLAIR, R. N. & YAZZIE, E. P. 1999. *Revitalizing indigenous languages.* Flagstaff, AZ: Northern Arizona University.

ROBINS, R. H., & UHLENBECK, E. M. 1991. *Endangered languages.* Oxford: Berg.

ROMAINE, S. 1989. 'Pidgins, creoles, immigrant and dying languages', in N. C. Dorian (ed.), *Investigating obsolescence: Studies in language contraction and death.* Cambridge: Cambridge University Press. 369–383.

ROMAINE, S. 2006. 'Planning for the survival of linguistic diversity', *Language Policy* 5(4). 443–475.

ROUQUETTE, J. 1980. *La littérature d'oc. Que sais-je?* Paris: PUF.

SANFORD, M. 1974. 'Revitalization movements as indicators of completed acculturation', *Comparative Studies in Society and History* 16(4). 504–518.

SCHIEFFELIN, B. B., & DOUCET, R. C. 1994. 'The "real" Haitian creole: Ideology, metalinguistics, and orthographic choice. *American Ethnologist* 21(1). 176–200.

SHANDLER, J. 2004. 'Postvernacular Yiddish language as a performance art', *The Drama Review* 48(1). 19–43.

SHANDLER, J. 2006. *Adventures in Yiddishland: Postvernacular language & culture.* Berkeley, CA: University of California Press.

SHIRREF, A. 1790. *Poems, chiefly in the Scottish dialect.* Edinburgh: D. Willison.
SHOEMAKER, N. 1991. 'From longhouse to loghouse: Household structure among the Senecas in 1900', *American Indian Quarterly* 15(3). 329–338.
SHUY, R. W. 2003. 'A brief history of American sociolinguistics 1949–1989', In C. Bratt Paulston & G. R. Tucker (eds.), *Sociolinguistics: The essential readings.* Oxford: Blackwell Publishing. 4–16.
SIBILLE, J. 2002. *Les langues régionales. Dominos.* Paris: Flammarion.
SIBILLE, J. 2007. L'occitan, qu'es aquò? *Langues et Cité*, (10), 2.
SILVERSTEIN, M. 1998. 'The uses and utility of ideology: A commentary', in B. B. Schieffelin, K. A. Woolard & P. V. Kroskrity (eds.), *Language ideologies, theory and practice.* Oxford: Oxford University Press. 123–145.
SILVERSTEIN, M. 2003. 'Indexical order and the dialectics of sociolinguistic life', *Language and Communication* 23(3–4). 193–229.
SILVERSTEIN, M. 2014. 'The race from place: Dialect eradication vs. the linguistic "authenticity" of terroir', in V. Lacoste, J. Leimgruber & T. Breyer (eds.), *Indexing authenticity: Sociolinguistic perspectives.* Berlin: Mouton de Gruyter. 159–187.
SKUTNABB-KANGAS, T. 2009. 'The stakes: Linguistic diversity, linguistic human rights and mothertongue based multilingual education or linguistic genocide, crimes against humanity and an even faster destruction of biodiversity and our planet', Keynote Presentation at Bamako International Forum on Multilingualism, Bamako, Mali. Bamako, Mali.
SNOW, D. A., SOULE, S. A., & KRIESI, H. 2004. 'Mapping the Terrain', in D. A. Snow, S. A. Soule & H. Kriesi (eds.), *The Blackwell companion to social movements.* Oxford: Blackwell. 3–16.
SPEAS, M. 2009. 'Someone else's language on the role of linguists in language revitalization', in J. Reyhner & L. Lockard (eds.), *Indigenous language revitalization. encouragement, guidance and lessons learned.* Flagstaff, AZ: Northern Arizona University. 23–36.
SPOLSKY, B. 1995. 'Conditions for language revitalization: A comparison of the cases of Hebrew and Maori', *Current Issues in Language and Society* 2(3). 177–201.
SPOLSKY, B. 2003. 'Reassessing Maori regeneration', *Language in Society* 32(4). 553–578.
SPOLSKY, B. 2008. 'Riding the tiger', in N. H. Hornberger (ed.), *Can schools save indigenous languages?, Policy and practice on four continents.* Basingstoke & New York: Palgrave MacMillan. 152–160.
SUMIEN, D. 2006. *La standardisation pluricentrique de l'occitan: nouvel enjeu sociolinguistique, développement du lexique et de la morphologie.* Turnhout: Brepols.
SUMIEN, D. 2009a. 'Classificacion dei dialèctes occitans', *Linguistica occitana*, 7. 1–56.
SUMIEN, D. 2009b. 'Comment rendre l'occitan disponible? Pédagogie et diglossie dans les écoles Calandretas', in P. Sauzet & F. Pic (eds.), *Politique*

linguistique et enseignement des langues de France. Paris: L'Harmattan. 67–86.

SUMIEN, D. 2012. 'Le catalogue des langues romanes: Clarifier les critères et les idéologies', *Revue des langues romanes* CXVI(1). 5–33.

SUSLAK, D. F. 2011. 'Ayapan echoes: Linguistic persistence and loss in Tabasco, Mexico', *American Anthropologist* 113(4). 569–581.

SWADESH, M. 1948. 'Sociologic notes on obsolescent languages', *International Journal of American Linguistics* 14(4). 226–235.

TEISSIER, O. 1894. *Poésies provençales de Robert Ruffi (XVIe siècle)*. Marseille: Librairie Provençale de V. Boy.

THIESSE, A.-M. 2001. 'Les deux identités de la France', *Modern & Contemporary France* 9(1). 9–18.

TOURAINE, A., DUBET, F., HEGEDUS, Z., & WIEVIORKA, M. 1981. *Le pays contre l'état: Luttes occitanes*. Paris: Seuil.

TOURTOULON, C. DE, & BRINGUIER, O. 1876. *Étude sur la limite géographique de la langue d'oc et de la langue d'oïl (avec une carte)*. Paris: Imprimerie Nationale.

TSUNODA, T. 2006. *Language endangerment and language revitalization: An introduction*. Berlin: Walter de Gruyter.

UNESCO. 2009. *UNESCO interactive atlas of the world's languages in danger*. Paris: UNESCO.

URLA, J. 2012. *Reclaiming Basque: Language, nation and cultural activism*. Reno & Las Vegas: *Reclaiming Basque: Language, Nation and Cultural Activism*. Reno, NV: Nevada University Press.

VALLVERDÚ, F. 1977. 'La normalitzacicó del català modern', *Treballs de Sociolingüística Catalana* 1. 147–155.

VALLVERDÚ, F. 1990. 'El concepte de "normalització lingüística" en els estudis sociolingüístics catalans', in G. Bazalgas, P. Gardy & P. Sauzet (eds.), *Per Robert Lafont*. Montpelhièr & Nimes: Centre d'Estudis Occitans & Vila de Nimes. 275–284.

WALLACE, A. F. C. 1952. 'Handsome lake and the great revival in the West', *American Quarterly* 4(2). 149–165.

WALLACE, A. F. C. 1956. 'Revitalization movements', *American Anthropologist* 58(2). 264–281.

WALLACE, A. F. C. 1970. *The death and rebirth of the Seneca*. New York: A. A. Knopf.

WALLACE, A. F. C. 2003. 'Introduction to part I: Processes of culture change', in R. S. Grumet & A. F. C. Wallace (eds.), *Revitalizations and mazeways: Essays on culture change* (Vol. 1). Lincoln, NE: University of Nebraska Press. 3–8.

WALLACE, A. F. C. 2004. 'Foreword', in M. E. Harkin (ed.), *Reassessing revitalization movements: Perspectives from North America and the Pacific Islands*. Lincoln, NE: University of Nebraska Press. vii–xi

WALSH, M. 2005. 'Will indigenous languages survive?', *Annual Review of Anthropology* 34. 293–315.

WARDHAUGH, R. 1987. *Languages in competition*. Oxford: Blackwell.

WEBER, E. 1976. *Peasants into Frenchmen: The modernization of rural France, 1870–1914*. Palo Alto, CA: Stanford University Press.

WEIR, L. 2008. 'The concept of truth regime', *Canadian Journal of Sociology/ Cahiers Canadiens de Sociologie* 33(2), 367–390.

WHITELEY, P. 2003. 'Do "language rights" serve indigenous interests? Some Hopi and other queries', *American Anthropologist* 105(4). 712–722.

WOODBURY, A. C. 2011. 'Language documentation', in P. K. Austin & J. Sallabank (eds.), *The Cambridge handbook of endangered languages*. Cambridge: Cambridge University Press. 159–186.

WOOLARD, K. A. 2004. 'Is the past a foreign country? Time, language origins, and the nation in early modern Spain', *Journal of Linguistic Anthropology* 14(1). 57–80.

WRIGHT, S. 2007. 'The right to speak one's own language: Reflections on theory and practice', *Language Policy* 6(2). 203–224.

YÚDICE, G. 2003. *The expediency of culture*. Durham, NC: Duke University Press.

ZANTEDESCHI, F. 2013. *Occitan: Une langue en quête d'une nation*. Pueglaurenç: IEO Edicions.

ZARETSKY, R. 2004. *Cock and bull stories: Folco de Baroncelli and the invention of the Camargue*. Lincoln, NE: University of Nebraska Press.

ŽIŽEK, S. 1997. 'Multiculturalism, or, the cultural logic of multinational capitalism', *New Left Review* I(225), 28–51.

INDEX